CANDIDATES FOR EUROPE

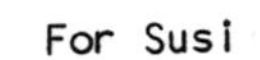
For Susi

Candidates for Europe

The British Experience

MARTIN HOLLAND
Department of Political Science
University of Canterbury
Christchurch, New Zealand

Gower

Published by
Gower Rublishing Company Limited,
Gower House, Croft Road, Aldershot, Hants GuII 3HR
ENGLAND

Gower Publishing Company,
Old Post Road
Brookfield
Vermont 05036
USA

British Library Cataloguing in Publication Data

Holland, Martin
Candidates for Europe : the British experience.
1. European Parliament——Elections, 1979
2. Nominations for office——Great Britain——History——20th Century 3. Elections——Great Britain——History——20th century
I. Title

324.941'0857 JN36

ISBN 0-566-00871-8

Printed in Great Britain by Paradigm Print, Gateshead, Tyne and Wear

Contents

LIST OF TABLES AND FIGURES

Figures

ACKNOWLEDGEMENTS

This book is based upon research undertaken for a Ph. D. thesis at the University of Exeter between 1978-1982. I wish to thank the Conservative, Labour and Liberal parties for their assistance as well as all the aspirants, candidates, agents and activists who cooperated by completing questionnaires. I owe the greatest debt to Dr Michael Rush for his tireless and thoughtful supervision of the research, and to Sean Goddard for his excellent graphics. I am also grateful to the University of Exeter, University of Canterbury and to the Commission of the European Communities for their research support and funding.

Most of all I wish to thank my wife, Susi, for making everything seem worthwhile.

Publication supported by the Commission of the European Communities printing grant for university theses.

1 Introduction

Between 7-10 June 1979, one hundred and eleven million voters in the then nine Community countries took part in the first direct elections to the European Parliament. This study examines the recruitment and selection of British candidates for those elections. The prime concern of the analysis is to develop a theory of recruitment relevant to the British party system: Europe constituted the vehicle for this exercise but the European connection was a subsidiary theme. This restriction is not xenophobic in origin, but can be justified theoretically: the study of each country, rather than of the nine as a whole, was appropriate. National autonomy for each contesting party remained, despite the issuing of joint manifestoes by some transnational groupings. Each party was responsible for the selection of its own candidates. Essentially, the elections were

> national second-order elections. They are determined more by the domestic political cleavages than by alternatives originating in the EC...A first analysis of European election results satisfactorily justifies the assumption that European Parliament direct elections should be treated as nine simultaneous national second-order elections.(1)

The scope of this volume is also limited in terms of the parties analysed. Only the Conservative, Labour and Liberal parties are discussed in detail; they were the only ones to contest all seventy-eight mainland Euro-constituencies. The Scottish Nationalist Party and Plaid Cymru recruitment and selection procedures are not considered: the parties that contested the three Northern Ireland seats are similarly excluded from the analysis. The use of the Single Transferable Vote (STV) electoral system in Northern Ireland had significant implications for the selection process, but these fall beyond the scope of this study.

Three themes are examined. Firstly, a case-study of the selection process and recruitment of candidates for the first direct elections to the European Parliament is considered. Contrasts are drawn between each party's selection machinery and their respective levels of rank and file participation. These selection procedures are linked to a series of aspirant profiles that investigate the three stages of candidacy: those elected as Members of the European Parliament (MEPs); those selected as Prospective European Parliamentary Candidates (PEPCs); and, lastly, those individuals who aspired to be candidates but at some point in the selection process were rejected.(2) This elected/selected/rejected trichotomy constitutes a methodological innovation in Bristish political science and the testing of hypotheses generated from this division is the major focus of this study. The role of partisan 'gate-keeping' and selection criteria is also examined and the aggregated data constitutes a framework for future analysis of candidate or legislative conorts. The second theme is the construction of a model of recruitment specific to the election of British MEPs. The model has been designed to accommodate testable hypotheses which accurately reflect the data and offer comprehensive explanations. The application of the model helps to distinguish candidate studies from recuitment theory. The third theme emanates from the second. The problem of defining the optimal perspecitve for analysing the study of recruitment to British political parties is considered, and some progress made towards a general macro-theory of recruitment. This third objective is, however, very much a subsidiary goal.

Why do we study candidate recruitment? Firstly, any analysis of political systems has to incorporate the role of parties: the method of recruiting the leadership elites is a defining characteristic of political parties.(3) In liberal democratic systems in particular, Seligman regards the recruitment of candidates for elective office as their basic function and argues that a 'party that cannot attract and then nominate candidates surrenders its elemental opportunity for power'.(4) Secondly, political recruitment has important consequences for the operation of democracy and for a political system's stability. Czudnowski argues that recruitment constitutes the critical link between society and the political system; it is an essential democratic function aiding system maintenance and promoting continuity.(5) Arguably it is inter-elite competition, not public participation that forms the basis for stable democratic procedures.(6)

Thirdly, as Kim suggests, recruitment is even more crucial to democratic theories if we can demonstrate that it 'significantly affects the attitudes of legislators and thereby influences the functional and decisional outputs of a legislative system'.(7) Similarly, Marvick states

> political recruitment study is an empty and futile exercise if it merely asks 'Who Governs?' instead of asking how governance is shaped by the skills, contacts and values of those who participate...Its pay-off as a mode of inquiry comes when it helps the observer to anticipate what viewpoints are likely to be introduced into a political context by virtue of the pressence of political actors with particular kinds of credentials.(8)

Recruitment then, can help to explain change within the processes of decision-making: it may constitute a substantive determinant of legislative behaviour and outcomes. Simply, recruitment studies must examine how the selection of elected political elites effects the polity.

Fourthly, recruitment studies must attempt to resolve a fundamental problem. It is insufficient to describe how political leaders achieve elected office; recruitment theory has to postulate why. What distinguishes them from other non-political individuals? Is it education, status, personality, socialisation, occupation or opportunity? Recruitment analysis has to consider all such variables in explaining leadership cohorts. Lastly, the study of recruitment rather than elections, is the more fruitful perspective for explaining elected political elite composition. Selection is often tantamount to election in an electoral system that institutionalises incumbency through 'safe' seats.

Why is it important to study the selection of British candidates to the European Parliament? The attitudes, aspirations, policy positions of MEPs will help to determine the future development of the European Parliament. Despite the Parliament's restricted constitutional role, since direct election there have been examples where the collective action of MEPs has led to change. The most celebrated case was the rejection of the 1980 Budget Proposals. The study of recruitment will help to gauge and explain change. Is there support for a United States of Europe, control over the Commission, extension of the European Parliament's powers, or for a uniform electoral system? This study measures such policy positions for British MEPs, and for defeated and non-selected aspiring MEP candidates. Were the policy positions of MEPs similar or in opposition to those of their non-elected competitors? How would the European Parliament's role have developed had a different seventy-eight individuals been elected? While the British MEPs represent less than one fifth of the Parliament's members, their attitudes are of importance. For example, one can hypothesise about the consequences had the election produced a Labour rather than a Conservative landslide. The European Democrats may not have emerged as a political grouping, and the European Parliament would have been dominated by the Socialist group, within which the British Labour Party would possibly have been the largest component.(9) Thus the composition of the European Parliament and its policy outcomes can be seen as a result of the earlier intraparty selection procedures, moderated only by the election itself.

In short, the purpose of this study is to develop a framework for a cohort analysis of MEPs and the development of the European Parliament, as well as improve the status of recruitment theory and model-building.

Notes

(1) K. Reif and H. Schmitt, "Nine Second Order Elections: a conceptual framework for the analysis of European election results", European Journal of Political Research, vol. 8, 1980, p.3.

(2) Within the rejected aspirant category further sub-divisions

are possible. For example, in the discussion of Labour profiles, three rejected nominee categories are examined. However, for the purpose of simplicity, recruitment is treated as a three stage process unless otherwise stated.

(3) G.A. Almond and G.B. Powell Jnr., Comparative Politics: a developmental approach, Boston, Little Brown, 1966, p.118.

(4) L.G. Seligman, "Political Recruitment and Party Structure: a case-study", American Political Science Review, vol. 55, 1961, p.77.

(5) M.M. Czudnowski, "Political Recruitment", in F.I. Greenstein and N.W. Polsby (eds.), Handbook of Political Sience Vol. 2, Reading, Addison-Wesley, 1975, p.156.

(6) K. Prewitt, "Political Ambitions, Volunteerism and Electoral accountability", American Political Science Review, vol. 64, 1970, p.5.

(7) C.L. Kim, "Attitudinal Effects of Legislative Recruitment", Comparative Politics, vol. 7, 1974, p.109.

(8) D. Marvick, "Continuities in Recruitment Theory and Research: towards a new model", in H. Eulau and M.M. Czudnowski (eds.), Elite Recruitment in Democratic Polities, New York, Sage, 1976, pp.29-30.

(9) After the 1979 election the European Democrats were composed of sixty British Conservatives, one Official Ulster Unionist, two Danish Konservative Folkieparti and one Danish Centrum Demokraterne.

2 Political recruitment and candidate studies: A search for a model

Political recruitment and candidate studies are not synonymous, although all too often they are treated as such. The pioneering work of both Rush and Ranney in the 1960s heralded a plethora of candidate studies that focused upon those who contested for election to local and national office.(1) In contrast, only limited and superficial attention has been paid to the study of the recruitment process within British political parties: that is, the process whereby individuals contend for candidacy.

The distinction between recruitment and candidate analysis is of fundamental importance, yet one that has been widely neglected. Recruitment for political office is an on-going process encapsulating the complete universe of candidate selection: it is dynamic not static. Recruitment is best conceptualised as a spectrum along which all the elements of the selection process can be located: it traces the path of a specified group of individuals from their initial motivation for running, through the various (local and central) screening mechanisms, and if successful, to their selection and possible election. A fuller understanding of how and why political parties attract, select and promote certain individuals while rejecting others, demands a sequential approach linking each inter-acting variable in a causal model.

The traditional 'candidate study' only isolates those selected by their party. This constitutes just a single phase of the total process, focusing on selected political elite composition rather than recruitment. It may be methodologically easier to restrict analysis to selected candidates (or in extreme case, simply to 'winners'), but there has been an unwarranted concentration on this aspect of research. It represents a valid and useful approach but not a sufficient one; it fails to investigate those factors that exist beneath the facade of candidacy and can tell us very little about how those chosen candidates came to be selected, and nothing about those who aspired but failed to be selected. Research must go beyond selected candidates and investigate non-selected aspirants: only from this perspective can the scope and impact of political recruitment be appreciated. Such a synthesis encompassing the extremes of the recruitment/ candidacy continuum is absent from British recruitment literature.

How far can the established texts on recruitment within British political parties be of use in this new endeavour? Both Ranney and Rush provide exhaustive and explicit analyses of the important structural variables that determine the selection of Conservative and Labour prospective parliamentary candidates. The actual 'machinery of selection' is stressed, and rightly so: it limits and shapes all other considerations, especially the delicate centre-constituency relationship. Structural explanations represent the core of any adequate model of recruitment for British political parties.(2) However, these types of analyses are 'impressionistic' and can only speculate about the preferences of selectors by examining the features of the candidates actually chosen. Both Rush and Ranney infer plausible elements of an initial model and emphasise the role played by competing screening agencies. While they discuss these factors both knowledgeably and intimately, neither possessed the necessary data to test such hypotheses. Failed aspirants (i.e. those individuals who contested for selection but were rejected at some stage in the screening process) were not the focus of their study.

The utility of traditional candidate studies is limited. As Mellors conjectured, they maybe no more than 'an entertaining exercise in social arithmetic'.(3) Profiles of legislators - that is, successfully elected candidates - which are dependent almost entirely on demographic variables are, at best, only partially germane to the wider problems of candidate selection. Farlie and Budge go as far as to suggest that it is 'not obvious from investigations what attitudes the standard background characteristics indicate ... it is misleading to compile standard social background data on different elite groups in order to infer their political preferences and attitudes'.(4) Cameos of individual MPs, or their aggregated characteristics, are legitimate and valid areas of inquiry but they do not constitute recruitment theory. Such studies do contribute to a fuller understanding of the process, but they are firmly tied to the far end of the recruitment spectrum.

In his analysis of both local government and MEP recruitment, Gordon initially appeared to comprehend the need for a new inclusive research strategy.(5) He notes that

> it is probably tautological to simply study political recruitment in terms of those who are elected. Political recruitment should be seen as a dynamic process which usually takes place over a period of time. Ideally then a research strategy would examine the different hurdles through which individuals move and the filtering effect at each stage.(6)

Gordon reminds us that 'it is important to look at these steps to political recruitment because they pinpoint the sources in recruitment of interesting patterns of office-holders' characteristics and behaviour'.(7) To examine officer-holders in isolation offers no basis from which to develop comparative analysis; only be juxtaposing them with both non-elected and non-selected candidates can recruitment studies hope to progress beyond its current status of a superficial check-list of socio-economic similarities. While Gordon clearly states the central problem for contemporary research, neither at the local nor European level, can he provide any data substantiating his conceptual plea: only candidates, not the pool of aspirants, are analysed.

Collins, in his consideration of local councillor recruitment suggests 'the components at least of a causal model', although it remains untested empirically.(8) He argues that recruiting agencies, or 'gate-keepers', must be identified and where possible surveyed and analysed. But Collins is guilty of an elementary error. When discussing criteria recruiters use in selecting candidates he argues that 'this can be devised from who the recruiters eventually choose.'(9) Often the candidate finally chosen bears little or no resemblance to the initial criteria used by recruiters: supply and demand are limiting factors. Only by analysing recruiting agents can we test hypotheses.

The most distinctive, if descriptive, approach to gate-keeping has been adopted by Paterson. He focused on the 'selectorate', or the inner-party elite that determines candidate choice either through the formal channels of preliminary screening selection committees, or via more informal elite caucuses.(10) While Paterson's treatment of the topic is journalistic and lacks substantiated analysis, he has contributed to the development of recruitment theory by emphasising the crucial role played by intra-party mechanisms. A related theme was investigated by Fairlie: she was the first to systemically study the gate-keeping role played by party agents and secretaries.(11) Her findings were, however, inconclusive.

The most significant theoretical critique of the 'impressionistic' character of existing studies has been provided by Bochel and Denver.(12) They argue that past research has been guilty of unwarranted concentration on the end product, the 'candidate', to the almost total neglect of the actual process of political recruitment. They emphasize quite rightly, that the gate-keeping role performed by local party activists, their preferences and the selection criteria employed, are all crucial variables limiting the choice presented to the electorate and have, therefore, a direct impact upon parliamentary representation. While their research adds much needed empirical data on gate-keeping characteristics (in this case for Labour Party selections) Bochel and Denver fail to provide a comprehensive recruitment framework within which to locate their analysis. Examining the qualities sought by gate-keepers is an important aspect of any recruitment study: however, it only constitutes a partial explanation. Bochel and Denver focus on selectors' perceptions at the expense of any consideration of those aspirants from among whom the gate-keepers choose. Hills' examination of candidates for local political office displays a similar methodological weakness. Having drawn attention to factors that act to discourage women recruits and to the static nature of past research, Hills is unable to provide the necessary empirical data to account for this phenomenon. Her explanation for this omission is that 'no records are kept of women turned down by selection panels. Hence the actual size of the pool of potential women candidates is unknown'.(13) What has to be known is who the competing aspirants are and whether they vary in terms of their political or socio-economic profiles. Simply, does the criteria stated by the gatekeepers actually conform to the candidate chosen? To answer these fundamental questions a comprehensive model of recruitment is required if anything more than a blurred 'snap-shot of a race taken at the finish line' is to be realised.(14)

To summarise, British recruitment studies have yet to resolve the fragmented and partial nature of their research. While a number of writers are aware of the methodological and theoretical imperatives necessary for the construction of a recruitment model, all of them have consistently failed to apply these conceptual demands to their research design. There is a glaring absence of the kind of data required to test recruitment, as opposed to candidate, hypotheses. The little analytic work that has been attempted is largely impressionistic, non-testable and relates to recruitment for local rather than national political office. While practical considerations often dictate the area of research (the higher the level of office, the greater the problems of accessibility), it is essential that model construction accurately interprets reality and that reality is not distorted to fit the demands of a model. As Marvick warns, 'models of political recruitment have been largely tailored to fit the data obtainable. Conceptual frameworks often seem to have been fashioned to display research findings obtained by inquiries remarkable for their pragmatic design'.(15)

A CONCEPTUAL AND METHODOLOGICAL CUE: AMERICAN RECRUITMENT LITERATURE

In the absence of an extensive body of recruitment theory specific to British politics, the prolific American recruitment literature offers guidance in developing a more scientific research strategy. Six approaches can be delineated: socialisation and background characteristics; the impact of the electoral environment; the effects of nominating systems; initial recruitment stimuli; gate-keeping and screening criteria; and motivation and ambition theories and the related structure of political opportunities. The classification of recruitment factors helps to structure a complex environment and serves as a useful heuristic cue for the construction of a recruitment model.

a) Socialisation and background characteristics: As in the British literature, socio-economic characteristics of candidates have been exhaustively documented. However, whereas in Britain background variables tend to be used in a simple arithmetic manner, American political science has sought to discover theoretical hypotheses related to these factors; but as Prewitt warns, 'the social bias in political recruitment is... just the starting point for analysis'.(16) All too often it is given the status of an explanatory variable without adequate justification. Age, sex, education, occupation, status and previous political involvement have all been used as partial explanations of attitudes and behaviour: however, the evidence of causal linkage is ambiguous.(17) Czudnowski has drawn attention to an as yet unresolved theoretical problem. He argues that 'the occupational background of any category of officeholders is not *per se*, a recruitment variable'; more explicitly, 'there is a critical gap in theorizing about elite recruitment because no researchable hypotheses have been offered to explain why only some members of a social category, group or occupation with recruitment relevant characteristics seek a political career while others do not'.(18)

Are background factors really associated with the recruitment process or are they no more than easily accessible statistics, and therefore deemed to be pertinent? Only by adopting the research strategy argued here and by testing the background characteristics of selected candidates against those of failed aspirants can we measure observable differences and infer selection biases. A general statement of causation, however, is not possible. Background variables do not offer a theory; they are not in themselves sufficient, although they may be indicators of differential access to the political opportunity structure.

A related method of analysis, the concept of 'brokerage occupations', was first utilised by Jacob. He defined initial recruitment 'as a process by which individuals possessing certain personality traits and occupying specified social positions in the community are screened by political institutions for elective office'.(19) This definition acknowledges the inter-relationships of psychological, institutional and occupational variables, but stresses 'the occupational role an individual plays in his daily life: the politician emerges only from those roles which teach him political skills and provide him with opportunities to enter the political arena'.(20) Jacob delineates the parameters of a brokerage role as those occupations that 'frequently place their practitioners into a bargaining role where they deal with outsiders (non-subordinates) and try to reach a mutually satisfying agreement'.(21) Such occupations help to develop many of the 'skills' a politician needs, generate political contacts and entrees, and are often at the fringe of politics. As a conceptual tool, the brokerage role has been a popular and successful recruitment variable for American politics. In a British context the concept of brokerage can only be applied with modifications. An implicit characteristic of Jacob's concept is that brokerage roles should allow easy transference from an occupation to political candidacy. For Jacob, the occupation of lawyer typifies this property. In British recruitment the teaching profession also seems to possess this attribute. The time and resource flexibility produced by this profession appears to be a distinct advantage in securing initial recruitment, particularly in the Labour and Liberal parties. The brokerage concept is of utility but only with the following amendment: the dominant criterion becomes the ability to switch from an occupation to a political role.

Occupational categories tend to be static. One attempt to produce a longitudinal analysis focused upon the role of socialisation in promoting political recruitment. Prewitt drew attention to the need to couple social background data with socialisation theories; together they represent the foundations of his recruitment model. Socialisation is used to identify and explain the politically active stratum of society. Prewitt believes that formative socialisation shapes and limits the pool of potential recruits. But socialisation theories are not complete explanations; they are simply another element of the recruitment model. In addition, while the value of this approach is accepted, practical research methodology may prohibit the measurement of these components empirically.

A related avenue of explanation that can more easily be investigated deals with apprenticeship of aspiring candidates: these may be a consequence of, or help to reinforce, socialisation experiences. Czudnowski regards apprenticeship roles as critical linkage positions in communication networks.(22) When applied to British recruitment studies this method of explanation seems to offer plausible hypotheses. In particular, Bochel found that aspiring Labour councillors had to serve an apprenticeship in terms of local party activity.(23) Similar apprenticeship hypotheses must be included in any model of British political recruitment.

b) The impact of the electoral environment: Parties are the primary mechanism for successful recruitment in both the UK and America, regulating the supply of elected representatives. The electoral environment in which candidate selection operates is a crucial recruitment variable as the perceptions of both selectors and aspirants are often shaped by a consituency's electoral status. The need to encapsulate this perspective within recruitment models has been stressed by Seligman, who emphasised electoral competitiveness and Black, who argued that candidacy could be seen as a function of constituency size and competition for the office.(24) It would be misleading to conclude that electoral status has been totally absent from British candidate studies: Stanyer for example, has drawn attention to this component.(25)

A further electoral factor that must be considered is that the electoral system employed determines more than winners and losers; it has consequences for the whole recruitment procedure. The system in operation will help to shape the behaviour of both candidates and selectors. Recruitment strategies are dissimilar in multimember PR and single member single ballot constituency systems. The electoral system influences 'the degree of party control of nominations (and)...the type of goal orientations that prevail in the process'.(26) Two final components that affect recruitment are incumbency and since 1981, the process of mandatory reselection in the Labour Party. Incumbency limits the process of political recruitment whereas reselection purposefully promotes such opportunities.

The electoral status of a constituency, the national electoral system as well as incumbency are further components in a model of candidate recruitment. Their importance is not confined to the actual election itself, but influences both candidates' initial motivations and ambitions and, the recuiters' perceptions and selection criteria.

c) The effects of nominating systems: Like political science in general, American recruitment studies have moved away from legal, constitutional or institutional approaches towards an analysis of less formal processes. However, as Tobin and Keynes point out 'although one cannot deny the significance of sociological or psychological variables in explaining political recruitment and selection, formal selection criteria such as a state's nominating system can also influence the processes of recruitment and selection'.(27) It is mistaken to ignore structural institutional mechanisms: the recruitment system adopted shapes and confines all other inputs by defining the parameters of candidacy. As early a 1959 Seligman contended that there had been an unwarranted 'neglect of selection routes and channels of ascent... the 'who' has been stressed to the neglect of the 'how' of recruitment'.(28) In a similar vein, Czudnowski stresses the importance of considering 'recruitment ladders' and regards party control over eligibility and selection as a major component in his model. Similarly, Snowiss considers recruitment in relation to party organisation, suggesting that the degree of party control over candidate eligibility and criteria of selection constitutes a cross-cutting variable.(29)

Check lists of rules or procedural descriptions, like socio-economic characteristics, are an essential aspect of candidate selection. Ideally, these factors should be used in conjunction with psychological, motivational and other informal variables to produce an eclectic theory of recruitment. The fault of past research has been that in most cases recruitment analysis has only used structures and mechanisms to explain selection outcomes. Inferences rather than testable hypotheses have been employed. Data designed to repair this omission must focus on the mechanisms of party procedures, how they are interpreted and applied and what the consequences are for centralisation or local selection autonomy.

d) Initial recruitment stimuli: The isolation, measurement and classification of initial recruitment stimuli is methodologically difficult. Seligman has offered the most commonly employed four-fold classification: self-recruitment; sponsorship or agency; conscription; and co-option.(30) Self-recruitment means that the individual is the primary instigator of his candidacy: sponsorship can be by any intra-party group or faction; conscription occurs where a loyal party worker is drafted, often as a token 'standard bearer'; and co-option involves enlisting an established political figure in order to strengthen party organisation and mass support.(31)

There are fundamental problems concerning the self-recruitment category. Research findings relating to the percentage of candidates who consider themselves to be self-starters are likely to be inflated because individuals 'like to think of themselves as 'self-starters', a self-image, especially attractive to politicians, which precludes dependence on others'.(32) Most recruits are not pure self-starters but influenced by informal contacts with party recruiters. The identity of these agents and their promotion of candidates has to be explored. Once again, past research has tended to lack useable data to test the self-starter hypothesis. Despite the absence of an accepted typology, the attempt to classify recruitment mechanisms auxillary to the formal or institutional provisions heightens the potential explanatory nature of a recruitment model.

e) Recruiters, gate-keepers and screening criteria: Prior to the published research of Bochel and Denver the absence of a systematic examination of selection criteria constituted an important flaw in British candidate studies. The characteristics of selected candidates have been traced backwards to infer selection criteria, but such an exercise contains a *non sequitur*. The candidate that is eventually selected and the selection criteria used are often not coterminous. Two questions need to be asked. Firstly, who are the recruiting agents? Secondly, what criteria guide their choice?

The degree to which the nominating or selection process is open or closed obviously influences the operation of recruitmet agencies. The examination of internal party recruiters and screening agents is indispensable to any explanation of why potential candidates either become, or do not become, candidates for office.

Hunt and Pendley's 'Community Gate-keepers' is the best study of internal party screening mechanisms. They criticised recruitment theory as being 'overly reliant upon candidate based constructions of the recruitment process. Investigation of recruiters rather than candidates, is needed to provide a more complete perspective on community leadership selection'.(33) While the candidates' perception of the selection process is vital, an understanding of the recruiter's motivations and criteria is equally as indispensable. Only the examination of the gate-keeping process in conjunction with selected and non-selected candidate studies will succeed in clearly delineating the screening mechanisms distinctive to British recruitment and candidate selection. Furthermore, having identified recruiters, the next task is to describe each party's filtering process, which may often be formally or institutionally defined. Only then can the less tangible notion of selection criteria be examined.

It is best to conceptualise recruitment as a sequence of screenings. This filtering effect need not be limited to the later stages of selection, but can be applied to the entire recruitment spectrum. There is, however, a major limitation on the type of conclusion that may be drawn: the operation of criteria is not universal - it will vary from one setting to another. Consequently, aggregated generalisations and correlations may be inapplicable comparatively: each selection may be sui generis.

A final element that influences selection criteria is the open or closed nature of the recruitment system. Tobin and Keynes found that restrictive nominating systems enhance the party's recruitment control. Conversely, open nominating systems increase the access and influence of other organised and non-party groups. Dominant partisan gate-keeping is reduced and criteria less centralised. Thus institutional differences can inhibit other selection variables.

f) Personality, motivation and ambition theories: As noted in the earlier discussion of background variables, structural or socioeconomic hypotheses by themselves are inadequate explanations of recruitment. Personality, motivation and ambition theories offer a plausible explanation of why some individuals become politically active while others do not. Motivational arguments may be powerful, but their explanatory value is enhanced when placed in the context of other facilitating components. However, while there can be no doubt that personality factors constitute a necessary aspect of recruitment models, their exact role and importance is less easy to establish or to agree upon. Czudnowski's consideration of motivation and 'political personality' summarises the predicament. He states that 'the proposition that personality factors are likely to be a major recruitment relevant variable is intuitively appealing, but efforts to demonstrate the relevance of predispositions in recruitment have been neither numerous nor very successful'.(34) The problem is often a methodological one as motivational data tends to rely upon respondents' recall ability:

securing accurate data for past motivations is notoriously difficult. The respondent may genuinely have forgotten his initial stimulus, or be guilty of anticipated role socialisation: only with these reservations in mind, can the contribution made by psychological analysis be estimated accurately.

The most thoroughly researched psychological trait is that of ambition. For example, Schlesinger assumes that 'ambition lies at the heart of politics' and can be differentiated between discreet, static and progressive ambitions.(35) But ambition is not the sole motivation; it is curbed by the structure of opportunities open to the individual e.g., institutions, incumbency, age, party etc. More importantly, just as with all the other aspects of political recruitment discussed so far, little research has been conducted into the motivations or attitudes of unsuccessful candidates.

Lastly, the structure of political opportunities must be considered. This approach straddles all of the conceptual areas considered so far, from social background eligibility through the open or closed nature of nomination to the constraints upon ambition. Opportunity is related to the degree of risk and competition exhibited by a selection process, i.e., political opportunity is controlled by the supply of aspirants and the demand for new candidates. Hence political opportunity is not merely a structural component and its precise function remains largely unspecified. Black for example, is somewhat dismissive of the impact opportunity structure has upon recruitment. He argues that it 'does not cause either ambition or success; what it does is to determine indirectly the kind of men whom we will find in various types of office'.(36) He regards it very much as an auxiliary component. Conversely, Schlesinger regards ambition and opportunity structure as mutually supporting central elements. Its specific location with a recruitment model may be challenged but its value as an explanatory variable cannot.

To summarise, there is no single personality paradigm: rather 'it is likely that there is a syndrome of personality traits, which in various combinations are functional in various recruitment situations'.(37) Political science needs to test alternative personality hypotheses 'because politics abounds with instances in which political behaviour can be explained only if we have an account of the personal psychological variables that mediate between the stimuli of politics and the resulting behaviour'.(38) However, while Greenstein is correct in suggesting that if other variables are held constant we will find variation in behaviour possibly due to personality factors, Seligman warns against an over-reliance on a single mode of explication because,

> in interrelating political contexts with personality factors, the danger lies in using personality factors alone to explain recruitment, while neglecting both the larger and immediate political context that may facilitate or inhibit their expression...What concerns us is not political motivations...per se, but the part they play in recruitment and selection.(39)

Notes

(1) M. Rush, The Selection of Parliamentary Candidates, London, Nelson, 1969; A. Ranney, Pathways to Parliament: candidates selection in Britain, London, MacMillan, 1965.

(2) M. Holland, "The Selection of Parliamentary Candidates and the Impact of the European Elections", Parliamentary Affairs, vol. 24, 1981.

(3) C. Mellors, The British MP, Farnborough, Saxon House, 1978, p.1.

(4) D. Farlie and I. Budge, "Elite background and Issue Preferences: A Comparison of British and Foreign Data", British and Political Sociology Yearbook, vol. I, 1974, p.234.

(5) I. Gordon, "The Recruitment of Local Politicans: An Integrated Approach with some Preliminary Findings from a Study of Labour Councillors", Policy and Politics, vol. 7, 1979 and, The Recruitment of British Candidates for the European Parliament, Political Studies Association conference paper presented to the 'Political Leadership' panel, PSA conference, Hull University, 1981. These two articles are treated together as the framework for analysis employed in each was identical and the theoretical arguments duplicated virtually without alteration.

(6) Ibid., (1979), pp.2-3; (1981), p.3.

(7) Ibid., (1979), p.3; (1981), p.3.

(8) C.A. Collins, "Considerations on the Social Background and Motivation of Councillors", Policy and Politics, vol.6. 1979, p.443.

(9) Ibid., p.443.

(10) By way of illustration Paterson argues that 'an MP can be elected with a 10,000 or 20,000 majority, but owe the opportunity to stand for election on winning ticket to a handful of gentlemen assessing his worth over an after dinner Port with the President of the local Conservative Association, or to the deliberations of a sparsely attended Trade Union branch meeting', P. Paterson, The Selectorate - the case for primary elections in Britain, London, MacGibbon and Kee, 1967, p.12.

(11) L.D. Fairlie, "Candidate Selection Role Perceptions of Conservative and Labour Party Secretary/Agents", Political Studies, vol. 24, 1976 and, Secretary/Agents in the British Conservative and Labour Parties, unpublished Ph.D. dissertation, Indiana University, 1973.

(12) J. Bochel and D. Denver, "Candidate Selection in the Labour Party: What the Selectors Seek", British Journal of Political Science, vol. 13, 1983.

(13) J. Hills, "Life-style Constraints on formal Political Participation - why so few women local councillors in Britain?", Electoral Studies, vol. 2, 1983, p.41.

(14) M.M. Czudnowski, "Socio-cultural Variables and Legislative Recruitment", Comparative Politics, vol. 5, 1972, p. 564.

(15) D. Marvick, "Continuities in Recruitment Theory and Research: Toward a New Model" in Eulau and Czudnowski (eds.) Elite Recruitment in Democratic Polities, New York, Sage, 1976, p.40.

(16) K. Prewitt, The Recruitment of Political Leaders: A Study of Citizen Politicians, Indianapolis, Bobbs-Merrill, 1970, p.47, (author's italics).

(17) For example, see S.C. Patterson and G.R. Boynton, "Legisltive Recruitment in a Civic Culture", Social Science Quarterly, vol. 50, 1969; K. Prewitt and H. Eulau, "Social Biases in Leadership Selection, Political Recruitment and Electoral Context", Journal of Politics vol. 33, 1971; D.C. Schwartz, Political Recruitment: an essay in theory and research, unpublished Ph.D. thesis, M.I.T., 1965; and K. Prewitt, op.cit.

(18) M.M. Czudnowski "Political Recruitment", in F.I. Greenstein and N.W. Polsby, (eds.), Handbook of Political Science, vol. II, Reading, Addison-Wesley, 1975, p.209.

(19) H. Jacob, "The Initial Recruitment of Elected Officials in the US - a Model", Journal of Politics, vol. 24, 1962, p. 703.

(20) Ibid., p.709.

(21) Ibid., p.709.

(22) M.M. Czudnowski, "Towards a New Research Strategy for the Comparative Study of Political Recruitment", International Political Science Association, Eight World Congress, 1970.

(23) J.M. Bochel, "The Recruitment of Local Councillors - a case study", Political Studies, vol. 14, 1966.

(24) L.G. Seligman, "Political Parties and the Recruitment of Political Leadership", in L.J. Edinger (ed.), Political Leadership in Industrialisd Societies, New York, Wiley, 1967; G.S. Black, "A Theory of Professionalisation in Politics", American Political Science Review, vol. 64, 1970.

(25) J. Stanyer, "Electors, Candidates and Councillors: some Technical Problems in the Study of Political Recruitment Processes in Local Government", Policy and Politics, vol. 6, 1977.

(26) M.M. Czudnowski, "Legislative Recruitment under PR in Israel: a model and a Case Study", Mid-West Journal of Political Science, vol. 14, 1970, p. 224.

(27) R.J. Tobin and E.E. Keynes, "Institutional Differences in the Recruitment Process: a four state study", American Journal of Political Science, vol. 19, 1975. p.668.

(28) L.G. Seligman, "A Prefactory Study of Leadership Selection in Oregon", Western Political Quarterly, vol. 12, 1959, p.153.

(29) L.M. Snowiss, "Congressional Recruitment and Representation", American Political Science Review, vol. 60, 1966.

(30) L.G. Seligman, in L.J. Edinger, op.cit., p. 312; - "Political Recruitment and Party Structure: A case study", American Political Science Review, vol. 55, 1961, p.85.

(31) Alternative categorisations have been offered by: C.L. Kim, J. Green and S.C. Patterson, "Partisanship in the Recruitment and Performance of American State Legislators" in, H. Eulau and M.M. Czudnowski (eds.), op.cit; K. Prewitt and H. Eulau "Social Biases in Leadership Selection, Political Recruitment and Electoral Context", Journal of Politics, vol. 33, 1971; C.L. Kim, "Attitudinal Effects of Legislative Recruitment", Comparative Politics, vol. 7, 1974; and Prewitt (1970), op.cit.

(32) K. Prewitt, (1970), op.cit., p.111.

(33) A.L. Hunt and R.C. Pendley, "Community Gate-Keepers: an examination of political recruiters", Mid-West Journal of Political Science, vol. 16, 1971, pp.411-412.

(34) M.M. Czudnowski, in: Greenstein and Polsby, op.cit., p. 218.

(35) J.A. Schlesinger, Ambition and Politics; political careers in the United States, Chicago, Rand McNally, 1966, pp.6-10. Discrete ambitions are where a candidate only seeks a particular office for one term only; static ambitions constitute a long term career in one particular office; and progressive ambitions indicate that the candidate aspires to win election to higher office successively.

(36) G.S. Black, "The Theory of Political Ambition: Career Choices and the Role of Structural Incentives", American Political Science Review, vol. 66, 1972, p.145.

(37) M.M. Czudnowski, in: Greenstein and Polsby, op.cit., p.218.

(38) F.I. Greenstein, "The Need for a Systematic Inquiry into Personality and Politics", Journal of Social Issues, vol. 24, 1968, p.13.

(39) L.G. Seligman, Recruiting Political Elites, New York, General Learning Press, 1971, p.4.

3 The MEP recruitment model

The preceding chapter has described six distinct (though often overlapping) approaches to the study of recruitment. This chapter utilises each of these perspectives to construct a model of recruitment for the European Parliament. While the model seeks to be exhaustive in its consideration of the recruitment process, its context is limited both geographically and temporally and it does not aspire to universality. It evaluates hypotheses of a comparative nature, but the primary purpose of the model is to explain British MEP selection for the first direct elections to the European Parliament.

A model is not a replica but a simplification of reality; it can only consider a limited number of variables as crucial, ignoring others that may be relevant to some degree. The more heuristic and powerful a model is, the more severely it will cut away unnecessary aspects of reality in order to highlight basic features that would otherwise be obscured. Simplicity need not imply superficiality: however, sophistication may need to be sacrificed for starkness, reality for comprehensibility. Yet, as Barry has indicted, although an exact fit between the deductions of a model and the facts cannot be expected, the less close the fit the less confidence we can have that the processes of the model approximate those of the real world.(1) Furthermore, he questions 'at what point does the price of unrealism paid for simplicity and deductive power become too high?'(2) The elements of the MEP model have been developed as a result of both fieldwork and theory, adding confidence to the belief that the units of analysis are accurate and appropriate, not contrived or imposed.

The approach to the process of recruitment argued here envisages layers or filters that successively reduce potential candidate cohorts. There is a gradual but continuing process of selection and elimintion which narrows the entire population to the few who hold office. Precise terminology is required to distinguish between the relative success rates and stages of candidacy.

Definitions of candidacy(3)

1. Winners (MEPs)	those individuals who were elected to a specific institution.
2. Candidates Winners and Losers Selected aspirants/ applicants	those individuals who contested the election irrespective of the result.
3. Non-selected aspirants/ applicants/nominees* rejected aspirants/ applicants/nominees*	those individuals who were denied access to the selection process, or who entered the selection process but were eliminated at some point prior to adoption.

* Labour Party only

To talk of an undifferentiated mass of 'candidates' is of limited value. It is essential to isolate the different recruitment stages posited in the model although obviously these three groups are not totally discrete. In addition, the 'black box' of inner party selection mechanisms is specified. It is within the crucial inner selection mechanisms that the important recruitment decisions are often made by actors other than the candidate. Only be dissecting the central and local party recruitment structures can a plausible account of British candidacy be approached. A limitation of the model is that it only focuses on those individuals engaged in competition for elected office; it does not attempt to explain what Prewitt labels 'the active political stratum', prior to candidacy.(4)

The accompanying figure represents the recruitment assumptions. The potential pool of aspirants are characterised by particular combinations of psychological predispositions, facilating or mediating components and background characteristics. While the causal roles played by motivation, ambition, socialisation and personality factors have been emphasised and their theoretical place in the model is unquestioned, their empirical testing by political scientists is less easily achieved. The facilitating or mediating components such as brokerage and apprenticeship roles are more readily quantifiable and accessible and are used as partial explanatory variables. Demographic information constitutes the third aspect of the potential aspiring candidate profile. The interrelated impact of these categories defines the initial size of the aspirant cohort.

The political opportunity structure is the second filtering stage. Access to the political system and where applicable, levels of incumbency, further reduce this elite group of motivated eligibles. This filtering or gate-keeping function is the central component of the model. Using Seligman's terminology an initial dichotomy can be made between those aspirants who are 'self-

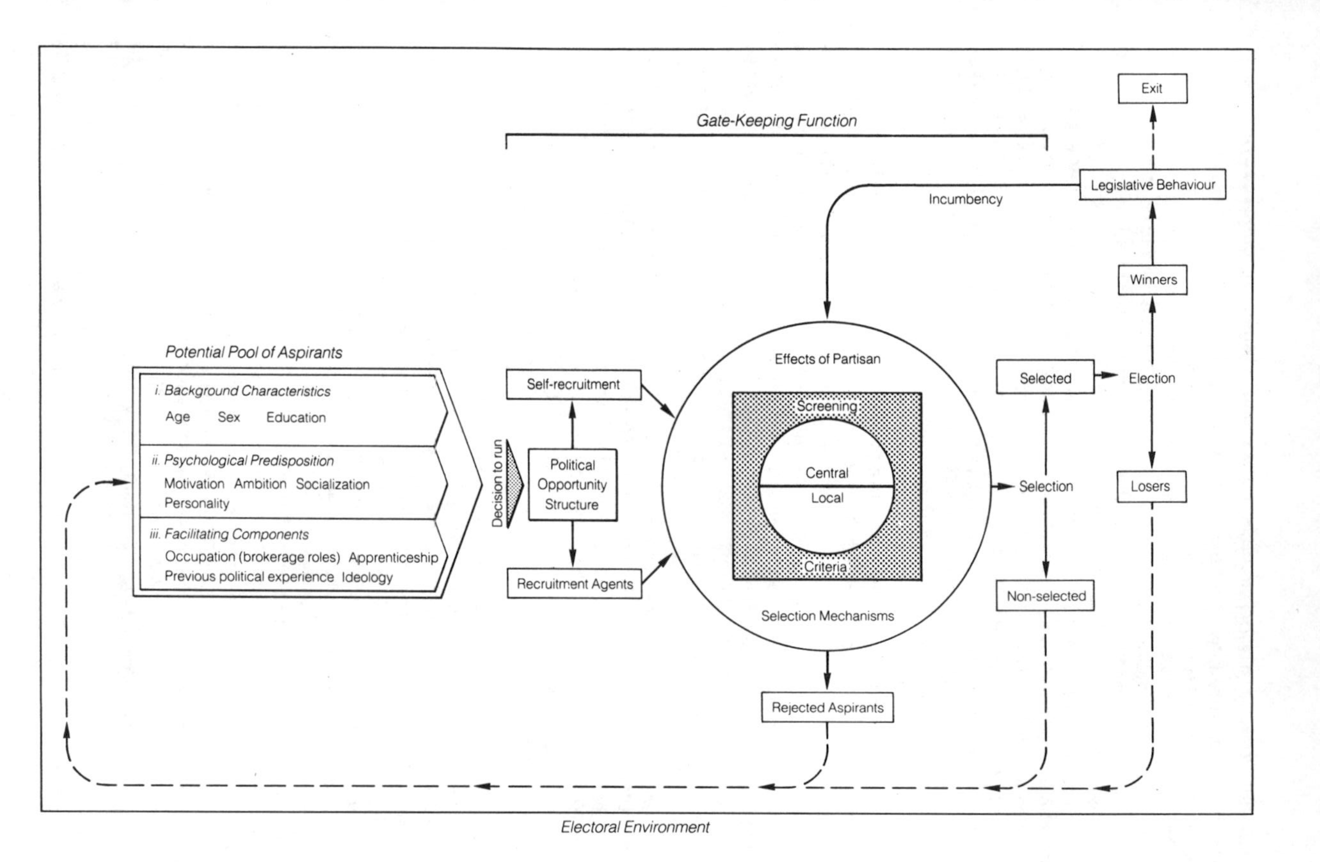

Figure 3.1 MEP Recruitment Model

starters' (those individuals not recruited by any external group) and those drafted by recruitment agents, via sponsorship, co-option or conscription. Thus the combined impact of personality attributes, occupational skills, background characteristics and the nature of the opportunity structure will have reduced the initial pool of aspirants prior to the formal gate-keeping selection process.

The contrasts and similarities in the selection machinery adopted by the Conservative, Labour and Liberal parties is a necessary aspect of the model. Description of central and local selection procedures is a prerequisite to further analysis: however, the emphasis is not simply upon institutional structures, but stresses the need to examine the criteria adopted by the consecutive screening agencies. At this stage, unsuitable aspirants are rejected from the process. The actual selection decision itself creates two categories for analysis - the unsuccessful candidate and the non-selected competitors. Similarly the election itself creates a winner/loser dichotomy among selected candidates. Thus three stages of candidacy can be examined - a) rejected aspirants, b) non-selected aspirants and c) winners and losers. Hypotheses will test for discernible patterns between these groups. Rejected and non-selected aspirants, as well as losers, may return to the potential pool of aspirants or decide to quit the candidate race either temporarily or permanently. (Here Stanyer's classifiction of persistent defeatist, one-off candidacies, and returners is of utility.) Why certain individuals possessing similar personality and background attributes do not enter the candidate process cannot, however, be tested for by this approach.

The penultimate phase of the model links recruitment to legislative behaviour. Finally, incumbency is seen as a means of by-passing the earlier recruitment hurdles, though this interpretation may require revision in the light of the procedures for the reselection of Labour MPs agreed at the 1980 party Conference: incumbency in the Labour party is now a less certain asset. The model does not posit a static set of relationships, but rather views the entire gate-keeping process and resultant cohort behaviour as being influenced by the constraining factor of the electoral environment. This environment may also effect the psychological predispositions and the facilitating or mediating components of potential aspirants.

The position of the facilitating or mediating characteristics in the model may cause certain problems. Are such factors as occupation, education or sex really recruitment relevant characteristics? Are they explanatory or spurious variables? They are placed at the formative end of the recruitment spectrum in order to express their impact on each subsequent stage of the model. For example, the criteria adopted by central or local selectors may be a consequence of profile characteristics: they will have a negative and positive impact. As stated earlier, by themselves such variables offer either insufficient or partial explantions, but to neglect them would constitute an unjustified omission. Finally, although the model has been described in a sequential manner, the precise linkages between variables are not necessarily linear. However, the model's simplifying assumptions treat the process in this simple causal way.

METHODOLOGY

Although the first direct election to the European Parliment offered methodological advantages, such as the lack of incumbent cohorts, it also created severe and more numerous restrictions.

Firstly, the problems relating to access to information were magnified. In comparison with the well-documented and procedurally established machinery for Westminster candidates, the arrangements for the selection of European candidates, for all parties, were rushed, experimental and somewhat ad hoc. It was not until November 1978 that the electoral boundaries were finalised; thus only at a very late stage were organisational structures established and the personnel involved determined. Often a fundamental research problem was simply to discover the appropriate body or individual responsible for a particular aspect of selection. Once this was achieved the familiar problems of confidentiality, internal party secrecy and suspicion had to be combatted. Actual access to information met with varying degrees of success. At one extreme virtually the complete cohort of Liberal aspirants was achieved (138 individuals with a respouse rate of 90.6 per cent): conversely, the most disappointing aspect of the research design was the failure to gain permission from Conservtive Central Office to survey their list of 'approved candidates'. However, 160 of their estimated total of 230-240 approved candidates were identified and surveyed (response rate 71.9 per cent).(5)

Data collection was by postal questionnaire, the technical difficulties of which are well known.(6) Limitations, both financial and of time, made this the only feasible methodology. The questionnaires were, by necessity, administered over a relatively long time span - from January to July 1979. The problems of valid comparison are acknowledged, particularly with reference to certain policy option questions, but this lengthy time-scale was unavoidable. The actual identification of the candidates was an incremental process. Each day saw new candidates being announced and included in the survey population: the interruption of the general election on 3 May further prolonged the process. Up to seven mailings were used in an attempt to secure a high response rate.(7)

Aspiring MEPs were identified in three ways: via the Euro-agents/secretaries for each party; through personal contacts with candidates and party workers; and by using party or intra-party group 'approved' lists.(8) The questionnaire data was supplemented by specific case-studies as well as by interviews with MEPs, defeated candidates, non-selected aspirants, agents and central and local gate-keepers.

Electoral status is a key variable within the model. As this study concerns the first direct election measures of electoral status or incumbency based on past results were not possible. To overcome this, October 1974 General Election figures were used and 'projected' status calculated. The electoral categories chosen duplicate those used for previous domestic studies: a five-fold classification based on incumbent status - marginal, semi-marginal, comfortable, safe and impregnable.(9) Thus, whenever electoral status or incumbency is discussed the terms refer to projected calculations.

COMMON ELEMENTS OF THE POLITICAL OPPORTUNITY STRUCTURE

Before the formal arrangements and the gate-keeping functions of each party are analysed certain features of the political opportunity structure which influenced the recruitment process irrespective of party are examined.

(i) Incumbency

The formal structure of political opportunity allowed open and free access to eligible aspirants. There were no incumbents: every Euro-constituency was selecting its first Prospective European Parliamentary Candidate (PEPC). In contrast, Westminister elections are dominated by the existing incumbent cohort: the 'safest' constituencies only rarely have the chance to exercise their selection prerogative.(10) The election of 7 June 1979 offered a rare opportunity to study an entire selection process from its inception in a comprehensive manner.

(ii) The electoral system

The electoral system is a crucial determinant of the candidates' opportunity structure. As noted earlier, whether the system is based on STV, national or regional lists, or single member constituencies will influence the direction and control of the recruitment process and the selection of the eventual candidates. Despite the publication of a White Paper that considered a variety of proportional systems, and the introduction of two bills into the Lords (advocating regional list and additional member systems) the simple majority single member electoral system was adopted.(11) Although the Houses of Parliament did not attempt to legislate directly in the area of candidate selection, the choice of electoral system was an important opportunity structure variable. The consequences of introducing a new electoral system might have been to distort the established constituency-centre party relationship.

Having adopted a single member system, the Boundary Commission's role of defining the composition of each Euro-constituency and subsequent electoral status was extremely influential. The Commissioners' conglomeration of contiguous Westminister constituencies into gargantuan hybrids, confined the potential outcomes to a definite spectrum, the two extremes representing Labour or Conservative landslides, with little room for a third party variable. While Britain is blessed with non-partisan cartography in that the Boundary Commissioners do not intentionally create party biases, this does not prevent them from determining a constituency's probable electoral status. The Commissioners' final recommendations were only published on 23 November 1978: no European district was composed of less than six parliamentary constituencies, the median being eight. Glasgow was the largest Euro-constituency linking thirteen Westminister seats.(12)

While voting behaviour of the electorate is the final determinant of electoral status, the framework created by the Boundary Commissioners was a significant mediating factor. The individual elector's perspective is shaped by a constituency's inherent status; the degree of marginality may inhibit or promote turn-out.

The election figures for October 1974 have been used as the measure for electoral status, rather than those of May 1979, or the actual European results of June 1979, because these were the only estimations of electoral status available to both selectors and aspirants during the selection process. The Boundary Commission's recommendations gave the projected outcomes shown in Table 3.1.

Table 3.1

Projected Electoral Status of Euro-constituencies

Electoral status	Conservative		Labour		SNP*/ Liberal		All	
	%	n	%	n	%	n	%	n
Marginal	23.5	8	14.6	6	33.3	1*	19.2	15
Semi-marginal	26.5	9	24.4	10	66.7	2*	26.9	21
Comfortable	35.3	12	26.8	11	-	-	29.5	23
Safe	14.7	5	22.0	9	-	0	18.0	14
Impregnable	-	0	12.2	5	-	0	6.4	5
	100.0	34	100.0	41	100.0	3	100.0	78

Projections based on May 1979 results reversed this Labour victory (Conservatives forty-nine, Labour twenty-nine and Liberals and SNP none): the actual European election result exaggerated the Conservative's lead, giving them sixty seats compared to Labour's seventeen and the SNP's single success. The role played by the Boundary Commission in determining Britain's electoral cartography was tempered by the volatility of the electorate and a nationally low turn-out favouring the Conservatives. A comparison of the October 1974 projections with the individual Euro-constituency results produced the following pattern. All six projected Labour marginals fell to the Conservatives, as did nine of the ten semi-marginals. The fate of those Labour seats defined as having a comfortable incumbent status was only slightly better: nearly three-quarters returned Conservative MEPs. Of the safe Labour seats only Liverpool fell to a Conservative, turning the 24.4 per cent Labour October majority into a 6.5 per cent deficit. All five impregnable Labour seats remained intact, although in every case their percentage lead was diminished: two of the three SNP seats fell to the Conservatives. No projected Conservtive seats fell to either Labour or the SNP: the Highlands and Island Euro-constituency was always regarded as an SNP seat.

While the October figures under-emphasised the Conservatives' ultimate success, the discrepancy does not detract from the importance of the Boundry Commission as a pertinent opportunity structure variable. The perceived electoral status of a seat, regardless of its accuracy, is a significant determinant of candidate recruitment.

(iii) The dual mandate

A further element of the formal political opportunity structure was the provision for the dual mandate. The Government White Paper, Direct Elections to the European Assembly urged the consideration of a compulsory dual mandate; i.e., membership of the Commons would be an essential condition for membership of the European Parliament. The implementation of such a proposal would have produced a highly restricted opportunity structure. The reasoning behind the suggestion stemmed from xenophobic and party political concerns: such a qualification, it was argued, would 'discourage the development in Britain of European parties with federalist aims which might undermine the position of our national parties'.(13) The European Assembly Act, 1978, made no legal provisions concerning the dual mandate: each party was left to decide its own policy. Thus, the openness of the opportuntiy structure varied due to each party's interpretation of the concept: the Liberals respresented the most open position, Labour the most restrictive, with the Conservatives occupying the central ground though leaning towards the Labour position. The party remains the most crucial determinant of the political opportunity structure for both national and transnational elections: the absence of independent MEP candidates underlined this characteristic. The openness of the opportunity structure must, therefore, be seen within the context of the party system.

Notes

(1) B. Barry, Sociologists, Economists and Democracy, London, Collier-Macmillan, 1970, p.176.

(2) Ibid., p.152.

(3) Obviously these groups are not mutually exclusive. There is one possible area of confusion: the Conservative party used the phrase 'approved list of European candidates' to refer to both selected and non-selected aspirants, rather than merely those who actually contested the election. Where the approved list is discussed, this more general interpretation of candidacy is used.

(4) K. Prewitt, The Recruitment of Political Leaders: A Study of Citizen Politicians, Indianapolis, Bobbs-Merril, 1970, p.10.

(5) The candidates for each party were divided into winners, losers and non-selected aspirants (including those non-respondents for whom basic data could be collected). Traditional background variables were established (age, sex, education previous political experience), plus policy preferences, role perceptions, pro/anti-EEC, group affiliations and the number of seat applications. For both the Conservative and Labour parties, candidates for all the seventy-eight English, Welsh and Scottish Euro-constituencies were considered. The survey of Liberal Candidates only covered England and Wales: the selection

system operated in Scotland was based on an electoral college and took place in January 1978: comparable data was unavailable.

(6) For a practical summary see: G. Hoinville, R. Jowell and Associates, Survey Research Practice, London, Heinemann Educational Books, 1977; C.A. Moser and G. Kalton, Survey Methods in Social Investigation, London, Heinemann Educational Books, (2nd Ed.), 1971,; W.J. Crotty, "The Utilisation of Mail Questionnaires and the Problems of a Representative Return Rate", Western Political Quarterly, vol. 19, 1966; S. Welch and J.G. Peters, "Some Problems of Stimulating Responses to Mailed Questionnaires", Political Methodology, vol. 4, 1977; P.L. Erdus and A.J. Morgan, Professional Mail Surveys, New York, McGraw-Hill, 1977.

(7) The anonymity of all respondents had to be guaranteed: thus none of the quotations taken from questionnaire responses acknowledge the identity of the original source.

(8) These were: the Co-operative Party Euro-Panel; Labour Common Market Safeguards Committee; the Liberal Party Organisation list of approved candidates for the European election; and, the Labour Party's 'List of Possible Candidates for the European Assembly Elections'.

(9) S.E. Finer, H.R. Berrington and D.J. Bartholomew, Backbench Opinion in the House of Commons 1955-59, London, Pergamon, 1961. The constituencies were divided into five categories: a) marginal - a majority of less than 5.0 per cent of the total votes cast; b) semi-marginal - between 5.0-10.9 per cent; c) comfortable - between 11.0-16.9 per cent; d) safe - between 17.0-30.0 per cent; and e) impregnable - over 30.0 per cent of the total votes cast. The same categories were used by Rush; Ranney, however, used a three-fold classification based on winnability.

(10) The position in the Labour party has changed since the introduction of mandatory reselection of MPs.

(11) For a fuller discussion of the legislative process see, M. Hagger, The UK Legislation of Direct Elections to the European Parliament, unpublished PSA conference paper, Sheffield, 1979; V. Herman and M. Hagger (eds.), The Legislation of Direct Elections to the European Parliament, Farnborough, Gower, 1980; D. Butler and D. Marquand, European Elections and British Politics, London, Longman, 1981; Direct Elections to the European Assembly, HMSO, London Cmnd 6768, April 1977, p.5; and, European Assembly Bill, 389 H.L. Deb., cc. 691-776, 390 H.C. Deb., cc. 791-865.

(12) Electoral quotas were set for the Euro-constituencies (516,436 for England, 473,256 for Scotland and 513,793 for Wales). The wide range in the number of parliamentary constituencies was a direct result of the unequal size of electorates which varied from 23,683 to 100,635 in England, 21,011 to 96,254 in Scotland and from 27,403 to 78,385 in Wales.

(13) Cmnd 6768, op.cit., Annex D., p.23.

4 The Conservative party: Recruitment and party organisation

THE POLITICAL OPPORTUNITY STRUCTURE

Despite the limited legislative restrictions how open were the recruitment channels in the Conservative party? The party's attitude towards the dual mandate was somewhat ambiguous. Although Mrs Thatcher favoured a direct personnel linkage between Westminster and the European Parliament, the party was generally against a dual mandated policy. Fourteen former nominated MEPs (ten MPs, four Peers), nine Westminister MPs and four Peers were included on the Conservative approved list: of these, ten were adopted as PEPCs (five MPs, five Peers) and nine elected as MEPs.(1) The remaining 261 Conservative MPs were strongly discouraged from standing as MEP candidates. While no established provisions applied, prospective parliamentary candidates were dissuaded from standing for Europe as well: PPCs who managed to gain selection were asked to resign from their Westminster constituency.(2) In general, age was not construed as a barrier to recruitment although especially young aspirants were often discouraged because of their lack of experience rather than simply their youth. Exceptionally elderly applicants were also viewed unfavourably. The age for approved candidates ranged from twenty-eight to sixty-seven; the median was forty-seven and the mean 44.3.

While the opportunity structure was accessible, it was not public. Central Office did not officially advertise for applicants for the European list. As is usual in the Conservative party, information about the selection process and how to get on the list was disseminated informally. In purely structural terms, the limiatation of the dual mandate was the only restriction: no other category of applicant was excluded and incumbency did not arise. However, the superficial appearance of openness has to be placed in context: the political opportunity structure was necessarily limited by both the central and local selection machinery. Each of

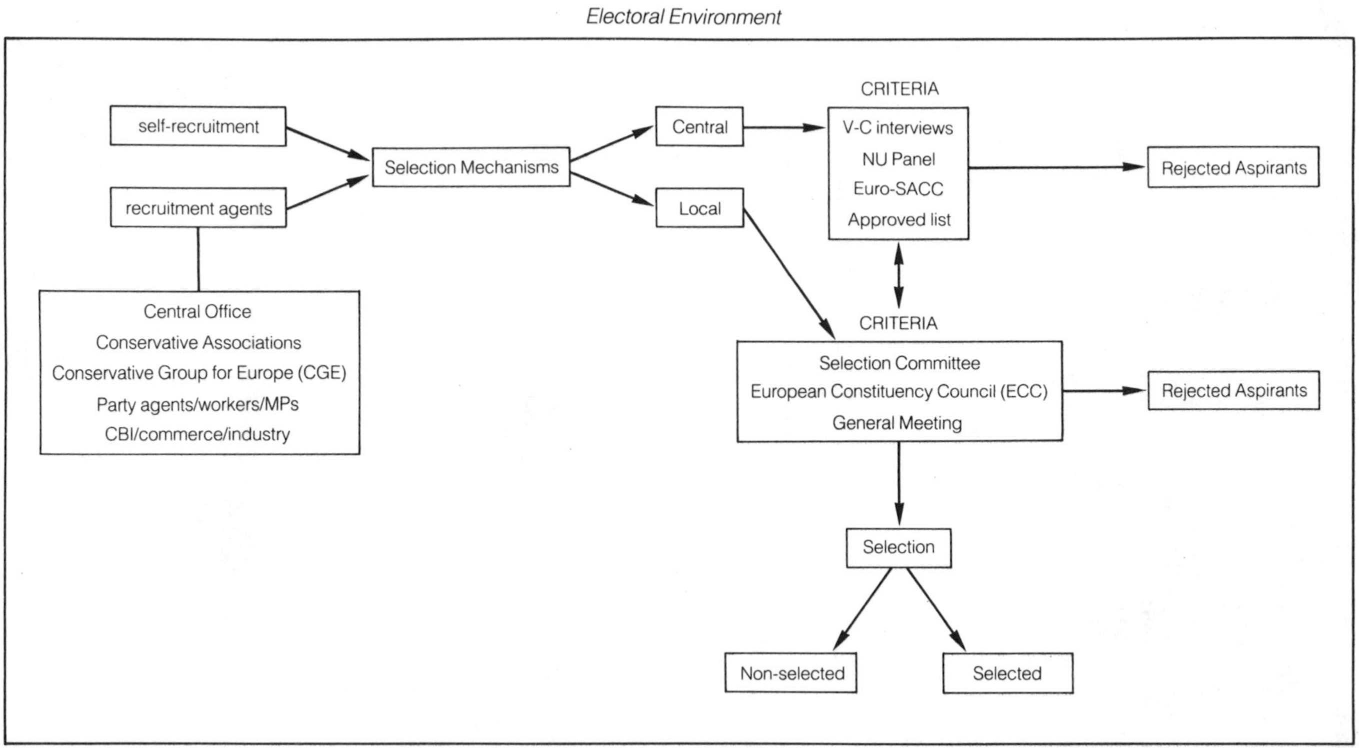

Figure 4.1 Application of the Gate-Keeping Function of the Model for Conservative Selections

these aspects of control are dealt with separately in this chapter.

Self Recruitment/Recruitment Agents

Figure 4.1 superimposes the Conservative selection procedure on the gate-keeping function of the recruitment model. The problems of identifying and defining self-recruitment or self- starters are substantial: the individual may find it difficult to isolate his initial recruitment stimulus, or spuriously translate all actions as originally self-motivated. In this respect, the data for Conservative aspirants may need to be treated with caution. Table 4.1 shows that 61.7 per cent of known cases believed the decision to run as an MEP to be exclusively their own idea. The catalyst of recruitment agents played a relatively minor role, although there is some evidence of the party activating certain candidacies, either through Central Office, the party leadership, constituency associations or sitting MPs.

Table 4.1

Initial Stimulus for European Candidacy

Stimulus	%	n
Own idea	61.7	50
Constituency Associations	5.0	4
Central Office/Party Leadership	6.2	5
Family/Friends	-	-
MPs	8.6	7
CBI/Chamber of Commerce/Employer	-	-
Own idea plus MP	6.2	5
Own idea/Central Office/Party Leadership	8.6	7
Other combinations	3.7	3
Not Known		37
	100.0	118
All self starters	76.5	62

The clearest example of the national party attempting to influence a local selection occurred over Paul Channon's candidacy. Channon was not on the original Central Office compiled list of approved European candidates; however, Mrs Thatcher personally asked Channon to enter the European arena on the understanding that, if elected, he would head the Conservative delegation in the European Parliament. Channon agreed to become a candidate, but only contested the Essex North-East Euro-constituency which contained his parliamentary seat of Southend West. It was hoped that this would placate the dual mandate critics.

By the time Channon's candidacy emerged the Essex North-East Euro-Constituency Council had already chosen their short-list, but they were persuaded to interview Channon and he was subsequently included on the short-list of three presented to the general meeting.(3) Opinion at the meeting was particularly hostile: Mrs Thatcher's interference with the convention of local selection autonomy was strongly resented and concern expressed over the dual mandate and Channon's motives for standing. The result of the first ballot gave David Curry an overall majority and Channon's European aspirations were ended.

The fact that the national party managed to manoeuvre Channon onto the short-list was remarkable, but that was the extent of their power: their influence could be permeate the general meeting. As for Westminster selections, too close an identification with Central Office, or to be dubbed the leadership's protege, can be tantamount to political suicide. The case of Channon bore out Rush's conclusion that 'the merest hint of such support is often enough to damn any candidate in the eyes of the local association'.(4) Hostility towards central interference, the meetings dislike of the dual mandate and the excellence of David Curry combined to produce the Conservative party's most embarrassing selection blunder.

In drawing up the approved list, Marcus Fox, the party Vice-Chairman in charge of candidates, wanted to create what he considered to be a 'balanced' list. During his period as party Vice-Chairman he had streamlined the parliamentary list in an attempt 'to change the face of the Conservative party in Westminster ... to get a better balance'.(5) He did not want the European list to be dominated by the stereo-type Conservative candidate, and thus canvassed for applicants from a diverse range of professions. To this end, the Confederation of British Industry, and the Association of British Chamber of Commerce were asked to encourage suitable individuals. The composition of the elected Conservative MEPs suggests that the informal recruitment agencies were successful in attracting individuals from outside the normal channels of recruitment and constituted an important departure from previous parliamentary practice.

Formal Selection Procedures

The procedure adopted for the selection of European candidates was developed through the experience gained from Westminster selections: in general, the machinery employed paralleled the domestic example and the centralisation/local autonomy relationship duplicated. The absence of a party constitution does not result in undue diversification: as Rush points out, 'the vast majority of Conservative associations select their candidates by a fairly uniform procedure, but it is uniformity imposed by advice and long usage and not constitutional obligation'.(6) This statement was as equally valid for the Conservative European selection procedure. The lack of formal constitutional imperatives is misleading: the procedural structure for the selection of European candidates was uniform, variations occurring only where the advisory guidelines, set out in the model rules, allowed for individual interpretation. The resultant differences were largely ones of detail.

Figure 4.1 demonstrates the initial dichotomy within the selection mechanism, distinguishing central and local machinery. Within each level there were filtering stages that ultimatley determined which individuals were to be selected and which rejected: the following four sections concentrate on this process.

(a) Central selection mechanisms

The appproved list: Any discussion of the Conservatives' European selection procedure must commence with an analysis of the initial centralised control of candidate choice. The existence of a centrally compiled register or list of candidates who have been vetted and approved has been a common feature of Parliamentary selections. The National Union, the voluntary arm of the party, first established a Standing Advisory Committee on Candidates (SACC) in 1935.(7) The committee sought to control the quality of future MPs by ensuring that all aspiring candidates had their names on an approved list. The list constituted the pool of vetted aspirants that both maintained, yet often limited those eligible for recruitment to political office. While a PPC is not formally required to be on the Westminster list of approved candidates, in reality candidates from the list dominate.

Since this was the first direct election to the European Parliament an equivalent pool of available candidates did not exist: prior to 1979, the thirty-six MEPs had been dual mandated nominees, drawn from both the Lords and the Commons. The emergence of a directly elected Parliament necessitated consideration of how best to control the quality of candidates and produce the best selection method. These two priorities were often in conflict with the growing demands for wider participation in the selection process (both domestic and European).(8) The creation of a European list comparable to the Westminster example was believed to be the most efficient solution: Central Office, unfettered by existing aspirants, was presented with the unique opportunity of shaping the composition of this new list. Again, as this was the first election the organisational structure would be new and untested: the relatively small number of seats, the tight time schedule and the inexperience of most local associations in European affairs made it essential that Central Office impose a certain degree of order and control. It would have been confusing, possibly chaotic, had every interested aspirant been allowed to apply directly to each seat without any prior central screening mechanism. There needed to be organisational direction, though this would not necessarily involve procedural innovation.

Central Office limited the number of aspirants who were to be allowed to compete for adoption: the ratio of candidates on the list to seats was fractionally over 3:1. Even so, the number of approved candidates that applied to specific seats was substantial. Of all known cases, 20.0 per cent received between fifty and sixty-six applications, a further 20.0 per cent attracted a minimum of thirty. When compared to the number of applicants for seats in the Commons, the competition for Europe appears restrained: it is not unusual for a vacant Westminster seat to attract up to 400 hopefuls. Limiting the number of approved candidates to below 250 for seventy-eight European constituences demonstrated a much tigher control and central dominance of the European selection process than for its Westminster counterpart. In its own defence, Central Office could point out that if the approval process worked efficiently, every candidate on the list should have been a competent potential MEP and therefore a vast array of choice was unnecessary.

Most associations did not regard the central screening role as an encumbrance or a challenge to the established convention of local selection autonomy: the approved list was an essential aid. It was normal party procedure to use a list; the calibre of the European list was impressive and offered a wide choice of suitable tested individuals. Essentially, central selection was in harmony with local demands; it would be inaccurate to describe Central Office and local associations in conflict. They shared the same goal - the selection of the most able Conservative candidates.

European Constituency Councils were not sent a copy of the approved list. Only those applicants who intimated that they wished to apply for a certain seat had their names and biographical notes forwarded to that Euro-constituency by Central Office.(9) While no upper limit was fixed, Central Office suggested that approved candidates should not aply for more than fifteen seats. Not everyone obeyed this directive: indeed, a majority of respondents (54.1 per cent) stated that they were unaware of this unofficial maximum. One individual (who was subsequently elected) initially applied to what were, in his opinion, the thirty-seven safest Tory seats, although he was eventually restricted to twenty six by Central Office. Table 4.2 gives the distribution for the total number of seats each approved candidate applied to. 87.8 per cent kept within the suggested maximum of fifteen and 59.0 per cent limited themselves to fewer than ten applications.

Table 4.2

Number of Seat Applications for Candidates on the Approved List

No. of Seats	% of candidates	No. of candidates
1	6.0	5
2	4.8	4
3	8.4	7
4	7.2	6
5-9	32.5	27
10-15	28.9	24
16 and more	12.1	10
Not Known		35
	99.9	118

range = 1-37
median = 8.0
mean = 8.9

Candidates not on the approved list were not precluded from entering the selection process. They could apply directly to a

Euro-constituency and the frequency of such 'local' applications was substantial. A total of 101 non-approved aspirants applied to fifty of the seventy-eight British Euro-constituencies. However, the central party organisation did not abdicate its screening role. The advisory Model Rules state that 'should the selection committee wish to consider any of the local applicants further, then it shall submit the name(s) for consideration by the Euro-SACC'.(10) No candidate could be short-listed without prior approval of the Standing Advisory Committee on European Candidates, a similar provision as used for Westminster selections. Forty-one of the 101 local applicants were submitted for consideration by Euro-SACC; twenty-seven of these achieved approved status three of whom were adopted as PEPCs, and one, Paul Howell, elected as an MEP.

More importantly, the official guidelines state that 'the selection committee should not consider applicants who have already been interviewed by the Euro-SACC and who have not been included in the list of approvad candidates'.(11) Rejection by the central machinery proved a fatal blow, at least for aspirations for the first elections, in that none of those initially rejected by Central Office made a short-list. Any consideration of the candidate selection process for the European Parliament must appreciate the restraints imposed by the centrally approved list: it constituted the first hurdle along the route to political office.

Two final points need to be added. Firstly, the approved list was not a Central Office list, although administered by them. It was selected by a combination of National Union and Central Office representatives. Secondly, Central Office were responsible for compiling the complete British list. Despite the separate organisational structure of the Scottish Conservative Association, they agreed to use the list devised by Euro-SACC. In one sense there was a Scottish list within the British one: the Scottish Conservative Association made it clear that they were only prepared to consider applicants who possessed some Scottish credentials. Ironically, those candidates who could boast Scottish heritage were not prohibited from applying to English as well as to Scottish Euro-constituencies.

The party Vice-Chairman in charge of candidates: The precise influence of the party Vice-Chairman over selection for the Westminster approved list has been debated at length, most notably by Rush and McKenzie. The latter inferred that the views of the Vice-Chairman were paramount and his influence dictated the decisions of the final selection authority, the Standing Advisory Committee on Candidates. SACC, according to McKenzie, became merely a ratifying body, 'rubber-stamping' the Vice-Chairman's recommendtions.(12) Rush agreed that the advice of the Vice-Chairman is seldom rejected, but refused to relegate SACC to such puppet status. He argued that it is a necessary screening body, a safety check upon candidatures, and the absence of confrontation between SACC and the Vice-Chairman results from their common aims and similar criteria for evaluating candidate suitability.

Did the Vice-Chairman play a similar role in selecting candidates for the European approved list? In excess of 1,000 aspiring MEPs applied to Central Office for inclusion on the 'Approved European Candidates List': less than 250 achieved approved status. The central vetting process began with Marcus Fox, the then Vice-Chairman in charge of candidates. All would-be candidates for the list had to be interviewed initially by Fox; the interviews were in general, brief, lasting between fifteen to twenty minutes. Applicants for the list were seen from 1 February 1977 to as late as October 1978. The Vice-Chairman's role was to act as the first selection filter, vetoing those candidates he regarded as unsuitable. The authority of Marcus Fox, as in Westminster selections, was absolute; rejected applicants had no right of appeal. Over 300 individuals were excluded at this preliminary stage. One particularly disappointed interviewee publically voiced her objections:

> one harried back-bencher, with benefit of no formal application procedure, was expected, in 20 minutes conversation, to decide who was worthy to represent the Conservative electorate in Europe. With the best will in the world, no single man should have such a responsibility.(13)

The power wielded by Marcus Fox was substantial. The fact that a totally new list was being chosen and that numbers, were restricted, offered the Vice-Chairman the opportunity for greater involvement and influence. He was in the position to limit the options available to the second and third stages of approval, the National Union Panel and Euro-SACC. He may not have been explicitly able to promote a favourite son, but many aspiring political careers were, at his discretion, still-born.

Those candidates recommended by Fox were forwarded to the next stage in the central vetting process, the National Union panel interview. Prior to the interview candidates were asked to complete a formal application form; if a recommended candidate was not already on the Westminster list he was asked to complete a national as well as European form. The European application form was somewhat perfunctory. It consisted of basic background information - name , UK/European address, date and place of birth, nationality, title, marital status, and, perhaps surprisingly, only four questions designed to evaluate each applicant's European experience, qualifications and political views.(14) As a concluding rider to the application form, it was pointed out that if any applicant was an MP, he would be 'expected to vacate his seat at the following General Election subsequent to his election to the European Parliament'. This limited and undemanding application form was treated as an addition to the more detailed information covered by the Westminster form.

<u>The National Union Panel interview:</u> As for Westminster selections, the second filtering stage consisted of an interview by a panel of the National Union. This aspect of the selection process was poorly documented in 'Notes on Procedure' and has been dealt with only briefly in the standard texts. Prior to 1966, only MPs were involved in selection, but since 1972 the onus has fallen on the appointed members of the National Union, with MPs adopting a subsidiary role. This trend was reflected in the procedures implemented for Europe, where the Union played a major part in determining the composition of the list. The interviewing panel for European applicants was drawn from those with previous experience of the Westminster panel and those with special knowledge of European affairs. It consisted of twelve

parliamentarians (MPs/MEPs) and twelve members of the National Union who operated in differing teams of three with a National Union member in the chair. The composition of the panel was peculiar in one respect. Three of the parliamentary representatives were also aspiring candidates for the direct elections: all three were former appointed MEPs and as such were automatically placed on the European approved list. Thus while being aspirants they were also selectors, even if only at an early central stage.

Panel interviews were approximately thirty minutes in duration. The panel had five options: it could recommend that a candidate be a) included on the list; b) rejected; c) deferred; d) only considered by his local constituency, or e) recommended for a specific area. Recommendations were subject to the approval, or otherwise, of the full European Advisory Committee on Candidates. The panel was not redundant as a selection filter; it constituted an essential step in the selection process. No accurate figures for the panel's refusal rate were available, but one of the National Union's most experienced members estimated that 30.0 per cent of applicants were rejected at this stage, compared to an average of 70.0 per cent for Westminster. As an intermediary filter, the panel was primarily concerned with excluding those who were obviously unsuitable; borderline decisions were left to the full Euro-SACC. The panel did not in any sense merely 'rubber-stamp' the Vice-Chairman's choice.

<u>The Standing Advisory Committee on European Candidates</u>: Once again, the European provisions largely paralleled those devised for Westminster, with Euro-SACC duplicating the role established for the Standing Advisory Committee on Candidates for England and Wales. Euro-SACC considered those applicants recommended by the National Union panel. Applicants were not interviewed: decisions were based on biographical details, recommendations and the advice and information supplied by members of the Committee. As argued previously, one can contend that the approved list was determined more by the National Union than the central party organisation: Euro-SACC personnel were dominated by National Union representives. However, the influential role played by the party's Vice-Chairman in charge of candidates was often the deciding factor. He possessed the widest knowledge of the applicants and was the best equipped to evaluate a candidate. Yet, Euro-SACC was far from superfluous as McKenzie suggested its parliamentary predecessor was. In fact, Euro-SACC was under great pressure to reduce the size of the list and frequently refused to endorse the recommendations put forward by the National Union panel.

Applicants who secured approval were informed incrementally at the end of each month: however, once approved, candidates were instructed to keep this information confidential in order to prevent unfair lobbying by those who gained approval early in the process. It would be naive to assume that no pre-announcement lobbying occurred: the fact that applicants were not informed simultaneously was an important aspect of the recruitment process and had implications for the opportunity structure function of the model. Those guilty of breaking this confidence were liable to be expelled from the list: none were, although one individual was reprimanded by Central Office for such a breach. 11 December was the deadline by which approved candidates had to indicate which of the seventy-eight British Euro-constituencies they wished to apply to: Central Office forwarded the candidates' biographies to their chosen seats, setting the local selection machinery in motion.

Two variations to this selection procedure need to be noted. Firstly, the provisions for local non-approved candidates truncated this three stage process. Marcus Fox plus one member of the National Union panel constituted the screening body, recommending approval or rejection to Euro-SACC. Secondly, a number of Euro-Constituencies were unable to attract either sufficient suitable candidates, or found their short-lists depleted (a consequence of all seventy eight seats effectively selecting over the same six week period). Towards the end of the selection timetable approved candidates were notified by Central Office of any such vacancies and late applicants to the seats in question allowed. A formal list of reopened seats was not compiled, nor was this information uniformly supplied to every non-selected aspirant. Certain individuals were notified because they had originally intimated that they were willing to fight any seat: others took the initiative and approached Central Office or the relative ECCs directly.

Examples of re-opened applications tended to occur in the less desirable seats. The timing of selections was a crucial factor: it was realised that there would be a great fall-out of good aspirants who had unsuccessfully sought safer seats. Central Office asked those seats that were projected as secure Labour Euro-constituencies to select later in order to improve the choice of available applicants. For example, two Scottish seats had virtually no original applications; they waited until the more winnable Scottish seats had selected their PEPCs before inviting further applications. Similarly, two Midlands seats did not commence their selections until late February, thereby attracting a greater number of applications from failed aspirants. There was a clear pattern: the less attractive seats followed Central Office's request and selected later.

(b) Local selection mechanisms

The creation of the approved list of Conservative European candidates corresponds to the central gate-keeping function of the model. However, the more important influence was exerted at the local constituency level. The power of selection, or perhaps more importantly of exclusion, is exercised by the tiny minority of local party members who comprise the initial selection committee. It is these bodies that decide which candidates merit further consideration, and which are to be excluded. Both by formal and informal mechanisms the 'selectorate' nature of British candidate selection has long dominated Westminster politics; the trend was replicated for European selections.(15) Arguably, local gate-keepers have been more influential in determining the success or failure of political careers than any election result. Adoption for a safe seat is usually the beginning of a continuous and lengthy parliamentary career. How did the 'selectorate' process operate for European candidates?

The selection committee: The Model Rules state that the European Constituency Council, composed of six representatives per parliamentary constituency within the Euro-boundary, was the governing body of each Euro-constituency. It was the responsibility of the ECC to form a selection committee (the recommended number was two representatives per association). Thus, as in selection for the House of Commons, the crucial decision of whether to interview or reject an applicant (a judgement based solely upon biographical details) was concentrated in the hands of a very small local inner party caucus.

The number of applications received by each seat was directly related to electoral status. The mean for all Labour seats was 14.7 compared with that of 42.2 for all projected Conservative seats.(16) Although significant, electoral status was not the only factor: other criteria, such as local ties or central location played a role. For example, marginal and semi-marginal London Euro-constituencies tended to attract a disproportionately high level of applicants. However, the general pattern was that selection committees' screening potential increased in relation to a seat's winnability and the corresponding number of applicants.

Of greater importance was the number that actually managed to secure an interview with the selection committee, rather than the total number of applicants. For example, at Thames Valley (the most popular seat in terms of applications), only thirteen of the original sixty-seven hopefuls were actually given the further opportunity to contest for selection: conversely, the Surrey selection committee saw thirty-two candidates. Lancashire East was the only Conservative selection committee to interview every applicant, though this only invovled eight individuals.

Table 4.3

Number of Aspirants Interviewed by Selection Committee

No. Interviewed	% of Seats	No. of Seats
2-5	11.3	7
6-10	35.5	22
11-15	22.6	14
16-20	25.8	16
21 and more	4.8	3
Not Known		16
	100.0	78

By the very act of drawing up a short-list, the selection committee's power extended beyond this first pre-selection screening. From those interviewed, they decided which appeared before the European Constituency Council, the intermediate of the three selection stages. The Model Rules advised that 'not less than five applicants' be interviewed by the ECC: this often proved impossible due to lack of interested candidates. Only one of the four Welsh constituencies received more than four applications and over one quarter of Euro-constituencies failed to meet this requirement.

The European Constituency Council: The ECC was equivalent to a parliamentary constituency executive commitee; it constituted the second local gate-keeping or filtering mechanism. The Model Rules suggested that the ECC be composed of six representatives from each UK constituency within the Euro-boundary.(17) Its crucial function in relation to candidate selection was 'to agree the constitution of the selection committee and the procedure for the adoption of a Prospective Candidate and to proceed with interviews and to make recommendations to a General Meeting in accordance with the 'Notes on Procedure' issued by the Standing Advisory Committee on Candidates'.(18) Where situations demanded (such as a lack of applicants from whom to choose) the selection committee and ECC stages were fused.

Table 4.4

ECC Interviews

No. Interviewed	% of Seats	No. of Seats
3	16.1	10
4	9.7	6
5	38.7	24
6	19.4	12
7 and more	16.1	10
Not Known		16
	100.0	78

General Meeting Short-Lists

Size of Short-List		
2	9.9	7
3	78.9	56
4	8.4	6
5	2.8	2
Not known		7
	100.0	78

Each stage of the local screening machinery increased the number of those involved in the gate-keeping process, though the numbers from which to choose correspondingly diminished. The ECC was responsible for selecting 'at least three applicants' from amongst those recommended by the selection committee to appear before a general meeting of representatives of the constituency associations, the final selection hurdle. The general meeting was not a primary of all eligible party members. All but seven of the known cases followed the party's directive to select at least three individuals to contest the general meeting. Only two seats (both Scottish) intentionally restricted their short-lists to a choice of two: the remaining five Euro-constituencies all suffered from the problem of 'disappearing' short-lists. With all seventy-eight European selections taking place within six weeks, overlapping short-lists were inevitable. Thus, Mid and West Wales, South-East Wales and Kent West all lost one individual from their respective short-lists and Leeds saw two from their short-list of four selected for other seats prior to the general meeting. Lincolnshire had the misfortune of losing the greatest number of short-listed applicants. Of the five interviewed by the ECC, two were selected elsewhere and one withdrew his candidacy. The ECC were thus left with just two on their short-list and no suitable reserves.

The general meeting: At this third and final stage of the local selection process each parliamentary association was allowed equal representation, with a suggested minimum number of twenty-five voting representatives each. Selection was to be by exhaustive ballot, the winning candidate needing to secure 50 per cent plus one of the votes cast. Thus, only after the vast majority of applicants had been filtered out did the rank and file party membership (even in a limited sense) become involved. Furthermore, there was great variation between Euro-constituencies in the number of general meeting representatives allowed per Parliamentary constituency.

Table 4.5

Number of Representatives per Association Attending the European General Meeting

No. of Representatives per association	%	No. of Seats
less than 25	11.4	8
25	58.6	41
26-100	25.7	18
51-100	4.3	3
Not known		8
	100.0	78

Of the eight seats that failed to allow a minimum of twenty-five representatives, four were in Scotland and only one of them a projected Conservative seat, and then only a marginal. Perhaps in these less winnable constituencies participation by the rank and file was difficult to stimulate. The physical size of the Scottish

Euro-seats may also have been an explanatory factor. At the positive end of the participation scale, seven Euro-constituencies allowed 300 or more members to engage in the selection of their European Parliamentary candidate. Essex North East and Bedfordshire both decided upon seventy representatives per association; Hertfordshire favoured wider involvement, quadrupling the recommended minimum number allowing its component associations to each send a hundred representatives. Table 4.6 gives the distribution for the maximum possible size of European general meetings (the number of representatives multiplied by the number of Westminster seats within each Euro-constituency).

Table 4.6

Potential Maximum Size of General Meetings

Max No. of Representatives	%	No. of seats
150 and less	7.0	5
175-199	14.1	10
200	26.8	19
201-225	19.7	14
226-250	12.7	9
251-300	4.2	3
301-350	9.9	7
351 and above	5.6	4
Not known		7
	100.0	78

In comparison to Westminster selections a trend towards openness, at least at the final general meeting stage, can be seen. What is more, the opportunity for greater participation was eagerly accepted by party members. Despite the less than enthusiastic stance by the Conservative leadership concerning the EEC in general, and the elections in particular, the turn-out figures for general meetings were impressive. Over one-quarter realised more than 90.0 per cent involvement by eligible participants, with almost two-thirds above 70.0 per cent (see Table 4.7).

There was also a pronounced relationship between attendance at general meetings and electoral status.(19) The mean attendance percentage for projected Labour seats was 68.9 and 81.6 for Conservative Euro-constituencies. Only Labour marginals exhibited a mean percentage attendance score comparable to that of the Conservative incumbent seats. The previous findings relating to applicant numbers paralleled those for representative attendance figures. Impregnable and safe Labour seats attracted the fewest applicants and had the worst attended general meetings. In the securer Conservative seats, where selection was often tantamount to

Table 4.7

Percentage turn-out of Representatives at General Meetings

% Turn-out	% of seats	No. of seats
100-91	26.1	18
90-81	15.9	11
80-71	23.2	16
70-61	17.4	12
60-51	11.6	8
50 and below	5.8	4
Not known		9
	100.0	78

election, the representatives actively exercised their selection prerogative. However, even in impregnable Labour heartlands, the mean percentage scores were respectable.(20)

The local selection of all the Conservative European prospective candidates took place during the first three months of 1979. The first constituency to complete its selection was Cambridgeshire on 20 January, the last Cleveland, on 31 March. Twelve seats chose during January, a further twenty-one within the first week of February: all bar thirteen had selected their PEPC's before the beginning of March. The three week period from 31 January to 21 February was the most compact, with fifty-one selections taking place (see Figure 4.2). The immediate problems of selection committee, ECC and general meeting clashes were severe, allowing the lottery aspect of European candidacy to emerge. For example, on 3 February, six seats all had their general meetings - four were comfortable Conservative seats, one a semi-marginal and another a projected Labour marginal. In marked contrast to the incremental process for adopting PPCs for Westminster, European candidate options were limited by the time factor.

Table 4.8

General Meeting Timetable by Electoral Status

Date	Labour					Conservative				SNP		
Selection by	I	S	C	SM	M	M	SM	C	S	M/SM	%	N
9 Feb	1	0	2	5	4	6	7	9	2	0	(46.7)	36
18 Feb	0	1	3	4	2	1	1	2	3	1	(23.4)	18
28 Feb	1	4	2	1	0	0	1	1	0	0	(13.0)	10
31 March	3	4	3	0	0	1	0	0	0	2	(16.9)	13
	5	9	10	10	6	8	9	12	5	3	100.0	77

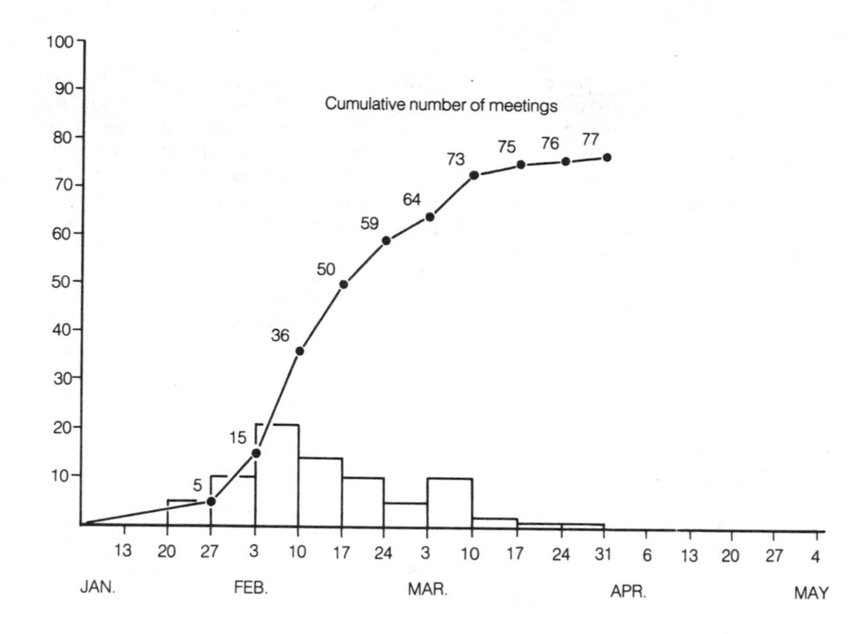

Figure 4.2 General Meetings by Time

It was the least winnable Labour seats that selected latest; only one projected socialist marginal or semi-marginal held its general meeting after 18 February, compared to eighteen (62.5 per cent) of the twenty-four impregnable, safe or comfortable Labour Euro-constitituencies. Conservative seats, regardless of electoral status, generally selected before 18 February (75.0 per cent). Only one of the last fifteen seats to select was a projected Conservative victory, and then only a marginal. Conversely, only two of the first ten seats to select were Labour-held, both semi-marginals.

To summarise, electoral status played a significant role: firstly, as an explanation for differing application levels; secondly, in relation to general meeting representative attendance; and thirdly, as an indicator of a constituency's selection timetable. As advised by Central Office, the least desirable seats chose later.

SELECTION CRITERIA

The procedural machinery for the selection of European candidates created the structural framework within which the central and local selection criteria operated. While the Model Rules mechanistically limited candidacy, the individual decision-making criteria at each stage constituted the more persuasive variable.

Central

The party Vice-Chairman: There has always existed an aura of secrecy surrounding both the identity and the criteria for choosing the Conservative party's approved list of candidates for Westminster: the same was true for Europe. As already noted, Marcus Fox, the party Vice-Chairman, had the unique opportunity to create an approved list free from incumbents, and although his power was not absolute, his influence was substantial. Fox's aim was to create a 'balanced' list. Such a blend required the inclusion of individuals with a wide range of talents and involved recruiting people from non-political backgrounds.

Being on the Westminster list was not a necessary or sufficient prerequisite for obtaining European approval. Fox used two broad criteria for discriminating between the flood of applicants; some previous political involvement, and a European dimension. He was not prepared to encourage those lacking both qualities. However, applicants who lacked one qualification, but were impressive in some other area, were granted a National Union Panel interview: one such exception was Sir Henry Plumb. In this way achievers from outside party politics could be accommodated. Applicants who were still hostile to Britain's membership of the EEC were excluded from further consideration. Approved candidates had to be sympathetic to the concept of Europe, although a healthy scepticism was not discouraged. Indeed, idealistic 'Euro-fanatics' were less likely to be chosen than critical pragmatists. Fox believed that the final list contained a wide range of European attitudes, 'not just starry-eyed federalists'.(21)

No explicit barriers were created, either in terms of sex or age, although older applicants were advantaged by their potential for greater relevant experience. As already noted, the dual-mandate was restricted to certain individuals. Fox was concerned to produce a list that presented a full range of abilities and regional variation from which the local constituencies could choose. The prime aim was to select the best Conservative MEP team in the European Parliament, not simply to produce locally oriented MEPs: although the final local autonomy of choice remained, there was a degree of centralisation and a firm control of the list. In consequence, Fox believed the calibre of the European list was superior to that of its domestic fore-runner.

As on the parliamentary list, women were severely under-represented, accounting for approximately 15.0 per cent of approved candidates. However, it would be misplaced to accuse either the Vice-Chairman in particular, or Central Office in general, of any sexist discrimination. No figures were available relating to the number of female applicants compared to the percentage selected for the list; it may have been that women were relatively more successful than their male competitors. It would seem appealing to argue that discrimination was societal, linked to patterns of formative socialisation and the resultant imbalance in the list a consequential manifestation. In short, for a variety of reasons women were less likely to see themselves as possible candidates. One interesting feature is that approved female candidates were more likely to be single than their male counterparts (exactly half of the sixteen known approved listed women); the equivalent figure for men was 3.6 per cent. Furthermore, three of the married women aspirants had previously proved themselves as capable politicians, and thus diffused one of the traditional arguments against selecting a woman candidate, namely that family life would interfere with their political commitments.(22)

Salary was one further specific criterion considered by Fox. During the interviewing period for the approved list, there was speculation concerning the future salaries of MEPs: Fox did not want to recruit those individuals who were interested in the financial rewards of Europe. In December 1978 the heads of the national governments of the Nine met in Brussels and agreed that MEPs should receive the same salaries as national MPs from the same country and be subject to their own national rates of taxation. Thus the Parliament operated nine different rates of pay, the deciding criterion being nationality, not occupation. Only MEPs from Luxembourg were to earn less than British MEPs, whereas the net income for the two highest paid national MEPs (French and Belgian) was four times the British figure. Six of the approved Conservative candidates withdrew at this point. Marcus Fox argued that such a small number of withdrawals proved that the list had successfully selected the right applicants. Nor did he criticise the six who withdrew: they were 'people in the middle of their business careers, earning 10,000 pounds or 15,000 pounds a year with no other means of support'.(23)

Obviously the operating criteria at the initial selection stage were broad and not totally rigid. Certain basic qualities or attributes were sufficient: however, over 300 applicants failed to qualify for the National Union interview. The system was not without criticism. An article in The Daily Telegraph reported an under-current of discontent amongst some rejected applicants. It was argued that under the guidance of Marcus Fox, Central Office had 'actively discouraged those without European experience or beyond fifty from pursuing their ambitions'.(24) This latter claim seems unjust: 40.0per cent of the 122 approved candidates that were surveyed fell into the fifty to sixty-seven age bracket, one-quarter being over sixty. To discourage those without any European experience from standing as an MEP candidate seemed sensible rather than discriminatory, and supports the criteria outlined as relevant by Marcus Fox.

National Union Panel: The structure of the interviewing panels makes any discussion of selection criteria limited; generalisation rather than specific explanation is all that is possible. While a history of constituency work and a record of party affiliation were prerequisites for Westminster candidacy, evidence of such loyalty was not demanded from potential MEPs: being a 'Conservative' in the broadest sense was adequate. Thus the National Union panel considered applicants who were only peripherally connected with the party, and their deciding criteria were more fluid, but not in conflict with those employed by Fox. No formal guidelines were devised, but as a group the panel utilised similar collective criteria.

AGE - Applicants of all ages were considered, the youngest being twenty-five, the eldest a seventy-nine year old ex-MP; however, those under thirty tended to be discouraged unless they could offer an excepional contribution.

LANGUAGES - Competence in a second Community language was not a

formal requirement: capable linguists were very much the exception.
EUROPEAN COMMITMENT - A commitment to any European federal ideal was not regarded as a selection criterion and membership of the Conservative Group for Europe was not demanded; not professing 'European' beliefs was not a reason for exclusion from the list.
CONTRIBUTIONS - The theme of looking for achievers from outside politics was evident. Some contribution at a high level in the sphere that the applicant had developed his career was the overriding criterion; political contributions were of secondary importance.
FINANCIAL REWARD - Those thought to be seeking financial gain were refused admission to the list. Similarly, anyone who treated the European Parliament as a ladder to Westminster was omitted from consideration.
DUAL MANDATE - The National Union panel did not use this as a discriminating criterion. Indeed, several of their members were potentially dual mandated.
MARITAL STATUS - It is commonly suggested that single applicants are disadvantaged in domestic selections; being single was not a disadvantage for European candidates. Those applicants who were married were simply asked to state their spouse's attitude towards their candidacy.
LOYALTY TO THE LEADERSHIP - Questions were occasionally asked concerning an applicant's support of Mrs Thatcher. This was used as a criterion where it was thought the applicant was a former Heath supporter, or in some way hostile to the current leadership.

The compatible aims and criteria used by the National Union and Marcus Fox supports the earlier comments concerning the power of the Vice-Chairman in charge of candidates: agreement did not imply subservience, but that there existed widespread acceptence of the relevant criteria for evaluating candidate suitability.

So far, the Central Office perspective of the process has been discussed. How did this perspective compare to the comments of elected, selected and rejected applicants concerning the general central screening criteria? Adverse remarks by aspiring MEPs were rare: in general the central procedure was regarded as appropriate, satisfactory and efficient. The greatest criticism related to the short time span that covered the selection process. Although Central Office had been interviewing applicants since early 1977, there was a glut of candidacies in late 1978. This, coupled with the boundaries delay and the simultaneous local selection meetings led several approved listed candidates to criticise Central Office for poor planning.

Perhaps the most surprising finding was that some applicants felt the interviewers at Central Office knew little about the EEC, and that selection was determined more by domestic political considerations than European expertise. One successful candidate stated that 'the interviewing panels were far less expert than most of the interviewees ... The contrast was greater than for Westminster since people know less about the EEC'. The comments of an MEP from the South-East were in a similar vein:

> Selection (was) by a committee whose questions bore the vaguest relation to Europe. The most surrealistic interview I have ever undergone. The written evidence they had asked for had clearly not been read. All in all, Central Office at its

non-meritocratic worst...to get on the initial list was the worst sort of arbitrary selection.

Several approved candidates found the National Union panel parochial, often being more concerned with evaluating local political work, campaign experience and motivation than with any European dimension of candidacy.

More general criticisms were made relating to the lack of professionalism exhibited in the Central Office selection procedure. One MEP's scathing comment was that it seemed 'incompetent by comparison with industry, but probably enough adequate people get through. Some excellent ones fall by the wayside'. Another MEP was equally damning: 'much of the interviewing was of a style and nature that was incompetent and frequently infantile'. A non-selected approved candidate cited a similar complaint: he felt that his interview 'was amateurish in the extreme - neither party seemed to have any idea of what the Common Market actually was'. These isolated complaints were the exception; it would be wrong to conclude that there was a general level of criticism. The different centralised selection outcomes which may have seemed contradictory simply reflect the variations in National Union panel personnel. Any procedure involving the use of several ad hoc interviewing boards must inevitably produce a wide variation in the adoption and application of criteria.

Basic background information covering the 118 approved listed respondents offered a partial test for estimating the success of the selection criteria in shaping the eventual chosen approved list. Namely, in what sense was the Euro-list a balanced list? Did it contain a significant number of non-political achievers who possessed European expertise?

The problems of correctly classifying occupations are formidable. Mellor's discussion of the British MP, pinpointed the major difficulty as that of multiple occupations.(25) With this qualification in mind, each approved candidate was assigned to one of the twenty-seven Office of Population Censuses and Surveys (OPCS) occupational groups.(26) Less than 10.0 per cent of approved candidates fell outside the Administrator-Manager or Professional/Technical/ Artist categories (Groups XXIV, XXV).(27) The socio-economic homogeneity of the list is even more overwhelming when one realises that all the respondents classified in Groups I-XX were farm owners or farm managers, not manual workers. By simply looking at occupations we can go some way to testing whether the list matched Marcus Fox's desired criteria. Occupational group classifications are obviously not precise measures of 'achievement', but they are the best predictors available. However, without knowing the cohort characteristics of non-approved candidates, or approved non-respondents, the inferences drawn from the data can only be tentative. While the examination of approved candidates is preferable to simply looking at legislators as a means of recruitment analysis, the methodological goals of the study are only partially satisfied. It must also be realised that the data-set probably tends to over-represent selected applicants and MPs and under-represent the less well-known applicants.

With these reservations in mind, the pattern remains clear: 59.3 per cent of approved candidates came from the higher echelons of British society - MP/Peers, senior Civil Service, company directors, professional workers, merchant bankers, accountants, 'Eurocrats' and the legal profession. They were, to quote the 'Notes on Procedure', individuals who had 'already distinguished (themselves) in other fields'.(28) In terms of previous parliamentary experience the respondents surveyed appeared to partially fulfil the 'non-political achievers' criterion. Whilst 58.1 per cent had at some time been included on the Westminster list of approved candidates (40.5 per cent of whom were currently on the list), only sixteen (13.6 per cent) were MPs at the time of selection, ten of whom were on the European list by virtue of their former appointed MEP status. Central Office's policy of discouraging existing prospective parliamentary candidates standing for Europe was fully reflected in the total absence of PPCs from the approved list. Only Paul Howell was a PPC (Normantion) prior to his selection as PEPC for Norfolk. He, however, was not on the original approved list, but a local applicant.

Table 4.9 gives the distribution of elections fought by those on the approved list. Exactly 50.0 per cent had at some time been parliamentary candidates: of those unelected, seventeen had contested both the 1974 elections. In addition, eight of the approved list were Peers.

Table 4.9

Number of Elections Fought by Aspirants from the Approved List

	No. of elections fought	%	n
i) Non-elected Individuals	None	50.0	59
	1	12.7	15
	2	17.0	20
	3-5	3.4	4
ii) MPs	1-5	5.1	6
	6-7	3.4	4
	8 and more	4.2	5
iii) Former MPs	3	3.4	4
	11	0.8	1
		100.0	118

While Central Office did not require applicants for the approved list to have electoral experience, such experience was clearly advantageous, as was any parliamentary experience in either the Commons or the Lords. Whether successfully selected candidates or elected MEPs were drawn disproportionately from this politically experienced group will be examined later.

At the local level, 40.2 per cent of the approved list had fought a local government election, of whom 85.1 per cent had been elected.(29) Other forms of political involvement were primarily restricted to local constituency office holding. One approved candidate (who was later adopted) professed a somewhat unique relevant past contribution - former membership of the Labour Party!

How did the 'European dimension' criterion match the final approved list's characteristics? 64.8 per cent of respondents claimed membership of the European Movement, with 68.6 per cent members of the Conservative Group for Europe. Quite what either membership implied in terms of the candidate and the selectors' perception of the candidate, is not clear.(30) How well did the list correspond to the anti 'starry-eyed federalist' criterion outlined by Marcus Fox? There was a trend supporting moderate reform: less than one in ten felt that the powers of the EEC needed to be reduced in relation to domestic parliaments, but a majority, 57.1 per cent, were anti-federalist with only 28.6 per cent convinced pro-federalists. The existing powers of the European Parliament were generally regarded as inadequate. 73.6 per cent believed that the European Parliament should be given wider powers. In particular, over a quarter of respondents argued that the Parliament should be a legislative chamber with fiscal authority and have the right to select, not simply dismiss, the Commission. Only one respondent stated that he was an anti-Marketeer. One possibly surprising finding was that 15.1 per cent saw being on the European approved list as a route to Westminster and not a potential career in itself, in conflict with the National Union's aim of excluding all such political careerists.

A number of those on the approved list could be described as 'Eurocrats'. For example, Ben Patterson was Deputy head of the London Office of the European Parliament, Robert Sheaf held the equivalent post at the London Office of the Commission and Basil de Ferranti had served as President of the European Economic and Social Committee of the Commission. Six others had ties or former ties with the Commission. Derek Prag had been a civil servant in the Commission; Robert Battersby had been Principal Administrator; Anthony Simpson had worked for the legal service of the Commission; Stanley Johnson was a former head of the Environmental Pollution Division; and Andrew Pearce an official of the Customs Department of the Commission. Lastly, Robert Jackson had been Chef de Cabinet to the Chairman of the EEC's Social and Economic Committee between 1976-78; prior to this appointment, he worked for Sir Christopher Soames (as he was then) in the office of the Vice-Chairman of the Commission. All nine were elected on 7 June.

While not classified as Eurocrats, other applicants were obviously qualified in terms of their European experience. Sir Henry Plumb was President of the Comite des Organisations Professionalles Agricoles (COPA), and as such had had experience in negotiating within the EEC. John D. Taylor had sat on an agricultural working party of the European Community as an NFU representative: David Curry had been The Financial Times Brussels correspondent in 1975, and Christopher Prout and Clive Stanbrook, were experts on EEC law. Others had vague and undefined business ties with Europe. In addition to this group of people with European experience, obviously the former dual mandated MEPs must be included as having relevant European credentials.

There are no academic works relating to the socio-demographic composition of the Conservative party's approved list for

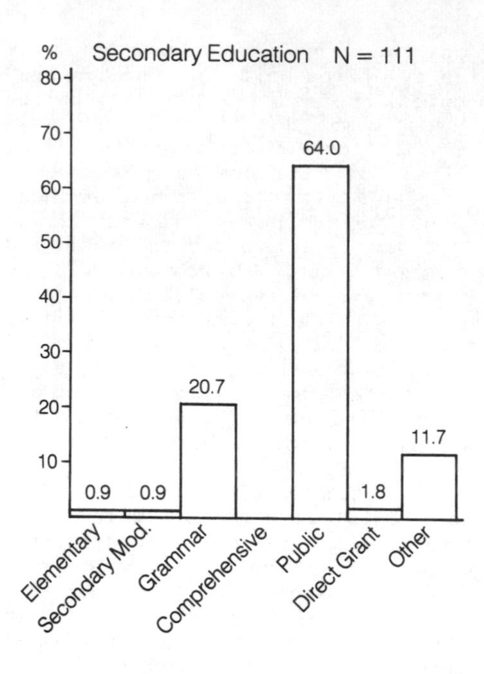

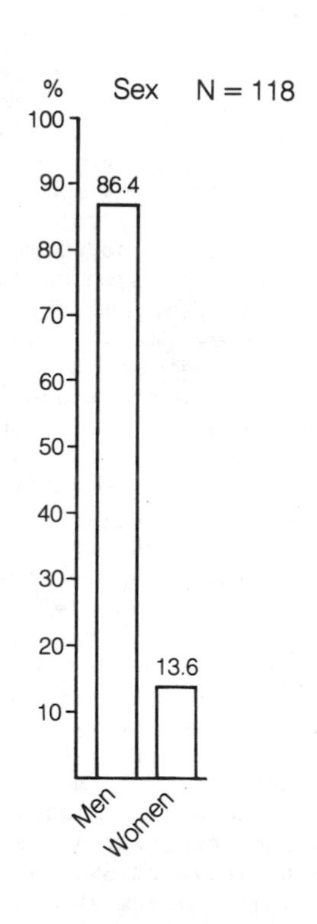

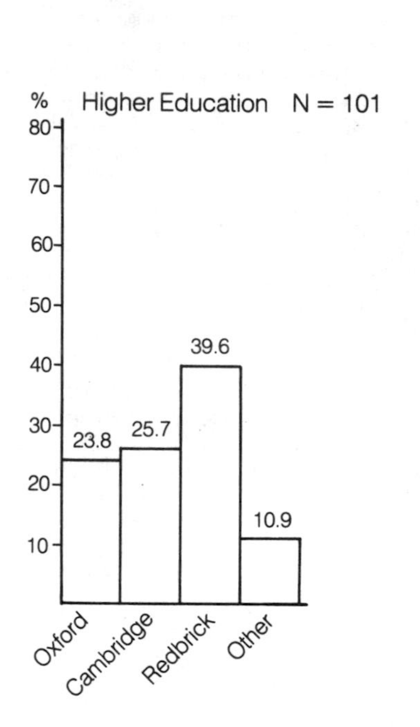

Figure 4.3 Background Characteristics of the Conservative Approved List

Westminster candidates, thus comparison with data for the European approved list was not possible. However, the following statistics give a base against which the profiles of selected, non-selected and elected cohorts can be matched. Figure 4.3 gives the educational skew for the approved list sample. Virtually two-thirds of the list were educated at a public school. What is more, 31.0 per cent of those educated at public schools attended one of the Clarendon schools.(31) 87.8 per cent of respondents received some form of higher education, predominantly at University level, and at Oxbridge in particular. 32.5 per cent of the list had received the combined benefits of a public school/Oxbridge education. The age range was considerable, from twenty eight to sixty nine.(32) Lastly, men dominated the list; of those approved candidates surveyed, only sixteen were women.

(c) Local selection criteria

The problems of delineating a coherent set of recruitment and selection criteria at the central level were formidable. Examination of the criteria used for seventy-eight different local selections compounds the problem: different ECCs valued different qualities and attributes. Although there is a sense in which each selection was unique, nevertheless certain broad patterns were evident.

The policy relating to the dual mandate was made centrally: MPs were not automatically debarred, but strongly discouraged except in particular instances. The local selection committees generally conformed to this central view. Butler and Marquand found that 'almost all the twelve Conservative MPs at Strasbourg were keen to continue with a dual mandate and there were at least a dozen who aspired to go to Strasbourg without giving up their Westminster seats'.(33) Twenty-eight European constituencies received applications from potential dual mandated MEPs. There were a number of examples where MPs were rejected despite (or perhaps because of) being the elected representative for a domestic seat within the Euro-constituency: this occurred in Devon, Sheffield, Suffolk, London Central, London North-West, Sussex East, Kent West and Salop and Stafford. There were no such objections at Wessex, where the MP for Dorset West was adopted as their dualmandated candidate. Three other MPs indicated they intended to resign their Westminster seats at the next available general election and seek selection as candidates for the European Parliament. Only one, Sir James Scott-Hopkins, was adopted by a Euro-constituency: the other two failed to get as far as the ECC interview stage.(34)

The position of Peers and the dual mandate was less contentious. Although members of the legislative branch of government, their non-elected status removed the problem of overlapping and possibly conflicting constituency commitments. Indeed, the House of Lords was mooted by some as the solution to the problem of linking MPs and MEPs institutionally by making MEPs members of the Upper House while in office. A peerage, however, was no more a guarantee of selection than was membership of the Commons. Specific barriers to selection were rare. Five Euro-constituencies regarded age as pertinent to selection, with one, refusing to consider applicants who fell outside the thirty to sixty year old bracket. Four other Euro-constituencies stated that only candidates from the approved list would be considered. However, the vast majority did not adopt negative criteria to exclude certain types of applicants.

How local associations would react to their new role as European selectors was unknown. As a method for gauging local gate-keeping, Euro-agents were asked to indicate the criteria used by their respective selection committees and ECCs for determining the composition of the final general meeting short list. The multiple responses are given in Table 4.10.

Table 4.10

Short-Listing Selection Criteria

N = 53

Criteria	%	n
Knowledge of the EEC	96.2	51
Previous Electoral Experience	56.6	30
Language Ability	54.7	29
Local Connections	47.2	25
Age	45.3	24
Industrial Expertise	35.8	19
Agricultural Expertise	34.0	18
Work Experience in the EEC	32.1	17
Marital Status	3.8	2
Sex	1.9	1

The seeming contradiction between the finding that only five Euro-constituencies used age as a barrier and the high percentage of responses for 'age' in Table 4.10 can be reconciled. The table refers to collective selection criteria in a positive sense; these ten items were not barriers for exclusion. Thus while age was deemed important in twenty-four Euro-constituencies, only in five instances was a candidate outside the chosen age range excluded automatically.

The examination of isolated criteria is not the most perceptive line of analysis: the combination of criteria is the more realistic evaluation. There was almost complete unanimity between Euro-constituencies, stressing 'knowledge of the EEC' as an essential criterion. This, together with previous electoral experience and language ability were the most commonly mentioned qualities, with connections with the local Euro-constituencies a close fourth. The absence of marital status or sex as pertinent criteria is an interesting departure from the findings for Westminster.

Electoral status was tested for as an explanation of differing selection criteria: the difference between projected incumbent Labour and Conservative seats was clear. It should not be surprising that Conservative seats (where the selectors were likely to be choosing a future MEP rather than just a candidate) displayed a greater concern for selecting someone who possessed language skills than those districts that were Labour held. Similarly, the opposite relationship for the criterion of former electoral experience seemed equally reasonable. Experience in fighting elections was regarded as a more important asset in those seats where the Conservatives were the challenging rather than incumbent party.

What criteria did the applicants themselves feel were being used by selection committee members? One MEP denied that there was any coherent logic underlying selection. He saw selection as based on 'luck - if you made the right speech at the right stage'. Another MEP supported this belief, describing the process as 'selection by attrition', with weather conditions and timetabling being the crucial criteria. Other candidates made specific complaints about the type of candidate being selected, thus implying criticism of the differentiating criteria employed by certain selectors. An adopted candidate for one of the southern seats attacked the aristocratic and sycophantic nature of the Conservative team: 'whilst having the final selection made by 250-400 people paid due regard to the democratic process, it put a premium on the ability of some candidates to charm their way to selection, particularly if they had a title'. Another PEPC argued that 'too many elderly people and not enough women or younger people (were) likely to be elected' whereas the prospective candidate for a London seat thought local selectors were 'too biased in favour of European technocrats, and not biased enough in favour of people with the hard experience of campaigning and constituency work'. One selected candidate questioned the whole competence of local selectors: she believed that 'in some cases the committees did not understand the questions they were asking, never mind the answers'.

That candidates' and selectors' criteria perceptions were in conflict should not be surprising. What looked organised and rational to the selectors may have appeared chaotic and haphazard to the applicants: nor is it surprising that non-selected aspirants were the more vociferous in their accusations. The most common criticism concerned the ability of selectors to evaluate applicants in terms of any European dimension. The comments of four rejected aspirants from the approved list illustrate the point. One, a rejected European aspirant and MP, felt that the 'standard of questioning was below the quality expected and was very often derived from beliefs about Europe rather than facts'. Another disappointed applicant recounted a similar experience,

> although it is very democratic process, I think too much power is left to local constituency committees ... Central Office thought that their intervention would have been looked upon with disfavour, whereas I found many cases where it was said that it would have been welcomed as local people often had little knowledge of what qualifications would be most useful in Europe.

A third restated this view more forcefully: 'the local selection committees were low in their knowledge of the requirements of an effective MEP and had little conceptual appreciation of the role or relevance of the MEP to their constituencies'. Lastly, a fourth rejected applicant argued that the qualities used by certain selectors were unreal and 'many had scant European knowledge and just imagined the candidate could speak half a dozen Euro-languages'.

Conclusions

The formal structures for the selection of European candidates generally mirrored those used for Westminster selections in the Conservative party. Access to the political opportunity structure was centrally controlled. The overwhelming majority of aspirants were drawn from the European approved list designed by the party Vice-Chairman, the National Union and Euro-SACC: 'local' aspirants were the exception. A small number of dual mandated candidates were encouraged to stand, although in general the party was opposed to this duplication of roles. Within this central framework the local autonomy of selection was preserved and representative participation vigorous. The final choice of candidate was firmly in the hands of each Euro-constituency.

At both the central and local levels, selection criteria were developed and the gate-keeping aspects of the process dominated. The central criteria, epitomized by Marcus Fox, disadvantaged 'starrey-eyed' federalists in favour of pragmatists with European and/or political experience. At the local level, whilst criteria varied between Euro-constituencies common features were evident. In particular, knowledge of the EEC, previous electoral experience and language ability were cited as relevant consideraions: neither marital status or sex were important selection criteria.

Notes

(1) One further MP, Paul Channon, was later recruited by the party leadership as the potential head of the Conservative delegation in Europe. However, he failed to secure selection in his local Euro-constituency of Essex North East and withdrew from the selection competition. Similarly, Geoffrey Rippon who had initially declined to allow his name to be included on the approved list, was the subject of much last minute subterfuge as Central Office attempted, albeit unsuccessfully, to secure his selection in a safe seat.

(2) One example occurred in Norfolk where Paul Howell was selected. He was the adopted candidate for Normanton but resigned prior to seeking Euro-SACC's approval of his European candidacy.

(3) The comments of the ECC chairman were as follows: 'I was approached by the Tory Party Chairman, Lord Thorneycroft, and was asked if Mr Channon could be a late addition', Essex County Standard, 9.2.1977.

(4) M. Rush, The Selection of Parliamentary Candidates, London, Nelson, 1969, p.21.

(5) The Guardian, 22.2.1979, p.5. Such streamlining or pruning is a common feature of post-election procedures in the Conservative party, although successive Vice-Chairman have given the impression that such an operation is an organisational innovation. See M. Rush, "Political Recruitment, Representation and Participation", in J.P. Mackintosh (ed.), People and Parliament, Farnborough, Saxon

House 1978, p.19.

(6) M. Rush (1969), *op.cit.*, p.14.

(7) *Ibid.*, p.15.

(8) M. Holland, "The Selection of Parliamentary Candidates, contemporary developmnts and the impact of the European elections", *Parliamentary Affairs*, vol. 34, 1981.

(9) This duplicates the contemporary procedure for Westminster selections - see M. Rush, "Political Recruitment" in J.P. Mackintosh (ed.), *op.cit.*

(10) Preparing for the European Elections, Conservative Central Office, 1978, p.9.

(11) *Ibid.*, p.9.

(12) R.T. Mckenzie, *British Political Parties*, (2nd ed.), London, Heinnemann, 1963, p.21.

(13) *The Daily Telegraph*, J. Reneson Keen, "Letters To The Editor", 25.1.1979.

(14) The four 'European' questions were:

1. Have you lived or worked in any of the eight other countries of the EEC or have you had any professional dealings with them? Please give details.
2. Which, if any, European languages do you speak well and to what degree of fluency?
3. What other interests, qualifications or experience do you have which might qualify you for membership of the European Parliament?
4. How do you see the Community developing a) in the short-term? b) in the long-term?

(15) P. Paterson, *The Selectorate: the Case for Primary Elections in Britain*, London, MacGibbon and Kee, 1967.

(16) The actual distributions for applications by electoral status were: projected Labour seats - impregnable, 8.6; safe, 11.9, comfortable 17.0; semi-marginal, 12.1; marginal, 23.8; projected Conservative seats - marginal, 34.7; semi-marginal, 41.7; comfortable, 42.6; safe, 52.4.

(17) *Preparing for the European Elections*, *op.cit.*, pp4-5. In addition, one UK Member of Parliament, chairman, Hon. treasurer and Central Office agent or deputy Central Office agent for the area concerned, plus a maximum of four non-voting co-opted members could attend, all in an advisory capacity.

(18) *Ibid.*, p.6.

(19) The mean percentage attendance at general meetings by electoral status were: projected Labour seats - impregnable, 60.4; safe, 62.7; comfortable 70.9; semi-marginal, 69.6; marginal, 81.1; projected Conservative seats - marginal 85.5; semi-marginal, 80.0; comfortable, 92.0; safe, 91.6.

(20) If the lowest figure of 36.0 per cent attendance in one Welsh Euro-constituency is excluded the mean for this group rises to 65.0 per cent. The mean scores for the four Welsh constituencies (irrespective of their electoral status) was the lowest statistic of all (56.6 per cent). Candidate applications for Wales were comparably low (mean = 4.25).

(21) Interview with Marcus Fox, party Vice-Chairman in charge of candidates, 1.3.1979.

(22) For comparative studies concerning the role of gender in the

selection process for Westminster candidates, see: J. Hills, "Candidates: the impact of of gender", *Parliamentary Affairs*, vol. 34., 1981; J. Rasmussen, "Women's Role in Contemporary British Politics", *Parliamentary Affairs*, vol.36., 1983; E. Vallance, "Women Candidates in the 1983 General Election", *Parliamentary Affairs*, vol.37., 1984; V. Randall, *Women and Politics*, London, MacMillan, 1982.

(23) *The Daily Telegraph*, 2.1.1979.

(24) *The Daily Telegraph*, 28.12.1978.

(25) C. Mellors, *The British MP*, Farnborough, Saxon House, 1978, p.59.

(26) *Classification of Occupations*, Office of Population Censuses and Surveys, London, HMSO, 1970. This classification is used by the British Election Study, Essex University. The following amendments were made: personnel managers, industrial relations advisors, 'Eurocrats', Peers, and marketing occupations were included in group XXIV; lecturers in higher education, company directors and merchant bankers group XXV.

(27) The actual distribution of the Conservative approved list by OPCS group was: Groups I-XX (manual, engineering, transport, industrial and agricultural workers) 3.4 per cent; Groups - XXI-III and XXVII (Clerical, Sales, Service, unclassified) 5.9 per cent; Group XXIV (Adminisrators and Managers) 33.9 per cent; Group XXV (Professional, Technical Workers and Artists) 56.8 per cent.

(28) *Notes on Procedure for the Adoption of Conservative Candidates in England and Wales*, Conservative and Unionist Central Office, 1978, p.5.

(29) n = 117; 47.

(30) n = 68; 72.

(31) Eleven from Eton, three each from Harrow and Westminster, two from Rugby and one apiece from Shrewsbury, Merchant Taylors and Winchester, leaving Charterhouse and St. Paul's the odd men out with no European approved candidates.

(32) mean = 46.9; median = 49; n = 118. Actual distribution was: 0-39 years, 23.7 per cent; 40-49, 32.2 per cent; 50-59, 30.5 per cent; and 60 and above, 13.6 per cent.

(33) D. Butler and D. Marquand, *European Elections and British Politics*, London, Longman, 1981.

(34) Their ages, seventy-two and seventy-three were a major disadvantage for both candidates. One of the Euro-constituencies involved applied an age restriction (over sixty) to automatically exclude certain applicants.

5 Conservative candidate and aspirant profiles

This study has been highly critical of the inadequacy of past approaches to the process of recruitment in British politics. This chapter posits a remedy and examines data for Conservative aspirants in relation to the MEP model. The guiding hypothesis is that there are significant differences and similarities between elected, selected and rejected aspirants.

Prospective European Parliamentary Candidates and Rejected Aspirants

What variables can be used as plausible explanations of why certain aspirants were selected to stand as Conservative candidates for the European Parliament whilst others were rejected? Do these two groups (PEPCs and rejected aspirants/applicants display any significant differences that might be used as part of a wider explanation?(1) While this chapter focuses purely upon aspirant and candidate characteristics, the analysis must not be divorced from the description of the selection process and the evaluation of criteria previously discussed. Four areas are examined to test for differences in recruitment relevant variables; background characteristics; previous electoral experience; the European dimension; and motivation and ambition.

a) Background characteristics: Consideration of biographical characteristics is the traditional basis for candidate analysis. As such, they represent the initial starting point for more elaborate inquiry; they do not, in themselves, constitute a sufficient explanation of political candidacy. Mellors has warned against the over-ambitious goals of this approach: 'It is a short step from arguing that the social profile of our political leaders is an important way of understanding the opportunities available for political recruitment to suggesting that a set of socio-economic background variables are the main causal factor in the attitudes and preferences adopted by these leaders'.(2)

Comparison of the age distribution between selected and rejected aspirants produced a positive relationship: while the age range was similar for both groups, PEPCs were considerably younger than their non-selected colleagues. Whereas applicants in their forties were as likely to be selected as rejected, 35.9 per cent of adopted candidates were aged under forty, compared with only 9.3 per cent of failed aspirants. Conversely, only 7.7 per cent of PEPCs were aged sixty or more in contrast to the non-selected group of whom more than one in five were over sixty. Inferences can be drawn from these age characteristics: relative youth did not seem to be a selection disadvantage, whereas relative old age may have been.

The sex distribution for selected and rejected aspirants displayed no significant differences. For both groups the paucity of female contenders was evident: only one in eight PEPCs and one in nine rejected applicants were women: being married was the norm for all applicants. Although public school was the typical form of secondary education irrespective of selection status, those who failed to gain a seat were predominantly public school products. The similiarity of both groups was also evident in higher education: approximately nine out of ten had undertaken tertiary training, almost exclusively at University. Lastly, just over one third of both groups had a public school/Oxbridge background.

The occupational distribution for non-selected applicants may have been distorted by the disproportionate number of MPs in the survey population. With this reservation in mind, the OPCS categories produced the following occupational groupings. Both selected and non-selected applicants were drawn from the higher echelons of British society: 85.9 per cent of PEPCs and 94.5 per cent of rejected applicants came from the two highest socio-economic groups. The range of occupations made comparison difficult: however, the following interesting characteristics emerged. The most favoured occupations for successful selection were that of 'Eurocrat', farmer, author/journalist and 'professional worker'. All eight 'Euro-crats' were chosen as PEPCs, as were all seven farmers and all twelve individuals classified simply as professional workers: all bar one author/journalist gained adoption. Conversely, company directors, MPs and senior civil servants were the least favoured occupations. In summary, age and occupation were the most distinctive background characteristics for differentiating PEPCs from rejected applicants.

(b) Previous electoral experience: The majority of both selected and non-selected applicants had, at some time, been on the approved list for Westminster candidates, with approximately four out of ten still on the domestic list at the time of their selection for Europe.(3) Five MPs, Sir Brandon Rhys Williams, Tom Normanton, James Scott-Hopkins, Jim Spicer and Elaine Kellet-Bowman were all adopted, leaving the remaining twelve MPs in the rejected aspirant category. 47.4 per cent of PEPCs had stood as parliamentary candidates for Westminster, although just seven of thirty seven former Westminster candidates had ever been members of the House of Commons: the five serving MPs plus Lord Harmer Nicholls and Basil de Ferranti. There was a similar degree of campaign experience among the rejected aspirants. In addition to the twelve sitting

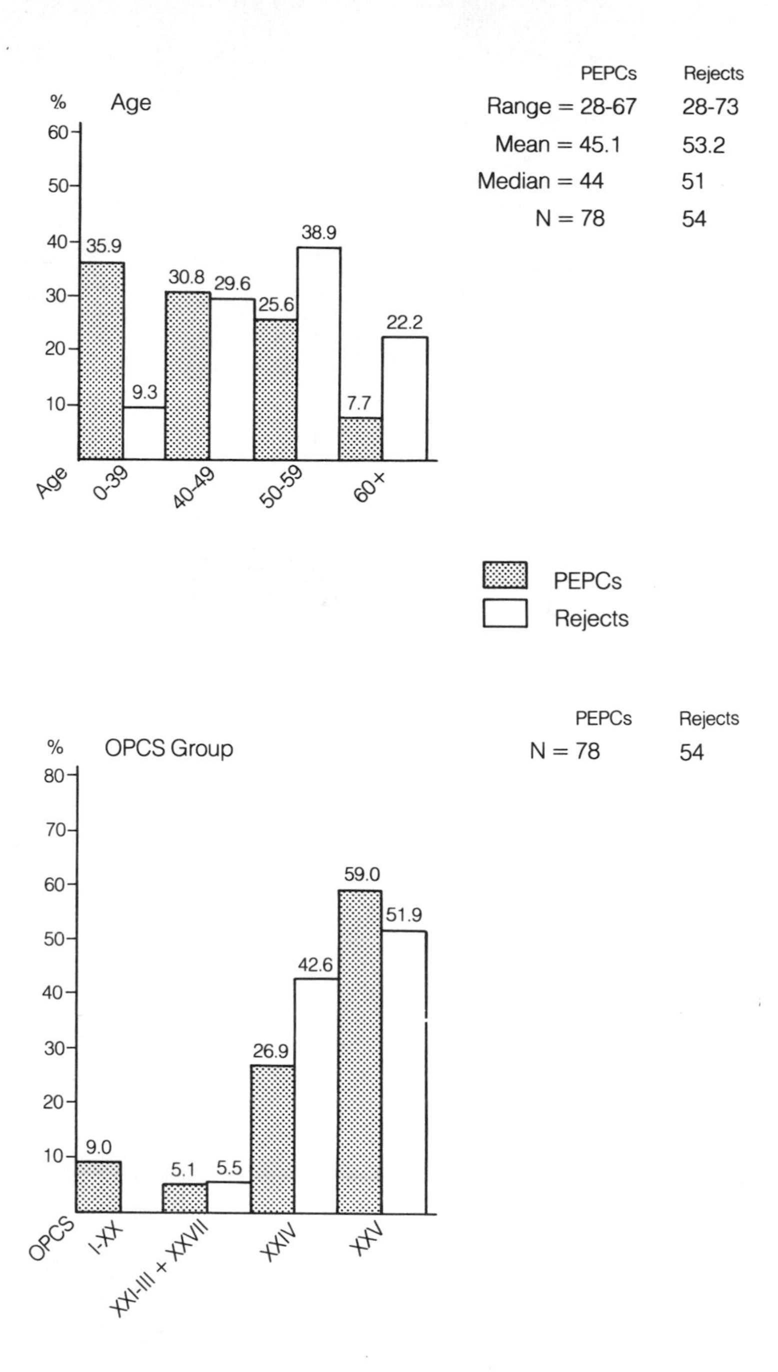

Figure 5.1 Background Characteristics of Conservative PEPCs and Rejected Aspirants

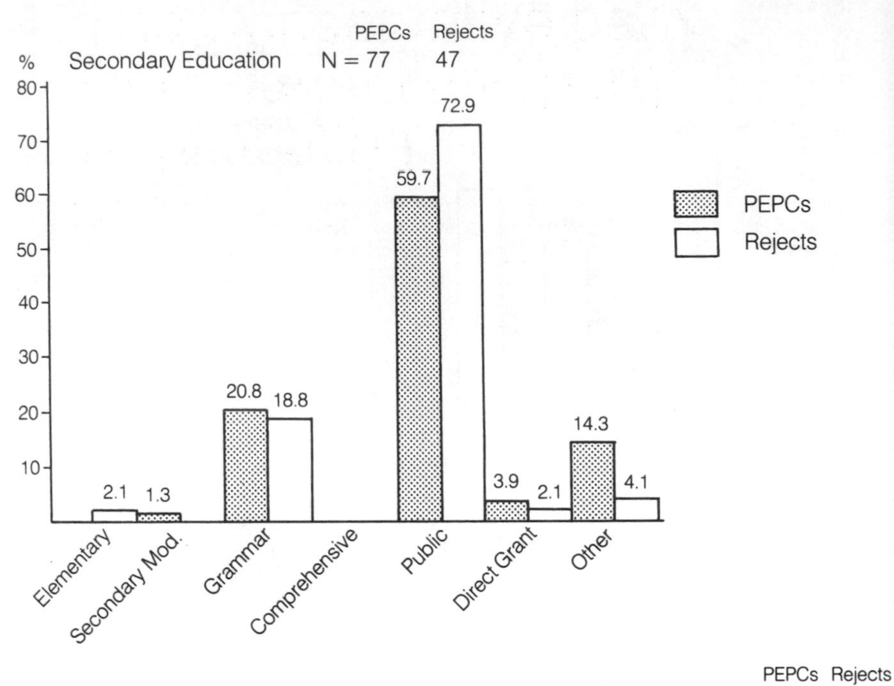

PEPCs Rejects
% Secondary Education N = 77 47
80
70
60
50
40
30
20
10
72.9
59.7
20.8 18.8
14.3
2.1 1.3
3.9 2.1
4.1
PEPCs
Rejects
Elementary
Secondary Mod.
Grammar
Comprehensive
Public
Direct Grant
Other

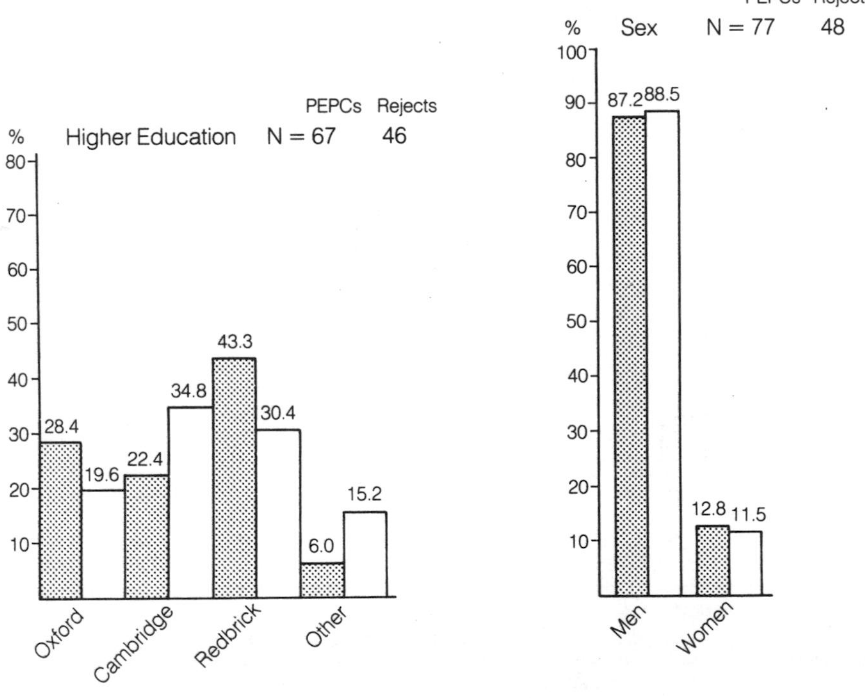

PEPCs Rejects
% Higher Education N = 67 46
80
70
60
50
40
30
20
10
43.3
34.8
28.4
30.4
22.4
19.6
15.2
6.0
Oxford
Cambridge
Redbrick
Other
PEPCs Rejects
% Sex N = 77 48
100
90
80
70
60
50
40
30
20
10
87.2 88.5
12.8 11.5
Men
Women

MPs, a further twelve aspirants had at some time fought a general election, although only two had been elected. Despite the success of five of their parliamentary colleagues, rejected MPs seem to have been handicapped by the reluctance of local selectors to choose potentially dual-mandated candidates. Five of the eight peers who sought selection were chosen as candidates.

There was virtually no difference in the local government experience of the two aspirant groups: 40.3 per cent of the selected and 42.6 per cent of the non-selected category had contested at least one local government election and the means for years service as councillors were almost identical.(4) In terms of apprenticeship roles, given that involvement at the local association level was the most common activity irrespective of selection, PEPCs tended to be more involved at the national office level.

12.8 per cent of PEPCs compared with only 3.8 per cent of rejects were local candidates whose names were not on the original list of Conservative approved candidates. Geography seems to have been an important factor: five of the eight Scottish Euro-constituencies selected local applicants. All five were subsequently approved by Euro-SACC. Electoral status also appears to have played a role: the least winnable seats often had to co-opt or recruit local 'flagwavers'. Seven of the Euro-constituencies that selected local applicants were projected Labour seats, two were regarded as potential SNP victories and just one, a projected Conservative seat, and then only a marginal.

Thus, as was found for background characteristics, there appeared to be little real difference in the previous political experience of selected and non-selected aspirants. However, the bias in favour of MPs in the non-selected sample make conclusions tentative. The most unexpected finding was the high percentage of PEPCs who were not drawn from the party's list of approved European candidates.

(c) The European dimension: Those chosen to stand as Conservative European candidates were more likely to belong to both the European Movement and the Conservative Group for Europe.(5) However, rejected aspirants were more federalist orientated than PEPCs, and wished to see the *status quo* retained in terms of EEC power and supra-nationalism (see Table 5.1). This tendency may have been an important selection variable: local selectors' suspicion of any federal implications may have excluded, *a priori*, any applicant who espoused such a policy. Yet the data presents seemingly contradictory statements in that PEPCs rather than failed applicants wished to promote a trans-national party system and extend the powers of the European Parliament. Adopted candidates also tended to stress the economic dimension of the Community, predominantly favouring monetary union: a bare majority of both groups favoured a uniform electoral system for the 1984 elections.

In summary PEPCs can be characterised as supporting the existing balance of power between the EEC and national Parliaments: fedralism was frowned upon, but developments within the existing legal framework encouraged. They favoured monetary union, the move towards a national party system and common electoral system, and the exercise of parliamentary democracy. In contrast, the majority

Table 5.1

Attitudes to Six Community Issues by Adoption Status

Issues		PEPCs n	PEPCs %	Rejects n	Rejects %
The creation of a European Federal State	Favour	8	15.4	14	51.9
	against	32	61.5	12	44.4
	unsure	12	23.1	1	3.7
		52		27	
Reduction in the powers of the EEC over national parliaments	Favour	-	-	7	28.8
	against	52	98.1	18	72.0
	unsure	1	1.9	-	-
		53		25	
The development of a Trans-national party system	Favour	38	76.0	18	69.2
	against	8	16.0	8	30.8
	unsure	4	8.0	-	-
		50		26	
An increase in the powers of the European Parliament	Favour	41	74.5	18	66.7
	against	10	18.2	8	29.6
	unsure	4	7.3	1	3.7
		55		27	
Monetary union	Favour	49	87.5	19	70.4
	against	3	5.4	6	22.2
	unsure	4	7.1	2	7.4
		56		27	
Uniform electoral system for the 1984 direct elections	Favour	29	53.7	14	53.8
	against	18	33.3	12	46.2
	unsure	7	13.0	-	-
		54		26	

(though a slender one) of rejected aspirants looked forward to a European federal state, and while they supported the other five European issues analysed, their level of support was less than that found for PEPCs.

(d) Motivation and ambition: All those surveyed were asked to indicate whether the initial decision to run as a potential MEP candidate was their own idea or stimulated by an external recruitment agent, such as Central Office, a constituency association, an MP or industry. A majority of PEPCs and non-selected applicants believed that it was their own idea to run for Europe, either exclusively, or in conjunction with a secondary recruitment stimulus: 76.6 per cent of PEPCs and 62.5 per cent of rejected applicants claimed some measure of personal motivation. The most pronounced difference was that non-selected aspirants were twice as likely to have been encouraged to stand by an MP as were PEPCs, although even 15.6 per cent of adopted candidates mentioned that an MP played an influential role.

Table 5.2

Initial Stimulus for Candidacy by Adoption Status

PEPCs N = 64 Rejects N = 24

Stimulus	PEPCs %	Rejects %
Constituency Association	6.2	-
Central Office/Party Leadership	7.8	12.5
Own Idea	64.0	58.3
Own Idea & Central Office/Leadership	6.3	-
MP	7.8	16.7
MP & Own Idea	6.3	4.2
MP & Constituency Association	1.6	8.3
	100.0	100.0
All Self Starters	76.6	62.5

Ambition is one of the most intangible and least quantifiable recruitment relevant variables, but one that is essential to any conceptualisation of why individuals enter politics. Limited by the methodological possibilities of a postal questionnaire, only broad and relatively unsophisticated indicators of ambition could be used. Respondents were asked an open-ended question: the responses fell into three broad categories, distinguishing European, personal and political based motivations.

PEPCs were twice as likely to mention a European based reason for their candidacy as were rejected applicants. The belief that Britain's economic survival depended on Europe was a typical PEPC attitude. In addition, PEPCs were more likely to cite the Labour

Table 5.3

Reasons for Running as an MEP Aspirant by Adoption Status

PEPCs N = 78 Rejects N = 54

Reason	PEPCs %	PEPCs subtotal	Rejects %	Rejects subtotal
a) European:				
wish to see a united Europe	5.1)		1.9)	
UK's future is in Europe	21.8)		5.6)	
belief in a European ideal	11.5)	50.0	9.3)	26.1
peace/defence in Europe	3.9)		5.6)	
promote and protect democracy	1.3)		-)	
Labour's anti EEC approach/socialism	6.4)		3.7)	
b) Personal:				
possess the right personal qualities	20.5)		11.1)	
can contribute something	5.1)	39.7	12.9)	35.1
history of job involvement in Europe	14.1)		11.1)	
c) Political				
failed as a Westminster candidate	6.4)		1.9)	
wanted to enter politics	11.5)		9.2)	
represent an area	5.1)	28.2	-)	24.2
MP/MEP dual mandate link	2.6)		5.6)	
promised an important post if elected	-)		1.9)	
others	2.6)		5.6)	

Party's anti-EEC approach as a recruitment catalyst. For example, one PEPC professed 'disgust at the disgraceful performance by the British Labour government as an EEC member'. A more radical motivation for candidacy offered by one candidate was his 'concern about the drift of my country towards a full socialist state and the collapse of the rule of law'.

These motivational interpretations need to be balanced against the more ambitious personal reasons offered by over one-third of selected and non-selected aspirants. A greater percentage of PEPCs felt they possessed the necessary personal qualities to be an MEP: however, rejected applicants showed a greater propensity for believing that they had a relevant contribution to make to the Community.

The politically based reasons for candidacy suggested a similar interpretation to personal ambition: 17.9 per cent of PEPCs stated that one of their reasons for running was a desire to begin a political career, or resurrect a failed Westminster one. Thus one candidate admitted to having 'always had ambition to be an MP and since I am a committed European the European Parliament was the natural choice when it became available'. The candidate in question faced a double disappointment: he failed to win in June

1979 and at a subsequent Westminster election. One former Westminster candidate was exceptionally honest about his prime motivation: 'Having failed to get a seat for Westminster, it was natural to go for Europe. I may find that, in the end, I prefer it'.

Clear motivational differences for the two groups existed. For PEPCs the dominant reasons for running were linked with the development of Europe, with personal political ambition a secondary factor. Converseley, rejected applicants were more concerned with their political ambition than with any belief in the European ideal, although PEPCs were more likely to regard Europe as an opportunity to enter politics or alter an unsuccessful domestic politcal career.

As a related test for ambition, respondents were asked about the direction of their future careers. A greater proportion of adopted than rejected aspirants viewed service in the European Parliament as a route to Westminster rather than as a career objective in itself, constituting in Schlesinger's typology 'progressive ambitions'.(6) The comments of two PEPCs illustrate this point.

> I had hoped to find a winnable seat for the Westminster Parliament ... having failed to so, I felt that a seat in the European Parliament would give me more scope for political service ... I think service in Europe may help me to find a seat at Westminster later.

> Not having obtained a parliamentary candidacy, I recognised accepting nomination for a European seat would provide a 'short-cut' to future possible selection by having served an apprenticeship in what was considered an unwinnable seat.

In conclusion, the difference between the selected and rejected aspirants can be summarized as follows. PEPCs were the younger group, one-third being under forty with only six of the seventy-eight adopted candidates (7.7 per cent) aged over sixty; the comparable figures for rejected aspirants were 9.3 and 22.2 per cent. Exactly three-quarters of failed applicants were from the independent sector of secondary education compared to 63.6 per cent of selected candidates. Euro-crats, farmers, journalists and professional workers dominated the occupational categories of PEPCs, accounting for 42.4 per cent of the selected cohort - only one rejected applicant fell into these categories. Membership of the European Movement and the Conservative Group for Europe and a belief in the gradual development within the legal constraints of the EEC, but a rejection of any federal aspiration, all distinguish selected from non-selected applicants. Furthermore, this latter group can be characterised as motivated more by personal ambition than a desire to promote European unity. In contrast, PEPCs were more concerned with the idea of Europe, and/or beginning a new political career outside Westminster (whilst at the same time often regarding the job of MEP as a route to the House of Commons).

Winners and Losers - Elected Versus Defeated Candidates

The analysis of winners and losers suffered from the inevitably small population size of both groups. The 7 June election produced a sixty to eighteen split in favour of elected over defeated Conservative candidates: the scope for valid analysis was consequently restricted.

(a) Background characteristics: As already shown, selected candidates were a youthful group: those who lost in the June election tended to be even younger, with 44.4 per cent below forty and a mean age of 43.8. The figures for MEPs were 33.3 per cent and 44.6 respectively. Again bearing in mind that only ten women stood as PEPCs, a disproportionate number failed to gain election, implying a sexual bias in relation to the winnability of a seat: there was no difference for marital status. 63.3 per cent of MEPs attended public school, compared to less than half of the defeated candidates. Over 80.0 per cent of elected and defeated candidates had experienced some form of higher education: MEPs tended to be Oxbridge products whereas defeated PEPCs were more likely to have come from a redbrick university. Similarly, whilst 38.3 per cent of all MEPs could claim a public school/Oxbridge background, this fell to 23.5 per cent for defeated Conservative candidates.

The socio-economic skew for both winners and losers was quite dramatic: 72.2 per cent of defeated candidates came from the OPCS groups XXIV and XXV, compared to 91.7 per cent of elected MEPs. Given that those in category I were in fact landowning farmers, the domination of Conservative candidates from the 'elite' segments of British society was all but complete - only one MEP and five defeated candidates fell outside this classification. The occupational breakdown of these categories was as follows. All the MPs who stood were elected as were four of the five peers who fought; only one Euro-crat failed to become a MEP as did two of the eight members of the legal profession and three of the twelve candidates described as professional workers. Conversely, the three candidates from the education sector all lost.

(b) Previous electoral experience: 63.8 per cent of MEPs had at some time been on the Central Office list of approved candidates for Westminster, compared to exactly half of the defeated PEPCs. A similar percentage of both groups were still on the Westminster list at the time of the Euro-selections.(7) Defeated PEPCs had less experience in contesting British parliamentary elections: 38.9 per cent compared to 50.0 per cent of MEPs had fought at least one contest. None of the defeated PEPC had ever been elected, whereas two MEPs, in addition to the five dual-mandated MPs, had. In contrast to their less experience in parliamentary elections, a greater percentage of defeated candidates had fought a local election: 55.6 per cent compared with 35.6 per cent.(8) Although MEPs had a better election success rate, 80.0 per cent had contested no more than three local elections, whereas exactly half of the defeated PEPCs had fought between four and nine contests. The parochial trend displayed by losing European candidates was reinforced by the concentration of their experience at the local rather than national political office level. The majority of losers (62.5 per cent) had served their 'apprenticeship' locally in constituency Conservative associations, compared to 46.3 per cent of winners.(9) Lastly, five of the sixty MEPs and five of the eighteen losers were local applicants, not off the original approved list. The influence of electoral status was apparent: local candidates were generally favoured in the marginal or hopeless districts.

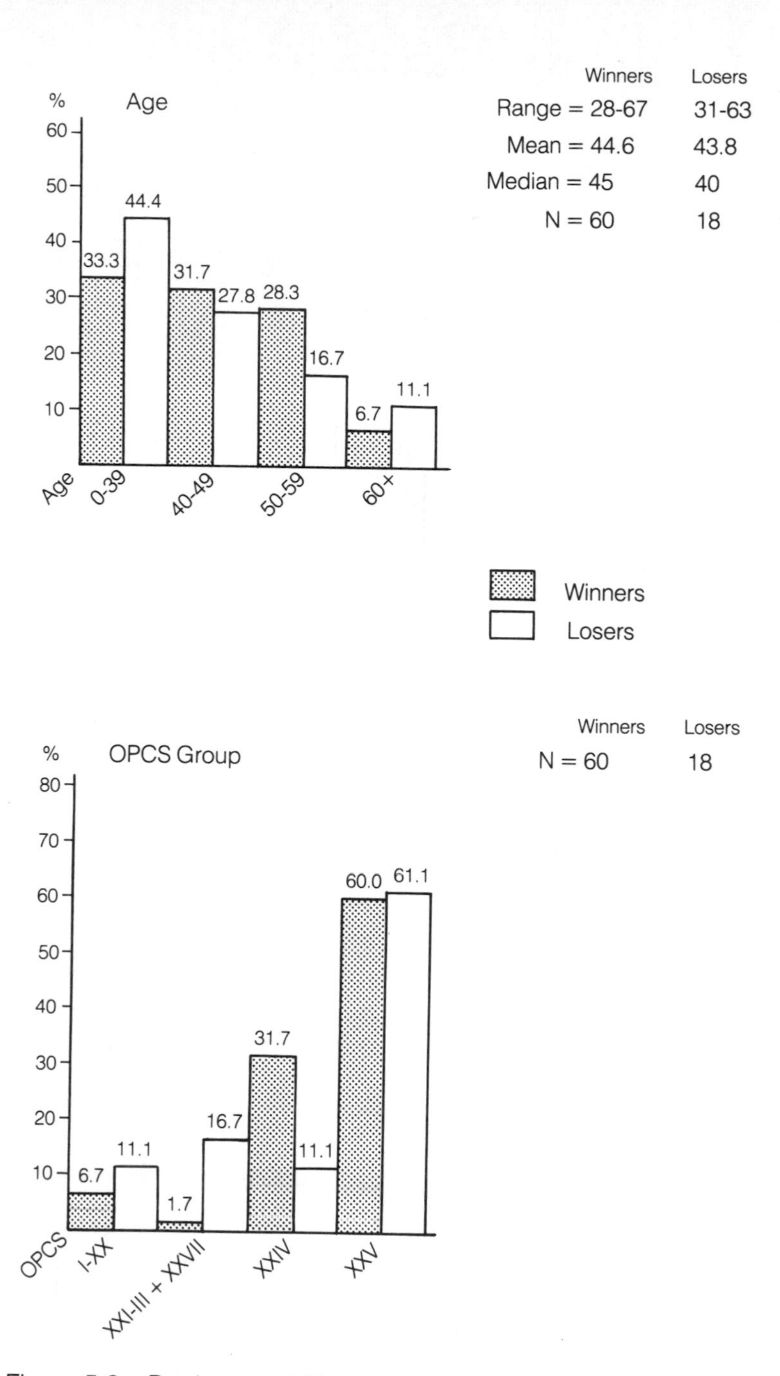

Figure 5.2 Background Characteristics of Winners and Losers

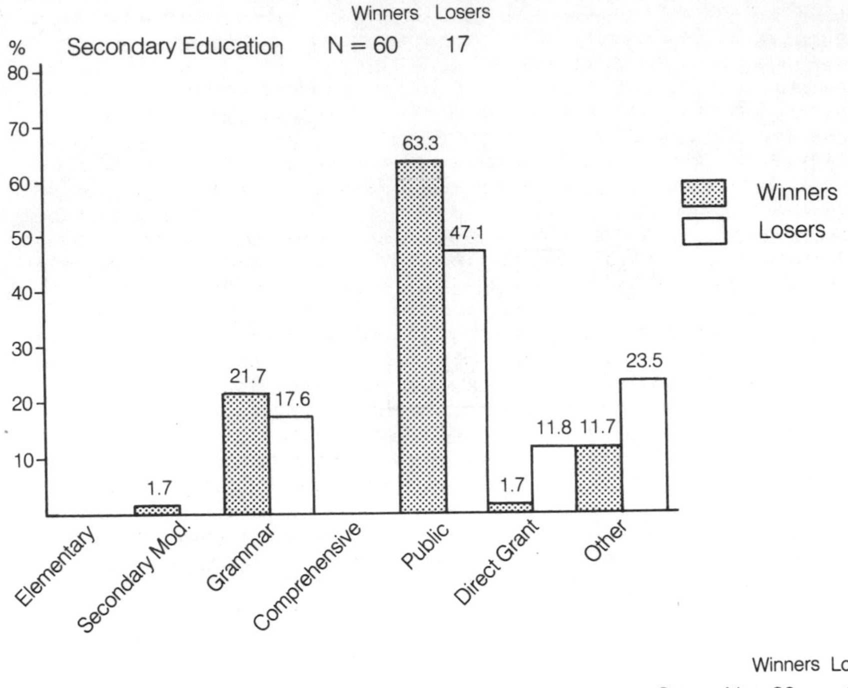
Winners Losers
% Secondary Education N = 60 17
80
70
60
50
40
30
20
10
63.3
47.1
21.7
17.6
1.7
1.7
11.8 11.7
23.5
Winners
Losers
Elementary
Secondary Mod.
Grammar
Comprehensive
Public
Direct Grant
Other

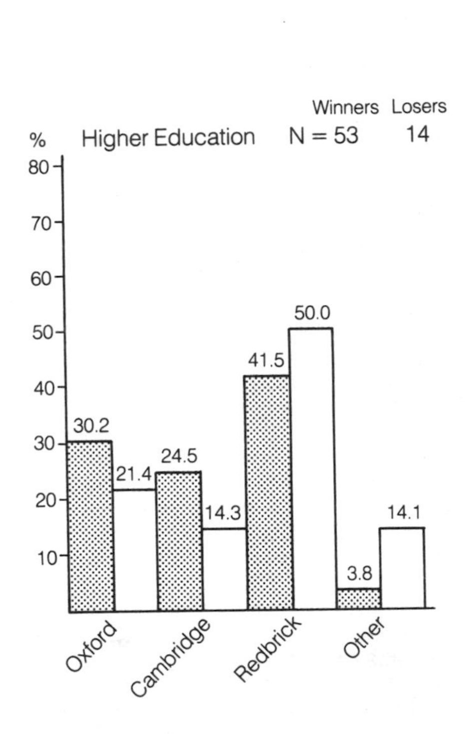
Winners Losers
% Higher Education N = 53 14
80
70
60
50
40
30
20
10
30.2
21.4
24.5
14.3
41.5
50.0
3.8
14.1
Oxford
Cambridge
Redbrick
Other

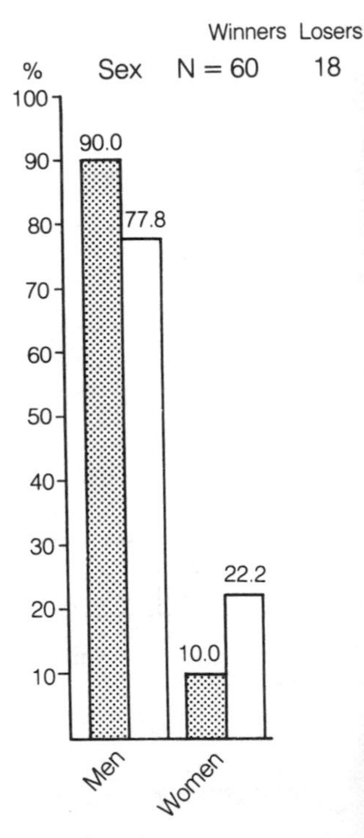
Winners Losers
% Sex N = 60 18
100
90
80
70
60
50
40
30
20
10
90.0
77.8
10.0
22.2
Men
Women

(c) The European dimension: Only tentative interpretations of the European attitudes of winners and losers can be offered due to variable response rates and small population size. All but one candidate (an MEP) were unanimous in their condemnation of any move on the part of national governments to reduce the role of the EEC, and three-quarters of both winners and losers wished to see an increase in the existing powers of the European Parliament. However, losing PEPCs tended to be more hostile to the idea of a European federal state, than those who were actually elected, yet paradoxically were more likely to favour the development of trans-national party system, the use of a uniform electoral procedure for the 1984 direct elections and monetary union.

(d) Motivation and ambition: The propensity for candidates to describe themselves as self-starters has already been mentioned. Of the four groups analysed so far, defeated candidates contained the lowest percentage of self-starters, with just 46.7 per cent claiming that it was their 'own idea' to run for the European Parliament; this compares with 69.4 per cent of elected MEPs. Furthermore, eight out of ten winners cited some degree of self-motivation compared with only two-thirds of losers. Of the remaining third, 20.0 per cent of defeated candidates stated that candidacy was suggested by their constituency association with 13.3 per cent mentioning Central Office/Party leadership as the recruitment catalyst. In contrast, the roles associated with Central Office and local Conservative associations were a minor recruitment variable for MEPs. The only substantial component other than self motivation was that played by MPs.

Losing candidates were far more likely to have been asked by Central Office to apply to specific Euro-constituencies: this happened in the case of seven of the eighteen Conservative losers, three of whom went on to be actually selected by the Euro-constituency in question. 82.4 per cent of MEP respondents stated that Central Office did not ask them to apply for any particular seats. This procedure does not imply any Central Office interference with local selection prerogatives: the role of the central party administration was personnel management and logistics - to help secure the widest possible candidate choice, not to directly determine adoption. The problem was that the least electorally winnable seats often found it difficult to attract a sufficient number of suitable applicants. Thus the majority of the seats that elected and defeated candidates were asked to apply to were projected Labour victories.

The reasons expressed by winners and losers explaining why they decided to run as aspirants produced the following motivational multiple response distribution. Candidates elected as MEPs tended to reflect the motivational patterns displayed by the PEPC cohort as a whole. The most commonly mentioned factors were European based, in particular the belief that the future of the UK was inextricably linked with Europe and a commitment to the European ideal. Personal reasons, namely confidence in one's own ability, personal qualities and relevant occupational experience, constituted the secondary set of motivational stimuli, with reasons derived from political ambitions firmly in third place. In contrast, defeated candidates were predominantly motivated by individual political ambitions. Exactly half explained their

Table 5.4

Initial Stimulus for Candidacy for Winners and Losers

MEPs N = 49 Defeated PEPCs N = 15

Stimulus	MEPs %	Defeated PEPCs %
Constituency Association	2.0	20.0
Central Office/Party Leadership	6.1	13.3
MP	10.2	-
Own Idea	69.4	46.7
Own Idea plus MP	6.1	6.7
Own Idea plus Central Office/Leadership	4.1	13.3
MP & Constituency Association	2.0	-
	99.9	100.0
All Self Starters	79.6	66.7

decision to enter the European selection process by referring to a previously failed or dormant political career. This pattern of political ambition was reinforced when one included the 16.7 per cent of respondents who mentioned their own personal qualities and abilities as a significant motivational factor. The contrast is not, however, complete: defeated candidates like their successful contemporaries displayed a strong tendency to claim some form of European idealism as a factor in prompting their candidacy.

Personal ambitions with regard to career objectives showed that the majority of winners and losers professed 'static' ambitions focusing their careers on continuing membership of the European Parliament after the 1984 direct elections (70.0 and 66.7 per cent respectively). One MEP could be classified as having a 'discrete' ambition - she intended to retire in 1984; another stated that his career plans depended on the financial remuneration of being a member. 28.6 per cent of losing candidates stated that they regarded their candidacy for Europe as a route to gaining selection for a winnable House of Commons seat: the figure for MEPs was somewhat lower at 19.6 per cent, but still accounted for a surprisingly large portion of winners. That over one if five respondents regarded the European Parliament as an apprenticeship for Westminser is an important recruitment finding. Six of the MEPs who regarded the House of Commons as their natural career goal were failed domestic PPCs, and one other had not contested an election. Three of the four losing candidates who wished to be MPs rather than MEPs had never been parliamentary candidates. Thus, both those who previously had been rejected by the British electorate and those aspiring to political life, hoped to use candidacy to the European Parliament as a pathway to the British legislature. This interpretation is supported by the conclusion of

Table 5.5

Reasons for Running for Winners and Losers

MEPs N = 60 Defeated PEPCs N = 18

Reason	MEPs %		Defeated PEPCs %	
a) European:				
wish to see a united Europe	6.7)		-)	
UK's future is in Europe	20.0)		27.8)	
belief in a European ideal	11.7)	51.8	11.1)	44.5
peace/defence in Europe	5.0)		-)	
promote and protect democracy	1.7)		-)	
Labour's anti EEC approach/socialism	6.7)		5.6)	
b) Personal:				
possess the right personal qualities	21.7)		16.7)	
can contribute something	5.0)	43.4	5.6)	27.9
history of job involvement in Europe	16.7)		5.6)	
c) Political				
failed as a Westminster candidate	1.7)		22.2)	
wanted to enter politics	6.7)		27.8)	
represent an area	3.3)	15.0	11.1)	61.1
MP/MEP dual mandate link	3.3)		-)	

the European Election Study; the first direct elections were 'second order elections', which primarily reflected a domestic rather than European dimension.(10)

As a supplementary measure, winners and losers were asked to indicate, if elected, whether they anticipated being an MEP on a full or part-time basis. Only 57.1 per cent of elected candidates and 69.2 per cent of losers regarded being a Euro-representative as a full-time commitment, infering that the European Parliament was seen by a substantal minority as a means to another goal, rather than a career in itself. In addition, the number of seat applications made by MEPs and defeated PEPCs were examined as a secondary indicator of ambition. The two groups were distinct. MEPs were far more likely to apply to a larger number of Euro-constituencies than losing candidates: one-quarter of the latter group applied to only one seat, with over half limiting themselves to a maximum of three districts. In contrast, the 70.6 per cent of MEPs applied to five or more seats. A mediating factor accounting for this difference was the high percentage of 'local' candidates in the defeated PEPC group.

Finally, every selected PEPC was asked to state what connections, if any, they had with their adopted Euro-constituency. There was no real difference in the responses of winners and losers - 50.0 per cent of the former and 47.1 per cent of the latter stated that they had no relationship with the area in question; 39.7 per cent of winners and 35.3 per cent of losers claimed that they worked, were residents or former residents in the area (rather than in the actual Euro-constituency). Losers were, however, more likely to have been adopted for a Euro-constituency where they had served as local government councillors or been PPCs.(11)

In conclusion, winners can be distinguished from losers by the following characteristics and attitudes. Losers tended to be the younger group, with just under half aged below forty; failed candidates were also significantly more likely to be female. In terms of education, MEPs were characterised by attendance at a public school and at Oxbridge; four out of ten were public school/Oxbridge products. The educational profile of losers showed that less than half had been to public school and that they were more likely to come from redbrick universities. Less than one quarter were public school/Oxbridge creations. MPs were an almost completely homogeneous socio-economic group, 91.7 per cent coming from OPCS occupational groups XXIV and XXV; losers, while predominantly drawn from these two classifications, were a less cohesive group. Typically, MEPs were drawn from the occupations of Euro-crat, MP/peer, professional workers and the legal profession: employment in the education sector coincided with defeat in the June election. MEPs were also the more politically experienced, both in terms of the number of general elections fought and actual parliamentary service. Defeated PEPCs tended to be more locally oriented. Firstly, they were more likely to have served their campaign apprenticeship fighting local government rather than Westminster elections. Secondly, they were more involved at the constituency Conservative association level than as national office holders. Thirdly, over a quarter of the losing candidates were 'local' in the sense that they were not on the original list of approved candidates, compared to less than 10.0 per cent of winners. With regard to European attitudes, MEPs were somewhat more pro-federalist, whereas losers tended to be less idealistic yet more progressive in their attitudes towards the more practical and immediate aspects of European harmonisation. Defeated PEPCs were split between self-starters and recruited candidates; MEPs were predominantly self-starters. A belief in Europe was the most common motivational factor mentioned by MEPs in explaning their candidacy, followed by personal qualities and qualifications with political ambitions a poor third. In direct contrast, defeated candidates became European aspirants in order to satisfy their political ambitions (which were often linked to Westminster rather than Strasbourg).

PEPCs by Electoral Status

So far, characteristics and attitude profiles of winners and losers, selected and rejected aspirants, have been compared and their differences and similarities noted. Although the winner/loser dichotomy is the traditional approach used in candidate studies, it may be a less appropriate or useful tool of analysis for the European elections, due to the disproportionate partisan turn-out and the peculiarly skewed results of the June poll. Thus the final candidate examination is based upon the October 1974 predictions of each Euro-constituencies electoral status. Recalling Seligman's inquiry, were Conservative selections affected where they had 'little hope or expectation of gaining a majority'?(12) The two major hypotheses under analysis were: did projected Conservative seats select different types of candidates to potentially Labour held areas? And, did impregnable, safe, comfortable, semi-marginal and marginal seats differ in their candidate choice for both Conservative and Labour Euro-constituencies?

(a) Background characteristics: The age distribution for candidacy displayed a general pattern related to the electoral status of Euro-constituencies. The youngest age category was the group most likely to represent a Labour seat: 67.9 per cent of this age category were chosen for Labour seats. The next youngest age group were also more likely to be chose for a non-Conservative area, with 62.5 per cent contesting either SNP or projected Labour districts. All the expected comfortable Labour Euro-constituencies selected candidates below forty-nine years of age; two-thirds of marginals, three-quarters of safe seats and 80.0 per cent of impregnable Labour strongholds also preferred candidates in this age range. The majority of fifty to fifty-nine years old secured adoption for projected Conservative districts. Those over sixty were just as likely to be picked for a Conservative as a non-Conservative seat (see Table 5.6).

As stressed throughout this chapter the dearth of female candidates for Europe was the most important finding relating to candidate gender even though the figures were higher than those for Westminster. Further analysis using electoral status as the dependent variable was revealing. Eight of the ten female Conservative candidates were adopted for projected Labour Euro-constituencies. What is more, the skew was towards the least winnable rather than marginal categories: five of the fifteen least winnable Labour seats chose women candidates. The only two women who were selected as PEPCs for Conservative seats were Elaine Kellet-Bowman MP, and Lady Elles, both of whom had proven records as politicians and parliamentarians. Both had also served as UK delegate members of the European Parliament.

The repeated occurrence of candidates from public schools restricted the analysis for education. Commenting on the distribution, the majority of projected Conservative seats (irrespective of electoral status) selected candidates with a public school background, whereas amongst non-Conservative areas, only Labour semi-marginal and SNP seats displayed a similar tendency. PEPCs not contesting a Conservative seat were more likely to be grammar school products, accounting for 68.8 per cent of candidates educated in this sector. Higher education reinforced the pattern. Every candidate adopted by a projected Conservative seat had been to university - what is more, the most desirable Conservative Euro-constituencies generally selected candidates with an Oxbridge degree: 80.0 per cent of candidates in projected Conservative seats had attended Oxbridge, compared to 27.8 per cent of candidates in projected Labour Euro-constituencies. Finally, 74.1 per cent of those who had received the benefits of a public school/Oxbridge education were chosen for Conservative districts, compared to only 28.6 per cent of those lacking this qualification.

Turning to occupations, all five MPs fought Conservative seats as did three of the five peers. Three-quarters of the Euro-crat category stood for similarly winnable Conservative Euro-constituencies. Rather surprisingly, the legal profession tended to be selected in non-Conservative seats and those employed in secondary and higher education were selected in the least winnable Labour areas. The only two university lecturers to gain selection, both of whom were women, were chosen to contest the sixty-sixth and the least winnable of the seventy-eight British Euro-constituencies. The only school teacher to stand as a Conservative PEPC, again a woman, fought the comfortable Labour seat of Strathclyde East. It is interesting to note that all three candidates drawn from the education sector were female, that they only contested virtually hopeless Euro-constituencies, and that none was chosen for English Euro-constituenices.

(b) <u>Previous electoral experience</u>: Over half of the candidates selected for projected Conservative seats had been on the list of approved Westminster candidates. For projected Labour seats, only marginal Euro-constituencies preferred to select candidates who did not have this minimal measure of former political activity. None of the candidates who contested the three SNP areas had ever attempted to run for the House of Commons. The distribution was altered when current membership of the domestic list was examined: 50.0 per cent of safe and comfortable Conservative Euro-constituencies chose candidates with this attribute, compared to 44.4 and 16.7 per cent for semi-marginals and marginals respectively. Only safe incumbent Labour seats had a bare majority of candidates from the national list.

58.8 per cent of candidates adopted for Conservative seats had fought at least one Westminster election, compared to 41.5 per cent of PEPCs who contested projected Labour Euro-constituencies. What is more, those in the latter group tended to have fought on fewer occasions - only 2.5 per cent as opposed to 17.1 per cent had fought between four and ten parliamentary elections respectively.(13) However, these figures were skewed by the inclusion of MPs in the projected Conservative seat category.

Only one candidate picked for a safe Conservative seat and only a third of each of the remaining Conservative categories had ever fought a local government election. Only in marginal and comfortable Labour seats were there a minority of candidates who had not been involved in elections at the local level. Overall, nearly twice as many Conservative candidates in projected Labour seats had experience at the local election level, 29.4 per cent compared with 51.2 per cent. Furthermore, no candidate from the projected Conservative seats had contested more than three local

Table 5.6

Age, Sex and Education of PEPCs by Electoral Status

	Conservative				Labour					SNP*	N	All	All	
AGE	S	C	SM	M	M	SM	C	S	I			Con	Lab	
28-39	2	4	2	1	3	3	6	4	3	0	28	9	19	
												32.1	67.9	row.%
												26.4	46.3	col.%
40-49	1	2	4	2	1	3	5	3	1	2	24	9	13	
												37.5	54.2	
												26.5	31.7	
50-59	1	5	3	4	2	2	0	1	1	1	20	13	6	
												65.0	30.0	
												38.2	14.6	
60 and over	1	1	0	1	0	2	0	1	0	0	6	3	3	
												50.0	50.0	
												8.8	7.3	
	5	12	9	8	6	10	11	9	5	3	78	34	41	
SEX														
Male	5	11	8	8	5	9	9	7	3	3	68	32	33	
Female	0	1	1	0	1	1	2	2	2	0	10	2	8	
											78	34	41	
SCHOOL														
Grammar	1	2	1	1	3	1	4	2	1	0	16	5	11	
Public	4	6	8	6	1	9	4	3	2	3	46	24	19	
Other	0	4	0	1	2	0	3	4	2	0	16	5	11	
HIGHER														
Oxford	4	7	2	2	1	0	0	0	3	0	19	15	4	
Cambridge	0	1	6	2	1	3	1	1	0	0	15	9	6	
Redbrick	0	2	0	4	1	6	8	5	2	1	29	6	22	
Other	0	0	0	0	1	1	0	2	0	0	4	0	4	
											67	30	36	

Key:
- I impregnable seat
- S safe seat
- C comfortable seat
- SM semi-marginal seat
- M marginal

* SNP seats are treated as a single category; in fact two were semi-marginals and one a marginal.

government elections; 50.0 per cent had fought only once. Conversely, 45.0 per cent of candidates from Labour Euro-constituencies had campaigned in between four and nine local council elections. Of those who ran, 60.0 per cent of individuals adopted for Conservative seats compared to 81.0 per cent from Labour and SNP seats were successfully elected to serve as local government councillors.

A major difference exposed by examining candidate characteristics against electoral status was the incidence of local non-approved selections in the less attractive seats. In the Euro-constituencies where the Conservatives had a minimum of 5.0 per cent over the second placed party, all twenty-six candidates were from the Central Office list (i.e., safe, comfortable and semi-marginal seats). The only case of a projected Conservative seat choosing a local rather than approved candidate was in the marginal Euro-consitituency of Norfolk. The remaining eight examples of local candidates all occurred in prospective Labour or SNP seats.

(c) The European dimension: There were no substantial differences in the distribution of European attitudes. Approximtely 60.0 per cent in both categories were against the creation of a federal state; unanimity existed for the issues of parliamentary power and a uniform electoral system, with attitudes towards monetary union only slighly less homogeneous. The only difference concerned the development of a transnational party system: 85.7 per cent of candidates selected for Conservative seats compared with 69.0 per cent in Labour and SNP areas favoured this innovation.

(d) Motivation and ambition: Candidates who managed to secure adoption for projected Conservative seats displayed a greater tendency to be self-starters (74.1 per cent compared to 56.8 per cent for Labour and SNP seat selections). These percentages rose to 85.2 and 74.3 respectively when multiple responses were considered. Except in marginals, a minimum of four out of five candidates in the Conservative Euro-constituencies were self motivated aspirants: only one individual stated that he was recruited by a Conservative constituency association or Central Office. Conversely 21.6 per cent of candidates adopted for projected non-Conservative Euro-constituencies traced their initial reason for running to these two recruitment agencies. Thus candidates in projected Conservative seats appeared to display greater self-motivated ambition, whereas recruitment by an external agent characterised candidates from non-Conservative seats. In particular, candidates who were finally selected for the least winnable Labour seats were more likely to have been directed to vacant Euro-constituencies.

Candidates who contested comfortable Conservative seats displayed a stronger tendency to explain their initial motivation for running by reference to a European or personal reason. Those from Conservative marginals were similarly motivated by a feeling for Europe, and those in Conservative semi-marginals by personal confidence and self-esteem. Candidates chosen for Conservative seats showed a greater reluctance to assign their motivational inspiration to a primarily 'political' motivation. In particular, only two candidates in this group ran because they 'wished to enter politics', and none as a result of a still-born Westminster career.

In contrast, all the candidates who stated that their main reason for running for the European Parliament was their failure to secure adoption (or election) as a domestic PPC, were selected for projected Labour-constituencies. In a similar vein, a significant number of candidates who stood in these Labour areas, saw candidacy for the European Parliament as a way of entering the realm of politics. As a group, Conservative candidates in Labour seats were three times more likely to assign a political reason as their motivational catalyst. However, for these candidates, like their counter parts in Conservative seats, a commitment to Europe constituted the most common motivational factor. In summary, both groups can be characterised as follows - candidates adopted for projected Conservative seats predominantly described their initial reason for running in terms of Europe or their personal qualities and qualifications. Candidates from Labour Euro-constituencies were even more likely to lay claim to a belief in Europe as their recruitment stimulus, with the personal qualities and political considerations in equal second place.

Electoral status had only a weak impact upon candidate career ambitions. Approximately seven out of ten candidates from both groups possessed static ambitions, although a greater number of candidates from the non-Conservative seats (particularly the less winnable ones) had progressive ambitions and regarded the European Parliament as a short-term goal in their longer career objective of becoming an MP. The total number of seats applied to and those short-listed for, were examined as a secondary measure of the impact of electoral status on ambition. Candidates who fought projected Labour seats tended to have applied to fewer Euro-constituencies during the recruitment process. 55.3 per cent limited themselves to five or less seat applications, compared to only 31.0 per cent of candidates from Conservative seats. The figures for between six to ten seat applications were 10.5 and 31.0 per cent respectively.

The difference in candidate profiles based on the criterion of electoral status can be summarized as follows. Candidates adopted by projected Conservative Euro-constituencies were more likely to be on the Central Office approved list, male, aged between fifty and sixty, educated in the private sector, Oxbridge products and classified in the OPCS occupational category XXIV. Being an MP coincided with adoption for a winnable Conservative seat, as did, to a lesser extent, the occupation of Euro-crat: they were more likely to have fought a Westminster election and have served the party at national office level. The only detected difference in attitudes was that more candidates adopted for Conservative seats favoured the development of a transnational party system. Typically, they were self starters, motivated by European beliefs and their own self esteem and were more likely to have applied to a greater number of Euro-constituencies. In contrast, candidates selected for non-Conservative seats were more likely to be local non-approved applicants, aged below forty, female, redbrick graduates, in the OPCS occupational category XXV (in particular teachers and the legal profession) and active at the local constituency association level. They had more experience in local government elections, and tended to see candidacy for the European Parliament as a substitute for a failed Westminster career, or as a route to becoming an MP. While they were predominantly self starters, candidates chosen for Labour seats also responded to external recruitment agents, such as Central Office, local associations and Members of Parliament.

Conclusion

Has the model's approach to the study of recruitment been of use, and to what extent have the objectives set out in Chapter 1 been achieved? Were there significant differences between elected, selected and rejected aspirants? Was electoral status a mediating factor? There were demonstrable differences between these aspirant cohorts for many of the major recruitment relevant variables, although often the most clear cut were for the more easily quantifiable background characteristics than for attitudes and motivations. However, even where the findings have been inconclusive, the approach remains defensible, the hypotheses not proven rather than rejected: partial explanations of this can be offered in support of the model.

Firstly, one militating factor that may have reduced the polarization of profile characteristics based on electoral status was that this was the first election to the European Parliament. There were no actual incumbent parties or candidates (only projected incumbency) and to a certain extent calculations of electoral status were thus less secure. Neither the Conservative party nor its candidates knew how the electorate would respond in a European election; domestic voting behaviour was the only guide and at best only a tentative estimation of a seat's marginality. The impressions candidates had of the winnability of Euro-constituencies may have been inflated. Very few seats were written off as hopeless as far as the candidates were concerned: 80.0 per cent of Conservatives who felt that their Euro-constituency was 'winnable' and 92.9 per cent who regarded their seat as 'marginal' fought what were projected Labour seats on October 1974 figures. Only eight candidates admitted to fighting what were electorally 'hopeless' Euro-constituencies. Thus candidates' interpretations of marginality were more optimistic (though perhaps more realistic) than the traditional calculations of electoral status.

Secondly, whilst the preceding sections have sought to expose differences, the similarities between winners and losers, rejected and selected aspirants are, in themselves, a useful comparative finding. The fact that these groups were similar in many ways is a comment upon the cohesive manner in which the Conservative party's approved list of European candidates was compiled. Despite Marcus Fox's plea to recruit from a wider non-political pool, the chosen aspirants tended to conform to a certain general pattern of attitudes and characteristics. Solutions to the approved list dilemma still remain largely intuitive. Was it that candidates without these group characteristics were rejected, or did they simply fail to emerge as aspirants, feeling themselves unqualified exactly because they did not match those qualities and attributes commonly held to be essential Conservative traits?

Aggregate analysis of individual responses can only indicate trends, not explicate laws. The preceding commentary has suggested such trends and supported the theoretical and methodological structure of the recruitment model.

Notes

(1) PEPCs (Prospective European Parliamentary Candidates) N = 78; rejected aspirants N = 52.
(2) C. Mellors, The British MP, Farnborough, Saxon House, 1978, p.2.
(3) PEPCs N = 46/76 (60.5 per cent); rejected aspirants N = 29/54 (53.7 per cent).
(4) PEPCs N = 31/77 (40.3 per cent); rejected aspirants N = 23/54 (42.6 per cent): PEPCs N = 23, range = 1-26, mean 8.8, median = 8; rejected aspirants N = 20, range = 2-24, mean = 9.1, median = 5.
(5) European Movement: PEPCs N = 53/78 (67.9 per cent), rejected aspirants N = 22/41 (53.7 per cent): Conservative Group for Europe, PEPCs N = 56/78 (71.8 per cent), rejected aspirants N = 21/41 (51.2 per cent).
(6) J.A. Schlesinger, Ambition and Politics; political careers in the United States, Rand McNally, 1966, p.10.
(7) MEPs N = 57 (42.1 per cent), defeated PEPCs N = 18 (44.4 per cent).
(8) MEPs N = 59, defeated PEPCs N = 18.
(9) MEPs N = 41, defeated PEPCs N = 16.
(10) K. Reif and H. Schmitt, "Nine Second Order Elections: a conceptual framework for the analysis of European election results", European Journal of Political Research, vol. 8, 1980, p.3.
(11) Defeated PEPCs - local government connection n = 2/27 (11.8 per cent), former PPC in Euro-constituency n = 2/17 (11.8 per cent): MEPs, local government connection n = 4/58 (6.9 per cent), former PPC n = 0 (0.0 per cent).
(12) L.G. Seligman, "Political Parties and the Recruitment of Political Leadership", in L.J. Edinger (ed.) Political Leadership in Industrialised Societies, New York, Wiley, 1967.
(13)

Number of Parliamentary Elections Contested by Electoral Status

	Conservative				Labour							
No. Elections	S	C	SM	M	M	SM	C	S	I	N	All Con	All Lab
1	2	2	1	1	1	1	1	0	1	10	6	4
2	0	3	2	1	1	3	2	2	1	15	6	9
3	0	2	0	0	0	1	2	0	0	5	2	3
4 and above	1	1	3	1	0	1	0	0	0	7	6	1
	3	8	6	3	2	6	5	2	2	37	20	17

6 The Labour party: Recruitment and party organisation

THE POLITICAL OPPORTUNITY STRUCTURE

All political parties were subject to three common restrictions on the political opportunity structure: incumbency, the electoral system and the dual mandate. The Labour party imposed additional formal restrictions for their own selections. Despite the 1975 Referendum result which produced a two to one majority in favour of membership, from 1976 onwards there was a continuous anti-EEC theme in both National Executive Committee (NEC) statements and Conference resolutions. For example, the 1978 composite resolution no. 42 was stridently anti-Community in tone and called upon the Labour party to 'reject any moves towards economic and monetary union and any other encroachments on the rights to self-government' and ultimately to 'transform the EEC into an enlarged, reformed and more flexible institution in which independent states can meet and discuss issues of mutual concern'.(1) Although the then Labour Government was unenthusiastic and despite this history of anti-EEC Conference resolutions, the Government felt bound by the provisions of the Treaty of Rome to hold direct elections. The NEC's decision to fight was for a different reason: the NEC felt no such legal obligation, but realised that it would be misguided to allow the elections to go uncontested. On 26 April 1978, the NEC issued the following statement:

> This National Executive Committee reaffirms its opposition to the principle of direct elections to the European Assembly, but in the event of the proposed bill being passed, the National Executive Committee would not wish to let the mounting feeling of dissatisfaction with the EEC go unrepresented and therefore believes that the Labour party should contest the elections.(2)

Just fourteen months before the election did the Labour party reluctantly agree to take part. This reticence had major implications for the recruitment process.

Once the decision to fight the election had been taken, the further question of the dual mandate had to be resolved. Were Labour MPs to be allowed to be European aspirants like their Conservative adversaries? Or would potential aspirants to political office be required to limit themselves to one institution only? An NEC bulletin sent to all Constituency Labour Parties (CLPs) in August 1978 stated that the NEC would refuse to 'endorse any candidature if the successful nominee has been elected to the current Parliament', and this was formalised in the NEC report presented to the 1978 conference which was approved by conference without dissent.(3) Sitting MPs who wished to run for the European Parliament had to declare that they would resign from Westminster at the next election before they could even technically be nominated for Europe. The deadline for this declaration was 1 November 1978: only two MPs did so by this date - Barbara Castle and Sir Geoffrey de Freitas, both of whom had planned, prior to the NEC ruling, to retire at the next general election. Colin Phipps, MP for Dudley West, also indicated that he would not seek re-election but did not announce this until 9 November. Such a guarantee avoided the embarrassment of a by-election to free European aspirants from their Westminster commitments. Other MPs were rumoured to have been interested in running for Europe, but only as dual-mandated individuals; they were not prepared to forfeit their domestic seats.(4)

The position for parliamentary candidates was less clearcut. Only at a very late stage, indeed only after the actual nomination process had begun, did the NEC decide that parliamentary candidates would be ineligible to stand as nominees for the European Parliament. The National Agent sent a letter to all CLP secretaries on 24 November clarifying the position. He stated that,

> the National Agent shall refuse validation of nomination forms in respect of prospective parliamentary candidature. This means that if a prospective parliamentary candidate is chosen by a constituency party as one of its nominees to be sent forward to the European Selection Organisation, at that stage, he or she must decide whether to withdraw from the propective parliamentary candidature or from the European selection.(5)

Labour Weekly reported that approximately eight Labour parliamentary candidates for Westminster had preferred to run for Europe and resigned their domestic candidacies.(6) One such example was Stuart Randall: he resigned as parliamentary candidate for South Worcestershire and was subsequently adopted for the Midlands West Euro-constituency, defeating Colin Phipps (the retiring MP for one of the parliamentary districts within the Euro-boundary) at the selection conference. Another was Mrs. Mary Panko who resigned her recent adoption as PPC for Aberdeenshire West for the European prospective candidacy at Mid-Scotland and Fife. Other parliamentary candidates who had intimated their interest in the European Parliament prior to the NEC decision to exclude them, withdrew their European candidature at an early stage.

Many would argue that to disqualify PPCs at such an early stage in the selection process was misguided and unjust. PPCs were asked to choose between a guaranteed Westminster candidacy and a European nomination without any guarantee of adoption. An alternative procedure would have been to allow PPCs to take part in the earlier stages of the European selection process, on the understanding that if selected they would be expected to resign their domestic commitments. The fact that the vast majority of PPCs who were nominted for Europe withdrew rather than resign their Westminster selections bears witness to the flaw in the NEC's position. Thus access to political opportunity within the Labour party was constitutionally restricted. NEC decisions outlawed both sitting members and aspirants to the House of Commons who had already been selected by CLPs. An important group of individuals with electoral experience and political skills were excluded from the European arena.

One other constitutional restriction on candidacy and the structure of political opportunity followed the parliamentary precedent; namely, that nominees were not members of any proscribed organisations and accepted the Constitution as well as the Standing Orders of the British Labour Party Group in the European Parliament. In addition, nominees had to be individual members of the party of at least two years' standing, and where eligible, members of a trade union affiliated to the Trades Union Congress or recognised by the TUC as a bona fide trade union.(7)

The timing of the European election had a major influence upon the openness of the candidate opportunity structure. It was widely believed that the then Prime Minster, James Callaghan, would call a general election in October 1978. Had this been the case, and had Labour faired badly, it is probable that a larger number of defeated MPs and parliamentary candidates would have emerged as European aspirants. With the General Election delayed until May 1979, the NEC ruling disqualified a large number of potential nominees. Only those parliamentary candidates in the less winnable Westminster constituencies would contemplate exchanging their chance of election to the House of Commons for the European lottery. Individuals who wished to fight the May 1979 local government elections were not prohibited from European candidature. All these factors combined to produce aspirants for the European Parliament who tended to be drawn from local rather than the national political level.

Self-Recruitment/Recruitment Agents

Figure 6.1 employs the structure of the general model to explain the Labour party's recruitment and selection process: the initial distinction is between self-starters and recruitment agents. As Table 6.1 indicates there were less pure self-starters among Labour aspirants than their Conservative rivals, although when the auxiliary categories combining 'own idea' with other external catalysts are included, a majority of Labour aspirants believed their recruitment was to some degree personally motivated (though the figure was still less than for Conservatives, 54.5 per cent compared with 61.7 per cent respectively). As in parliamentary selections, the role played by intra-party bodies as recruitment agents was substantial. The following are dealt with in detail - trade unions, the Co-operative Party, the Labour Common Market Safeguards Committee, the Labour Co-ordinating Committee, the Labour Committee for Europe, the European Movement and Constituency Labour Parties.

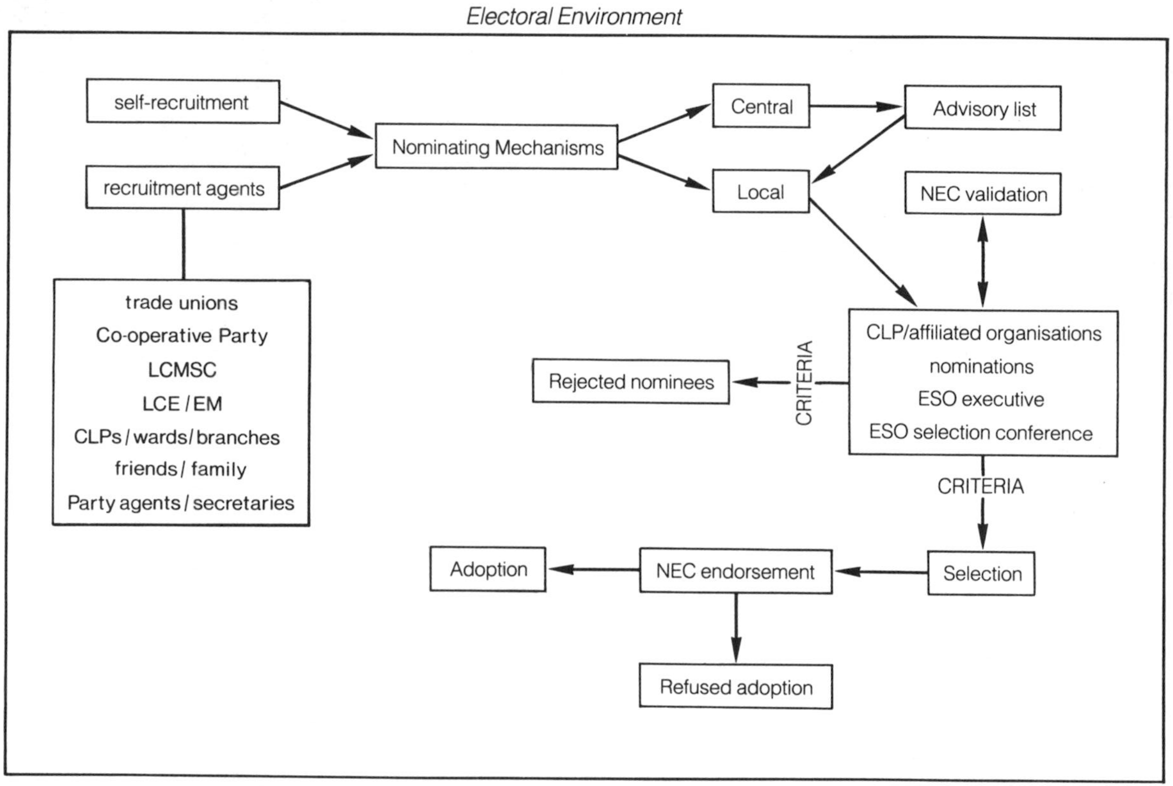

Electoral Environment

self-recruitment

recruitment agents

Nominating Mechanisms

Central

Local

Advisory list

NEC validation

trade unions
Co-operative Party
LCMSC
LCE / EM
CLPs / wards / branches
friends / family
Party agents / secretaries

CLP/affiliated organisations
nominations
ESO executive
ESO selection conference

CRITERIA

Rejected nominees

CRITERIA

Selection

NEC endorsement

Adoption

Refused adoption

Figure 6.1 Application of the Gate-Keeping Function of the Model for Labour Selections

Table 6.1

Initial Stimulus for European Candidacy

Stimulus	%	n
Own Idea	39.5	126
Constituency Labour Party (CLP)	25.1	80
Trade Union/Co-operative Party	8.8	28
Party Agents/Secretaries	1.3	4
Family/Friends	5.6	18
Own Idea plus CLP/Trade Union/Co-operative	10.3	33
Own Idea plus Family/Friends	4.7	15
CLP plus Trade Union/Co-operative	4.7	15
Not Known	-	68
	100.0	387
All Self Starters	54.5	174

Trade Unions: Trade Union sponsorship for parliamentary elections is a major source of and stimulus to recruitment. Examination of the figures relating to the number of sponsored candidates and sponsored elected MPs in the post-war period underlines the importance of this variable. Sponsored candidates have never accounted for less than one-fifth of all Labour candidates in the ten Westminster elections since 1945, and only once have they represented below one-third of elected Labour MPs. More significantly, the success rate for sponsored candidates has never fallen below 70.0 per cent.(8) These sponsored Westminster candidates were drawn from a nationally compiled 'A' List of Available Candidates which comprised candidates for whom trade unions were willing to accept financial responsibility. The financial advantage of selecting a sponsored nominee is obvious, and particularly seductive for the less prosperous Labour constituencies, although any mention at a selection conference of prospective sponsorship is strictly forbidden. However, as McLean suggests, it is impossible for selectors not to be aware of or to ignore the financial benefits of sponsorship.(9) As for all nominees, sponsored aspirants are subject to NEC validation and endorsement.

The area of sponsorship is controlled formally and through agreements between the unions and the Labour party. The 1913 Trade Union Act established the operation of political funds, and introduced a tight control of expenditure on 'political objects'. These provisions were complemented by the 1933 Hastings Agreement between the unions and the Labour party which set a fixed sum that unions could contribute to local parties that adopted sponsored candidates (it is updated periodically). It also allowed for trade unions to contribute to the election expenses where their sponsored candidate was adopted: unions pay 'a constituency 80.0 per cent of the limit laid down by the Representation of the People Acts'.(10) The provisions for Europe duplicated this parliamentary agreement.

Whereas the 'A' list of sponsored trade union aspirants is of some importance in domestic selection, such a list was absent for the European elections: this omission helped to weaken the centre's selection role in the Labour party, and constituted a major departure from Westminster procedure. Only three unions that sponsor parliamentary candidates agreed to extend sponsorship to European nominees: the Electrical Electronic Telecommunications and Plumbing Union (EETPU), the National Union of Mineworkers (NUM) and the Union of Post Office Workers (UPW). The EETPU forwarded nine names for inclusion on the Labour party's advisory list of possible candidates for the European Assembly; only one, Stuart Randall, was adopted. The NUM submitted four names for the list, but in addition were also prepared to support local members if adopted: only one individual, Michael Gallagher, secured adoption (and eventual election as the European member for Nottingham). The UPW was willing to sponsor candidates, but none of their nominees were successful, including the union's Deputy General Secretary, Norman Stagg, who failed to gain selection despite being nominated in four Euro-constituencies.

A number of other unions offered limited financial support, but not formal sponsorship. These were the Association of Scientific, Technical and Managerial Staffs (ASTMS); the Association of Professional, Executive, Clerical and Computer Staff (APEX); the National Union of Public Employees (NUPE); the Union of Shop, Distributive and Allied Workers (USDAW); the Amalgamated Union of Engineering Workers Union (AUEW); the General and Municipal Workers Union (GMWU) and the Associated Society of Locomotive Engineers and Firemen (AASLEF). The remaining unions who sponsor for Westminster did nothing to assist the election of their members to the European Parliament. Many cited the legal restraints of the 1913 Trade Union Act, the Hastings Agreement, or their internal rules relating to sponsorship, as prohibiting any involvement in candidate selection. For example, the Transport and General Workers Union (TGWU), the National Graphical Association (NGA), the Post Office Engineering Union (POEU) and the Iron and Steel Trades Confederation (ISTC) all found that their constitutions limited sponsorship to Westminster elections. A survey of the European election conducted by the Labour Committee for Europe confirmed this lack of union aid. They concluded that 'in general, trade union contributions were modest - save for two constituencies of which we are aware, when 5,000 pounds each was contributed'.(11) Even this sum was significantly less than the permitted 80.0 per cent of election expenses (which were in the region of 15,000 pounds) as directed by the NEC.

Thus the major unions who sponsor MPs tended to ignore Europe. Rush found that between 1950-1966, 69.5 per cent of all trade union candidates came from six unions - the TGWU, AEU, NUM, USDAW, the National Union of Railwaymen (NUR) and the National Union of General and Municipal Workers (NUGMW).(12) The Figures for sponsored candidates for the 1970 and October 1974 elections generally confirm this dominance with these six unions accounting for 65.7 and 63.8 per cent of all sponsored candidates respectively. In the case of the European election, however, only one candidate, Michael Gallagher (Nottingham) was sponsored by one of the six unions - the NUM. The contrast between the practice for Westminster and Europe was stark. Not only was there no formal list of trade union sponsored candidates, the major unions involved in parliamentary sponsorship ignored the European dimension, either because of their anti-EEC policy positions or constitutional rules. Thus a major source and agency for recruitment to the House of Commons was absent in the European recruitment and selection process.

The Co-operative party: Historically, there has been an uneasy and often tenuous relationship between the Labour party and the Co-operative party, especially in the area of sponsorship of parliamentary candidates. The works of Rush, Ranney, Patterson and Harrison all trace the development of formal agreements and comment on the informal intrigues that have coloured the two parties' relations since the Cheltenham Agreement of 1927.(13) The various agreements since that time, notably in 1946, 1958, 1960 and 1962, have imposed limits upon both the number and the type of constituencies in which 'Labour and Co-operative party' candidates could stand: in particular, the 1962 Agreement committed a high proportion of Co-operative candidates to fight less winnable constituencies. The situation since then has remained largely unchanged: the Agreement between the Labour and Co-operative parties (as amended July 1976) limited Co-operative party sponsored candidates to a maximum of thirty (including sitting MPs), distributed between 'favourable' and 'difficult' constituencies. These limitations, as well as the loser financial ties, distinguish Co-operative party from trade union sponsorship. Since the quota of thirty candidates was introduced (in 1964), it has never been filled, let alone exceeded.

Co-operative candidates for Westminster are drawn from their nationally approved panel: this practice was adopted for the European elections, although members of the Westminster panel were not automatically available for sponsorship for the European elections. The panel for the European Assembly consisting of thirty-eight aspirants was published on 12 December 1978; all were available for sponsorship subject to the National Executive Council of the Co-operative party agreement. However, for financial reasons, inclusion on the panel did not guarantee sponsorship. This financial constraint was evident in the selection process: of the six PEPCs who were on the Co-operative Panel only four received sponsorship (approx 3,500 pounds) and then only in respect of election expenditure.(14) The Labour party placed no limitation on the number of candidates that the Co-operative party was entitled to sponsor: the agreement related to parliamentary elections only. The absence of any formal agreement for the European elections was, perhaps, a consequence of the Labour party's late decision to contest the elections and the haste with which procedures were drawn up. In terms of distributing candidacies amongst the less winnable constituencies, there appeared to be an interesting departure from the Westminster practice. Rather than fighting projected Conservative seats, the four sponsored candidates were all nominated to and selected for projected Labour seats, ranging from the second most impregnable Labour bastion of Yorkshire South to the semi-marginal Cleveland. The principle of fighting both winnable and hopeless seats was not translated into practice.

All the Co-operative aspirants had to follow the selection procedure set out by the NEC of the Labour party; that is, nomination to an ESO was through affiliated bodies to CLP's, subject to validation and NEC endorsement. In general, the Co-operative party's impact as a recruitment agent was substantial, particularly when one contrasts it against the disinterest shwon by most trade unions. Their panel represented 9.9 per cent of all Labour aspirants, 5.1 per cent of selected PEPCs and 11.8 per cent of elected MEPs, a figure that was twice that for Co-operative sponsored MPs. However, neither trade unions nor the Co-operative party treated Europe as earnestly as they did their domestic obligations. Their muted participation detracted from vigour and energy of the recruitment process.

The Labour Common Market Safeguards Committee: The LCMSC was established immediately after the Referendum result of June 1975 as a small group of Labour party members who were opposed to Britain's membership of the EEC. By the time of the European selections, their number had swelled to one hundred, eighty-four of whom were MPs. The stated aim of the LCMSC was 'to safeguard Britain's interest and our socialist objectives now that we are in the Common Market, and in particular to hold the government to the promises and assurances which they gave during the Referendum'.(15)

The role played by the LCMSC in the recruitment process was of considerable importance, giving voice and support to the anti-Market theme within the party. However, the LCMSC was not a recruitment agent in the sense that the trade unions or Co-operative party were. It did not sponsor or directly recruit individuals as European nominees: it only offered support and a collective identity to those who were already self-motivated or recruited aspirants. The LCMSC should be regarded as an intra-party pressure group that tried to ensure the selection of labour PEPCs who were hostile to the EEC rather than as a stimulus or catalyst to political candidacy. However, its high public profile and concerted proselytizing efforts undoubtedly acted as a recruitment catalyst (nowever unintentional) for certain aspirants. Lmited funds and a volunteer based organisation prohibited any involvement in active recruitment. The budget for the pre-election financial year was a mere 1,200 pounds. However, there can be no doubt that the LCMSC had a selection impact that was far greater than its economic resources implied.

On 10 November 1978, the LCMSC issued a policy statement on the direct elections: it set out six principles on which it wished to see Labour's European candidates stand and called for a fundamental and radical change in Britain's relationship with the Community which reflected the policies endorsed by the 1978 Annual Conference.(16) More importantly, a covering letter circulated with the policy statement implied that ESO delegates should use these principles as their selection criterion. It stated that 'only by having candidates pledged to press for the reforms we advocate do we believe that anything substantial can be achieved. We therefore very much hope that you will be able to help us secure nominations for those who support our view'.(17) As a guide for CLPs who were looking for suitable anti-EEC nominees, the names, addresses and brief personal details of thirty-nine nominees from the Transport House advisory list of possible European nominees who supported the LCMSC statement were circulated with the covering letter and statement of policy. The statement and the list of supporters was published simultaneously in Tribune and Labour Weekly.(18) In response, the list of signatories had increased to ninety-four by the end of the year. However, this initial attempt to polarise the pro and anti European camps was merely the forerunner of a more orchestrated and pervasive attempt to influence the selection of Labour nominees.

The Labour Co-ordinating Committee: In January 1979, the Labour Co-ordinating Committee, in conjunction with the LCMSC, published an eleven point questionnaire designed to establish 'a candidate's knowledge of the [European] issues and his views as to the policies the Labour party should pursue'.(19) The questions were highly critical of British membership and focused on issues such as parliamentary sovereignty, federalism, UK budgetary contributions and the right of the annual conference to shape the party's European policy. The questionnaire, which was composed by Bryan Gould MP, first appeared in Labour Activist, the publication of the Labour Co-ordinating Committee, and was sent to all subscribers (circa 300) and LCMSC members. In addition it was sent to every CLP secretary and received coverage (and a degree of notoriety) in the national press, as well as being published in full in both Labour Weekly and Tribune.(20) It was suggested that these eleven questions be put to nominees at the selection conference stage 'or circulated to them in writing beforehand with a request for written replies by the time of the conference'.(21) The nominees' answers were to serve as policy commitments if elected. Iain Wrigglesworth, then Labour MP for Thornaby and a pro-Marketeer, denounced these proposals and especially the implied policy mandate of the questionnaire as 'offensive and deeply disturbing'.(22) Pro-Marketeers regarded this as a sinister anti-Market attempt to subvert the selection process; Wrigglesworth tried unsuccessfully to have the questionnaire banned by the party's general secretary, Ron Hayward.

Quite how influential the questionnaire was as a recruitment variable remains contentious: figures from the Labour nominees' data-set show that only a small minority (11.0 per cent) were asked to complete the questionnaire either orally at the selection meeting or in writing prior to the meeting. However, the general anti-EEC themes expressed by the Labour Co-ordinating Committee did dominate a significant proportion of questions at European selections.

As with the LCMSC policy statement, the Co-ordinating Committee's questionnaire was not intended to stimulate or lure nominees into the selection process, but rather to prevent the adoption of pro-European nominees within the existing aspirant cohort. The fact that neither organisation was mentioned as an initial recruitment stimulus supports this interpretation (see Table 6.1). However, the existence of the questionnaire, and the efforts of the LCMSC to make the pro-anti debate the major selection factor, were of importance at the intermediate rather than formative period of the recruitment process. Once the nominees had emerged at the CLP level, their overall position on Europe taken in conjunction with their association with the LCMSC/Labour Co-ordinating Committee, or their pro-European adversary, the Labour Committee for Europe, became a major selection factor.

The Labour Committee for Europe and the European Movement: Like its Conservative counterpart, the Conservative Group for Europe, the Labour Committee for Europe (LCE) was a constituent part of the non-partisan European Movement (EM). The European Movement denied any recruitment function only offering 'moral support and enthusiastic encouragement' and refused to sponsor any individual candidates. The actual financial ties between the European Movement and the Labour Committee for Europe were identical to those for the Conservative Group for Europe: as constituent parts of the Movement, both were given 6,500 pounds for the financial year ending 31 March 1979.(23)

The recruitment impact of the LCE, whilst muted, did appear to be more overt than that performed by any of the anti-EEC organisations. The LCE did not create a specific list of its nominees or advocate sponsorship; however, it did supply recommendations informally if approached by nominating organisations. At least two selected PEPCs received LCE grants for their election expenses and the LCE also urged its members to participate at the grassroots level of nomination. The greater financial resources of the LCE and organisational links with the European Movement made it a potentially stronger recruitment force. Although a smaller percentage of nominees claimed to be LCE as opposed to LCMSC members, the selection impact of this organisation should not be underestimated: in an internal party atmosphere hostile to the EEC and with only lukewarm NEC approval for contesting the elections, a surprisingly high number of candidates who were sympathetic to the aims of the Committee were adopted.

In summary, the pro-anti divide within the Labour party's recruitment and selection processes was of fundamental importance. Despite claims that the EEC was no longer an issue, that everyone had accepted the Referendum result and wished to see reform, behind this smokescreen the vying pro and anti factions fought with such intensity and bitterness that the European selection process offers one of the best examples of Labour Party factionalism and intra-party disputes. This antagonism helped to sow the initial seeds of a move towards the Social Democratic Party on the part of certain pro-Europeans. The existence of the LCMSC and the Labour Co-ordinating Committee on the one hand, and the Labour Committee for Europe on the other, exacerbated and guaranteed the dominance of this single criterion. However, the conclusion offered by Butler and Marquand remains perceptive: 'on the pro-Market as on the anti-market side, the picture was one of well-meaning confusion, rather than Machiavellian conspiratorial skill'.(24)

Constituency Labour Parties: One-quarter of Labour nominee respondents stated that their initial reason for running as an MEP aspirant was triggered by their local Constituency Labour Party (CLP), branch or ward. Individual measurement of this recruitment variable was not possible: all that can be said was that the local aspect of European candidacy reflected the Westminster example to a large degree. The greater emphasis placed on grassroots democracy within the Labour party inevitably led to a more parochial selection system. The formal selection procedures that accommodate this phenomenon are described in the following sections.

Formal Selection Procedures

(a) Central mechanisms:

As in the Conservative party, the broad structure for Westminster selections was used as the guide to establishing the organisation and procedures for choosing Labour candidates for the European Parliament.

The National Executive Committee (NEC): The Labour party's main objective in 1979 was to win the forthcoming General Election: the European election was of much lower priority and accounts for the NEC's limited role. As indicated previously, the most notable departure from domestic practice was the absence of a centrally compiled list of sponsored candidates, and the advisory nature of the one list of nominees that did exist. Although the Constituion and Standing Orders of the Labour Party are silent on the matter, for domestic selections the NEC is responsible for compiling and maintaining lists of possible candidates. The importance of these lists is demonstrated by the fact that candidates drawn from either the 'A' or 'B' list tend to dominate parliamentary selections. With no European equivalent of the 'A' list of sponsored aspirants, due to the trade unions' lack of interest or inability to sponsor, the financial burdens of candidacy fell principally upon local CLPs within each Euro-constituency, with the exception of the few individuals sponsored by either the Co-operative party, the NUM or EEPTU. Although there was no list exclusively for sponsored aspirants, individuals nominated by trade unions could be included on the advisory List of Possible Candidates for the European Assembly, and their nominated status advertised. Only two unions, the EEPTU and the NUM lent themselves to this option of advertising potential, though far from guaranteed, sponsorship.

There was a definite difference in the status of the domestic 'B' list and the advisory European or 'E' list. In their report to the 1960 Annual conference the NEC stated that the 'B' list consisted of 'members who have been approved by the NEC as suitable for consideration by constituency parties seeking a candidate'.(25) However, they still were 'subject to the same conditions under which endorsement is granted in other cases when their candidatures are submitted by CLPs after selection'.(26) Approval generally implied validation, but not endorsement. There were no such formal provisions for the prior approval of European nominees. The inferior status of the 'E' list was stressed as, 'the inclusion of a person's name in the list does not signify National Executive Committee approval to the nomination, nor does it give any guarantee of endorsement.'(27) The list was characteristic of the weaker central control displayed by the NEC with regard to the European candidatures in general.

The administrative compilation of the 'E' list was the extent of the NEC's involvement in this stage of the selection process and indicative of the party's general attitude and haste with which procedures were drawn up. Only in July 1978, less than a year before the election, did the National Agent write to CLP secretaries and affiliated organisations asking for nominations of available candidates to be submitted by eligible bodies. The actual compilation of the list was similar to that for Westminster: however, the major difference from the Westminster list was the clause that excluded MPs or endorsed candidates for parliamentary elections.

A final example of the _ad hoc_ approach adopted by the NEC towards the organisation of the 'E' list was its staggered publication and circulation. The original advisory list, consisting of one hundred names, was published and circulated on request to CLPs on 1 November 1978. A revised list with an additional eighty-eight names was made available on 20 November, and a third and final list of 248 possible candidates produced on 9 January 1979, nine days after the suggested deadline for all CLP nominations! The constrast between the rigorous central control over the Conservative approved list and the casual attitude displayed by the NEC towards European candidature was striking.

A second procedure under the auspices of the NEC was the process of validation: once again, the role performed by the NEC with regard to Westminster nominees was replicated for European aspirants. Although the National Agent, acting on behalf of the NEC, has the right to examine the validity of all nominations received prior to the short-listing stage of selection, in practice for both Westminster and Europe this requirement was largely an administrative obligation rather than an active gatekeeping function. According to the 'Rules', no parliamentary nomination was valid unless made on the appropriate form 'in terms prescribed by the NEC, bearing thereon the consent in writing of the member nominated'.(28) The regulations for European nominations followed this format. Instances of parliamentary nominations being refused validation are rare, and then usually only on technical grounds. Such technical grounds however, may be fabricated to disguise what were, in essence, political objections.(29) The Assistant National Agent responsible for overseeing the European selection procedures, refused to validate one CLP nomination because the nominee had failed to comply with Clause III-3 (b) of the _Constitution and Standing Orders of the Labour Party_ which requires party members, if eligible, to be members of a _bona fide_ trade union affiliated to the TUC, and thus consequently contravened Clause X-7 (a) of the Constitution which required the same qualification for parliamentary candidates. Rush's conclusion for parliamentary validations can be transferred without qualification to the European experience: validation remains the technical preliminary administrative check on candidate eligibility, nothing more.(30)

Although all short-listed nominees had to have been validated, the individual chosen by the European Selection Organisation had to apply for NEC endorsement before he or she could be officially adopted. The power of endorsement, like that of validation, is a procedural matter: except in very rare circumstances the political likes or dislikes of the NEC are not a factor: valid constitutional or technical reasons must be produced. Furthermore, the _Constitution and Standing Orders of the Labour Party_ state that no parliamentary candidature shall be endorsed until the National Executive Committee has received an undertaking by any one of its affiliated organisations that the election expenses of the candidate are guaranteed.(31) Technically, to secure endorsement candidates must comply with the requirements for validation (individual membership and trade union affiliation) and 'undertake to accept and act in harmony with the Standing Orders of the Parliamentary Labour Party'.(32) In accordance with the 1978 Annual Conference NEC recommendation that 'the procedures for the selection and re-selection of candidates should be the same as that for Parliamentary candidates', these Westminster provisions were translated to the European arena.(33)

It was not surprising that none of the seventy-eight Labour PEPCs were refused endorsement, although the National Agent in his role as European selections organiser for the NEC did occasionally stop the selection procedure or order that the short-listing be carried out again because of technical breaches in procedure. Again, the NEC's role for domestic candidatures was identical for Europe. Thus, examination of the three major areas of candidate selection for which the NEC were responsible, the approved lists, validation and endorsement, all demonstrated a reluctance on the part of the NEC to do anything more than the organisational minimum. Their impressive constitutional powers remained latent.

Other selection areas in which the NEC were involved were equally low-keyed. Firstly, the NEC's power of placement was even more restricted than the abortive efforts of Conservative Central Office to secure the adoption of Channon. The NEC did not attempt to influence the selection of any ESO candidates. Secondly, the literature sent out by the NEC relating to the European selection procedures was minimal. (This can be partially explained by the organisational pressures generated by the prospect of a general election, district council elections in England and Wales on 3 May and the 1 March referenda in Scotland and Wales.) Thirdly, not until 24 November was authorisation given for the establishment of ESOs. The candidates' dissatisfaction with the NEC's efforts were voiced at the pre-election conference at Birmingham: the NEC was castigated for allowing the campaign to be ill-prepared, rushed and under-financed, as well as being responsible for a general lack of consultation and co-ordination. One candidate was quoted as saying, 'it's not just the General Election that has been in the way. There has been a general meanness of spirit'.(34) The survey conducted by a working party of the Labour committee for Europe presented a more general and pervasive impression of hostility towards the NEC. Their questionnaire, sent out to all of Labour's seventy-eight PEPCs, was designed to investigate the 'disturbing reports from candidates, agents and others involved relating to the conduct and organisation of the recent European elections'.(35) It incurred the wrath of the anti-EEC element in the Party because of its pro-Market inferences and somewhat leading questions. In response to the question, 'What is your overall view about the role of the NEC during the campaign? (a) politically, (b) organisationally, (c) financially', the Committee found 'trenchant criticism' with regard to all three activities. The following extract from the report summarises their findings:

> Their [the NEC's] political role was summed up by one successful candidate (an historic anti-marketeer) who described their attitude by saying that the 'NEC never really seemed to want to fight the campaign at all'. Other less polite global assessments were 'bloody awful', 'inept', 'laughable', 'completely disinterested', 'were let down at

national level', 'schizophrenic', 'disastrous', 'confusion and division damaged our prospects' ... the services of Transport House to candidates were ineffective, negative, tardy and low standard.(36)

The report went on to cite the NEC's 'obvious lack of enthusiasm and negative approach' as a major reason for Labour's debacle in the election. The decision to pulp the original edition of the manifesto because it was entitled 'Labour in Europe' rather than the less committed 'Labour and Europe' was seen as characteristic of the NEC's confused and lack-lustre performance.

Lastly, NEC supervision at the constituency level was performed by their Regional Organisers. In essence, the Regional Organiser's role was to oversee the administrative aspects of selection, to ensure that rules and procedures were not infringed and to co-ordinate the organisation of selections. Once constituency nominations to the ESO had been submitted, the Regional Organiser was responsible for arranging validation and for convening the first meeting of delegates to the ESO itself.

In conclusion, the NEC's central selection procedures and mechanisms reflected their Westminster organisation role but, in its supervision of European selections, the NEC displayed even less control and involvement than that found by the leading authorities on the selection of MPs. The NEC initiated the organisational procedure, collated and coordinated the necessary administrative requirements, but did not perform any real gatekeeping function.

(b) Local selection mechanisms

In the Labour party, the European selection process used a three-tiered structure, both for nominees and delegates. The principle of delegate based grass-roots democracy extended from the branch or affiliated organisation level through to the newly-created ESOs.

Nomination: Reference to figure 6.2 illustrates the three-tiered procedure for the selection of Labour nominees. Each CLP Executive Committee was required to invite affiliated and party organisations entitled to appoint delegates to the General Committee to put forward nominees (provided it was made prior to the closing date for nominations), whereas the General Committee was not. No organisation could submit more than one nomination. According to the National Agent's guidelines, once all the nominations had been received, a special meeting of the CLP Executive Committee had to be convened. Prior to determining the composition of the short-list, the actual number of nominees to be forwarded to the ESO had to be decided, as did the precise balloting procedure. The Executive Committee had to 'decide whether they wish(ed) to recommend that the General Committee should forward one, two or three names to the ESO'.(37) It was then responsibile for recommending to the General Committee a short-list of those invited to appear before the CLP selection meeting. However, although the Executive Committee was responsible for short-listing, the General Committee had 'the power to accept, amend or reject the proposed short-list', and 'the final word on the composition of the short-list of nominees to be interviewed at the selection meeting'.(38) The actual selection meeting decided which of the CLP short-listed nominees would be submitted to the ESO, in

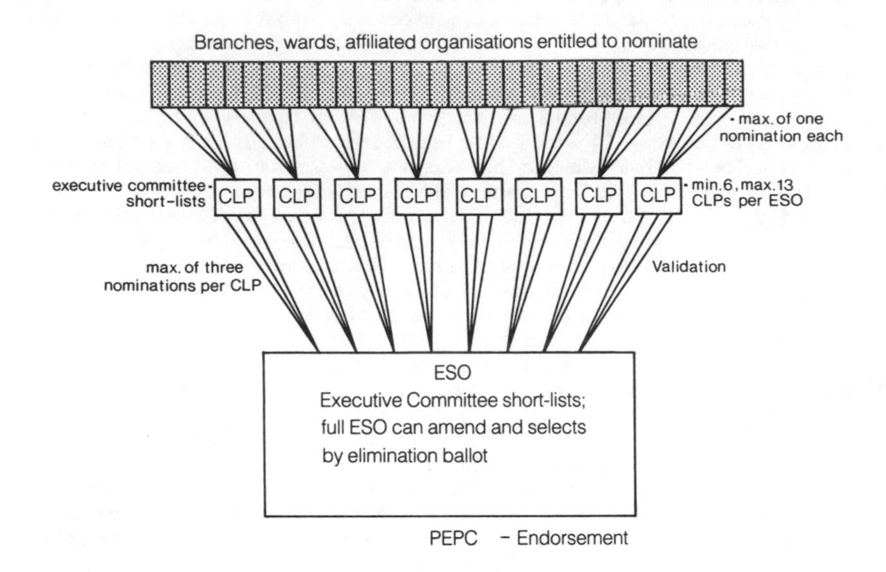

Figure 6.2 ESO Nomination Structure

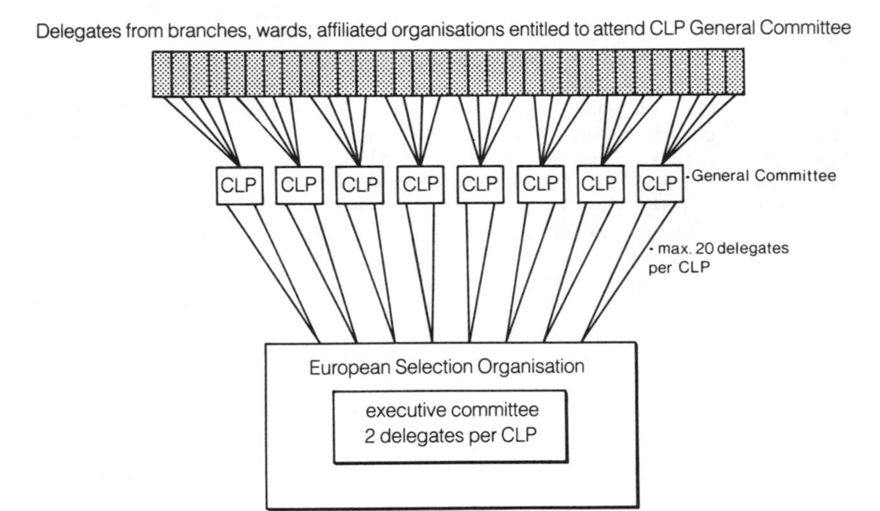

Figure 6.3 ESO Delegate Structure

accordance with the number determined by the Executive Committee. This nomination procedure allowed for a wide range in the potential maximum number of possible nominations. For example, the Euro-constituency of Glasgow contained thirteen parliamentary constituencies; had each exercised its right to submit three nominations to the ESO, the Executive Committe of the ESO would have been faced with a list of thirty-nine nominees.

Nominations submitted to the ESO level were not automatically placed on the ESO selection meeting short-list: the Executive Committee of the ESO chose the short-list, although their recommendation was subject to the approval or amendment of a larger meeting of the full ESO. The final selection of the candidate was made by a special meeting of the ESO, following the procedure set down for parliamentary candidates, namely selection by exhaustive ballot. Subject to NEC endorsement, the chosen candidate then became the PEPC for the Euro-consitituency in question.

Delegates: The delegate structure paralleled that for nominations (see Figure 6.3). The choice of delegates empowered to short-list nominees (at various stages in the nomination process) constituted one of the major gate-keeping variables within Labour's European selection procedure. The composition of CLP and ESO delegate bodies had a direct effect upon the eventual choice of nominees, often in a simple pro versus anti-Marketeer sense.

As Butler and Marquand suggest, the size of Euro-constituencies made it difficult for one group to dominate selections and partially explained why 'no selections were dominated by union influences'.(39) Delegates had to be individual members of the party and reside or be registered as electors in the constituency. Furthermore, the list of delegates and their addresses was read at the start of the General Committee meeting convened to consider the short-list; at this stage, every delegate had the right to challenge the credentials of any delegate. No delegates were admitted late to the selection meeting as voting members, if the first nominee had commenced his address. As stated in the previous section on nominations, at the CLP level it was the responsibility of the CLP Executive Committee to determine the number of nominees to be short-listed and submitted to the ESO, not the larger delegate body: exhaustive ballot by delegates determined which, if any, nominees were sent to the ESO.

The 1978 NEC Report to the party Conference stated that each ESO should be composed of an equal number of delegates from each CLP within the boundaries of the Euro-constituency, the number varying according 'to the the nature of the area, but in no case exceeding twenty delegates ... the delegates from each CLP shall be allocated between the party organisations and affiliated organisations as near as possible in the same proportion to the number of delegates appointed to the respective CLP General Committees'.(40) It was also recommended that the Executive Committee of the ESO have at least one member from each CLP. It was this body that was responsible for the important gatekeeping function of selection meeting short-listing (although the full ESO could, if it wished, amend their decision). The final choice between short-listed nominees was taken by ESO delegates at a special selection meeting (in practice the approval of the short-list and actual selection were often combined). As with parliamentary selections, the Labour party was committed to a delegate system, placing choice firmly in the hands of the local party, or at least in the hands of its chosen delegates.

How far were these procedural rules at the ESO and CLP levels, for both nominations and delegates, followed in practice? At the lower levels of the delegate structure (branch, ward, affiliated organisations to the CLP General Committee), the European provisions utilized the existing domestic arrangements. However, the conglomeration of between six and thirteen CLPs into new ESOs demanded a degree of flexibility in the number of delegates sent to each ESO: the Regional Organiser, after consultation with the CLPs within the Euro-boundary, decided on the size of the delegate body. The recommended maximum number of twenty delegates per CLP was adopted by the majority of ESOs (73.2 per cent of known cases).

Table 6.2

Size of CLP Delegate Bodies Sent to ESOs

No. of ESO delegates per CLP	%	No. of seats
12	9.9	7
14	2.8	2
15	11.3	8
16	2.8	2
20	73.2	52
Not Known		7
	100.0	78

In those cases that decided to have a reduced number of CLP delegates on the ESO, 'the nature of the area' was often the influential factor, both geographically and in terms of electoral status.(41) Thus all four Welsh Euro-constituencies and five of the most dispersed English Euro-constituencies chose between fourteen and sixteen delegates, seemingly because of the geographical factor. All the others were either safe or comfortable Conservative strongholds, areas where it was often difficult to maintain the existing local constituency organisations let alone support any new European structure. There was one exception to the ESO delegate selection meeting structure: this took place in the Highlands and Islands Euro-constituency - once again, geography was the deciding factor. Whilst this was physically the largest British Euro-constituency, it had the smallest electorate, 296,473, 37.4 per cent below the European electoral quota for Scotland. To overcome the dispersed nature of the ESO, selection was by a postal ballot rather than a delegate selection meeting, with each CLP allowed twenty votes.

In contrast to the Conservatives' General Meetings for representatives, the size of Labour's gate-keeping delegate bodies were limited constitutionally; in consequence, the potential maximum size of ESO selection meetings was generally smaller. 52.1 per cent of Conservative General Meetings had a potential representative maximum in excess of 200: the only Labour Euro-constituency to realise this number was Glasgow, where each of the thirteen parliamentary constituencies could nominate up to twenty delegates each.

Secondly, not only were Labour delegates less numerous, those eligible to participate were less likely to do so. Attendance figures for delegates at the final ESO selection meetings ranged from thirty-one to 179, with 56.7 per cent of selections being made by one hundred delegates or less.

Thirdly, the attendance totals of delegates as a percentage of the maximum possible eligible to vote at the ESO selection meeting produced the following distribution. When compared to the corresponding percentages of Conservative representative attendance, Labour delegates exhibited a lower level of turn-out; 82.6 per cent of Conservative General Meetings achieved a minimum of 61.0 per cent attendance; the figure for Labour was 52.3 per cent. These figures reflect the much lower level of interest in the European election shown by the Labour party. Electoral status also appeared to be related to delegate attendance. The three constituencies with the lowest ESO turn-out figures were ranked as the third, eight and eighteenth safest Conservative seats based on October 1974 results. The fourth, fifth and sixth ranked Conservative seats had turn-out figures of 40.6 per cent 35.8 per cent and 36.9 per cent. Conversely, all seven ESOs with more than 80.0 per cent delegate attendance were projected Labour strongholds. Labour's second most impregnable seat recorded the highest percentage turn-out of delegates (97.9 per cent); two other impregnable areas achieved 85.2 and 88.6 per cent attendance respectively; three safe areas 90.0, 91.8 and 82.1 per cent turn-outs and a comfortable seat 93.0 per cent. The high levels of participation displayed by Welsh ESOs reflected the strength of the local constituency parties.

This general trend was reinforced when every ESO percentage turn-out was tested against electoral status: Figure 6.4 constitutes a perfect rank order for mean percentage delegate attendance. The relationship between percentage delegate turn-out was both positive and constant: the more secure the seat for Labour, the greater the potential for high levels of delegate attendance; where Labour was contesting a hopeless Euro-constituency, mean attendance figures plummeted to below 50.0 per cent. This overall relationship paralleled that found for Conservative General Meeting attendance. However, in every case the mean scores, medians and ranges for Conservative representative turn-out were more impressive. For example, the mean attendance figure for Conservative representatives in safe Euro-constituencies was 94.7 per cent, whereas Labour delegates in comparable safe Labour seats only achieved a 78.9 per cent turn-out. Even Labour's impregnable seats fell short of the safe Conservative figure. The delegate participation figures for certain Euro-constituencies were skewed because specific CLPs only took a limited role, or occasionally no part at all in the European elections, due in most cases to their hostility to Britain's membership of the EEC. For example, in the Midlands West Euro-constituency, Walsall North CLP totally refused

Table 6.3

Potential Maximum Delegate Size of ESOs

Max. no. of delegates	%	No. of seats
84 - 100	11.3	8
101 - 125	15.5	11
126 - 150	35.2	25
151 - 175	21.1	15
176 - 200	15.5	11
201 and above	1.4	1
Not Known	-	7
	100.0	78

Attendance Figures for ESO Delegates

No of delegates	%	No. of ESOs
0 - 50	13.4	9
51 - 75	10.5	7
76 - 100	32.8	22
101 - 125	29.9	20
126 - 150	11.9	8
151 and above	1.5	1
Not Known		11
	100.0	78

Percentage Turn-out of ESO Delegates

% Turn-out of delegates	%	No. of Euro-seats
100 - 91	4.5	3
90 - 81	6.0	4
80 - 71	19.4	13
70 - 61	22.4	15
60 - 51	32.8	22
50 - 41	4.5	3
40 - 31	10.4	7
Not Known	-	9
	100.0	78

to participate; Lincoln CLP was similarly reported to have ignored the elections in protest.(42)

Returning to nominations, the following trends were evident; ESOs tended to receive fewer nominees than their Conservative counterparts: only fourteen Conservative Euro-Constituency Councils received ten or fewer applicants, whereas forty-five ESOs found themselves in this position. The two most popular ESOs were the comfortable Labour seat of London East which received twenty-one nominations, and its impregnable neighbour, London North East, which received seventeen. At the opposite end of the scale the third safest Conservative seat attracted only one nomination and the safest of all projected Conservative victories just two nominees. The mean number of nominations to all ESOs was 8.6.

Table 6.4

Total Number of CLP Nominees Forwarded to ESOs

No. of Nominees	%	No. ESOs
1 - 5	18.3	13
6 - 10	45.1	32
11 - 15	33.8	24
16 and above	2.8	2
Not Known	-	7
	100.0	78

That Labour nominees tended to restrict themselves to a smaller number of Euro-constituencies reflected the constitutional requirements of nomination (namely, that every aspirant had to be nominated by a local organisation affiliated to a CLP), the absence of an adequate approved list of available candidates (sponsored or unsponsored) and the general parochialism and lack of interest in the elections. Nonetheless, the dearth of Labour nominees to the CLP stage of the European selections was surprising: at the local level there was a plethora of eligible nominating bodies - branches, wards, affiliated organisations. There was a reluctance to nominate; consequently only a small minority of ESOs received the maximum number of three nominations from each CLP.

Labour aspirants, unlike their Conservative adversaries, could not apply directly to any Euro-constituency; nomination was internalised. Only well-known aspirants, or those with financial resources (either trade union or personal) could hope to be nominated in a large number of seats. In consequence, the application levels for the two parties were not directly comparable. These differences between the two and the reasons for these differences, however, were of major importance and had an impact upon the whole recruitment and selection process. Many nominees were critical of the extra hurdle created by the nomination structure and inferred that those with financial backing were advantaged.

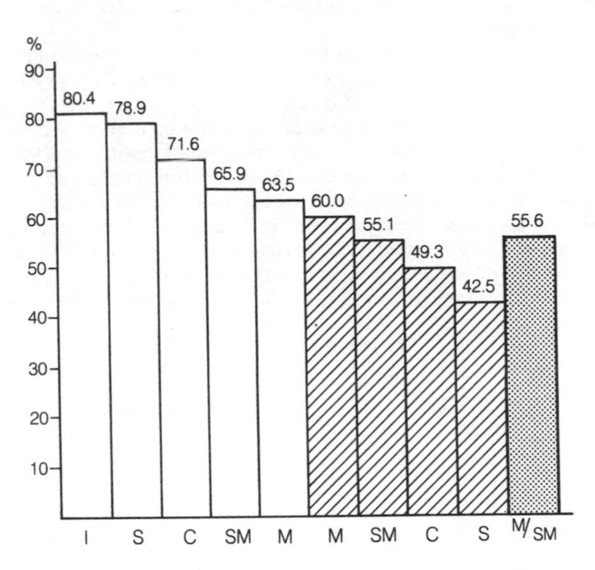

Figure 6.4 Mean Percentage Delegate ESO Attendance by Electoral Status

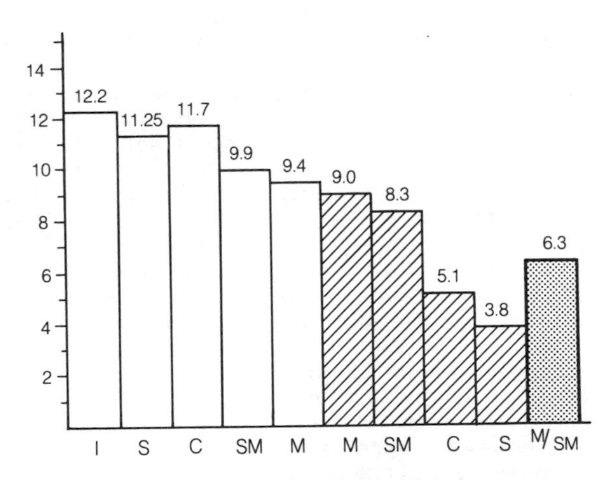

Figure 6.5 CLP Nominations to ESOs

Table 6.5

Size of ESO Short-Lists

No. on ESO short-list	%	No. of seats
1-3	8.5	6
4	14.1	10
5	25.4	18
6	36.6	26
7-10	15.4	11
Not Known	-	7
	100.0	78

As noted earlier, the ESO Executive Committees exhibited a predominantly benevolent attitude towards short-lists and tended to follow the principle of inclusion rather than exclusion. The largest Conservative short-list consisted of five candidates; over half the ESO selection meetings had the opportunity to choose from between six to ten nominees. Indeed, when the number of nominees short-listed was examined as a percentage of the total number of nominations submitted to each ESO, this inclusive policy was confirmed. Only 22.1 per cent of known cases chose to short-list less than half of all nominations received. It was common to short-list all nominees: this occurred in twenty-three Euro-constituencies (33.8 per cent). However, in two-thirds of Euro-constituencies the Executive Committee's short-listing power was not redundant. For example, Greater Manchester South reduced their short-list to five from fifteen, London North East to five from seventeen and London East rejected two-thirds of their twenty-one nominees. Although Executive Committee recommended short-lists had to be submitted to a full meeting of the ESO for approval or amendment, only two examples of amendment were found - at Midlands East and Essex South West.

Electoral status had a clear impact on nominations though the relationship was less dramatic than that found for Conservative applicants, but nonetheless constant in its direction. There was a slow decline in the mean number of CLP nominations as one moved away from the most winnable seats to those which were electorally hopeless. The three projected SNP seats were located at approximately the mid-point between the two extremes. (See Figure 6.5) The overall difference was most clearly illustrated by separating Conservative from Labour seats. The mean level of CLP nominations for projected Labour seats was 10.9 compared with 6.8 for Conservative seats. The effect of electoral status on the size of short-lists was less clear-cut. Although the least winnable seats tended to use smaller short-lists, this was often a consequence of their paucity of original nominees. Eighteen of the twenty-three ESOs to short-list all nominees were projected Conservative Euro-constituencies.

Finally, the selection procedure has to be put into context: the selection timetable drawn up by the National Agent bore no relation to the actual schedule implemented. The Labour party was the last of the major parties to establish its selection machinery. Originally, 31 December was set as the deadline for all CLP nominations and ESO selection meetings were to be no earlier than 15 January and no later than 28 February. A number of CLPs had to ask for an extension of the December deadline and the first ESO selection meeting did not take place until 9 February. This was at one of Labour's securest Euro-constituencies, Yorkshire South. Fifty-two of the seventy-eight ESOs had chosen a PEPC by the end of February, the original deadline for all selections. An exception was made for Scottish seats; because of the devolution referendum campaign selection was delayed until March. Selections for mainland seats were held between 4-15 March. The peculiar characteristics of the Highlands and Islands Euro-constituency demanded greater flexibility: their delegate postal ballot did not close until 7 April, giving time for both nominees to be interviewed by each of the component CLPs. The Welsh Referendum did not have the same delaying effect; the smaller number of Euro-constituencies and the lower priority placed on the question of Welsh devolution in the Labour party meant that it was practicable to run the campaign and Euro-selection organisation concurrently.

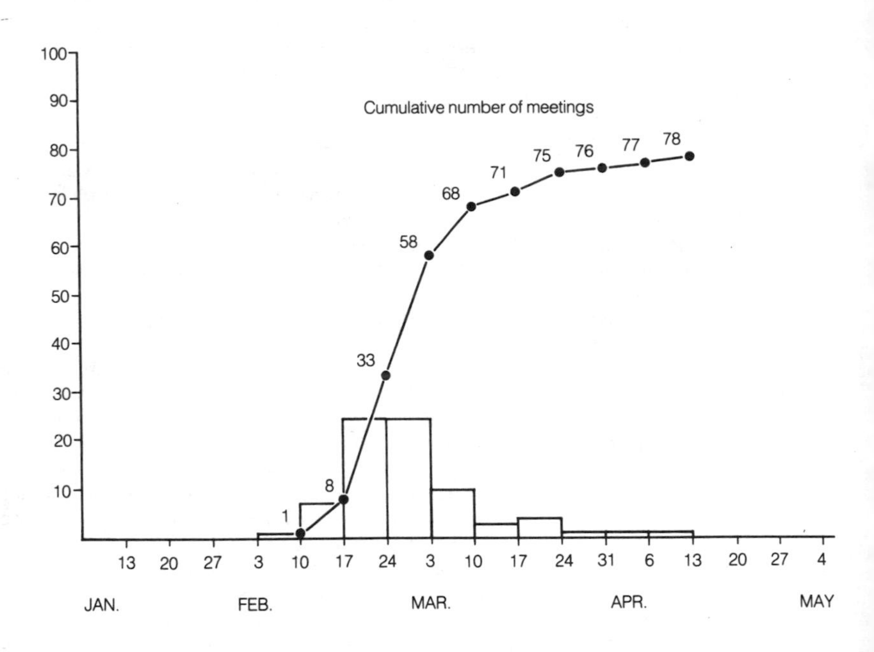

Figure 6.6 ESO Selection Meetings by Time

Electoral status was not a uniform predictor of selection dates. There was a surprising similarity between the selection timetables for both projected Labour and Conservative seats, although at the same time, interesting paradoxes within the electoral categories. While the majority of the more secure Labour seats tended to be the earliest to select, some were also amongst those ESOs which did not select until March. Projected Conservative seats were more likely to select later, but the difference was not as great as that displayed for the Conservative party selection timetable.

Comparison showed that thirty-six Conservative General Meetings had selected their candidates by the time Labour had chosen its first European candidate. However, intense selection during February reduced this lead, with the Conservatives having selected only twelve more candidates than Labour by the end of the month. Only two ESOs selected after the last Conservative General Meeting at Cleveland had chosen its candidate on 31 March (see Figures 4.2 and 6.6). Thus Labour's European selections were even more compressed than the Conservatives. This constituted another important selection variable as it tended to limit the potential for multiple nominations by simply restricting the number of ESO selection meetings an aspirant could physically attend. Of those who were nominated to an ESO, virtually seven out of every ten surveyed limited themselves to a single Euro-constituency. What is more only 17.0 per cent of nominees were short-listed for more than one ESO selection meeting.

Table 6.6

Number of ESO Nominations Per Aspirant

No. on ESO nominations	%	No. of nominees
1	67.6	234
2	16.8	58
3	5.5	19
4	4.3	15
5 - 15	5.8	20
None	-	86
	100.0	432

The comments offered by Butler and Marquand support these findings. They state that

> while many [candidates] were content to take their chances only in their own localities, some rushed around the country, addressing ward parties and union branches, deciding in the light of union timetables and personal enthusiasms, and sometimes conflicting reports on the state of opinion in different parties, which invitations to pursue and which to abandon.(43)

In addition, Butler and Marquand only identified two Labour

candidates as 'carpet-baggers', John Mills and Ernest Wistrich, who both fought 'hundreds of miles from home'.(44) An alternative index that could be used was the number and geographical spread of an individual's nominations. Thus amongst selected candidates, there were nine exceptions to the national pattern of nomination to a single Euro-constituency. John Mills was by far the most active in his search of a European seat: he was nominated in fifteen Euro-constituencies, seven of which were in London. Alf Lomas sought nomination at two of the Greater Manchester seats, and at seven of the London based areas. Basil Jeuda was involved in eight selection processes, though he concentrated on the Manchester seats and the surrounding Cheshire and Lancashire Euro-constituenies, as did Adrian Bailey who contested five ESO selections. Michael Walsh's seven nominations covered an area from Cumbria to Derbyshire, whereas Jim Daly limited his ambitions to six London seats and the adjoining Essex South West. Barbara Castle was promoted by supporters in six seats, dispersed between Manchester, Lancashire and London North East. John Dore was nominated in five seats which were geographically concentrated - London Central, West and North East, Hertfordshire and Bedfordshire. Lastly, Maeve Denby holds the honour of being nominated across the widest area, spreading from Essex South West, through London South West and Bedforshire, across to Bristol and finally up to Derbyshire where she was selected. There were more 'would be' carpet-baggers who failed to get picked: the most notable example was that of Ron Leighton. He contested five short-lists, but lost on each occasion. One possible explantion for his lack of success was that the later ESOs to select may have been aware of Leighton's earlier failures and were perhaps reluctant to pick a nominee who had been rejected so frequently elsewhere.(45) A further factor that may have made selection harder for Leighton was that all the seats he applied to were projected Labour victories. Leighton's European disappointments were, however, compensated for by his adoption and eventual election as Labour MP for Newham North East in May 1979.

These examples were the exception, not the rule: the general trend was for single nominations. Indeed, the cases cited above resemble Conservative applicant behaviour more closely than that of their Labour collegues. Obviously the factors mentioned earlier, namely constitutional restrictions on nominations, the absence of an approved list and parochialism were important limitations on recruitment. Even so, the compact ESO schedule was a relevant factor and, when considered in conjunction with these other factors, it helped to create a better understanding of the Labour party's selection procedure for Europe. In summary, the value of electoral status as an explanatory variable cannot be overstated. For both parties it was a crucial determinant and excellent predictor of delegtae/ representative turn-out, the levels of application/nomination and lastly, of the selection timetable of candidates for Europe.

SELECTION CRITERIA

Central

The absence of any centralised criteria for shaping the European aspirant cohort was the most striking feature of the Labour party's

European selection procedure; the NEC simply complied with its procedural obligations. For Westminster selections, the NEC possesses extensive constitutional powers, but can do little to establish any general criteria, either in shaping and designing the approved lists, or over the type of local nominee selected by CLPs. The extent of their power is to ensure the 'eligibility' of candidates as Labour PPCs in formal terms, namely via validation and endorsement, and in technical sense, by checking that the election expenses have been guaranteed and that procedures were conducted in accordance with party regulations. The NEC can do very little to influence selection criteria or candidate 'suitabiliy' as opposed to 'eligibility'; in practice they are not active gate-keepers.

Even this restrained control over Westminster selections was far more active than that exhibited by the NEC over Euro-selections. The exercise of technical powers was dealt with earlier and no examples of exclusion on political grounds were found. Indeed, the tolerance displayed towards certain candidacies was remarkable. On the one extreme, Terry Harrison, a member of the editiorial board of *Militant* and a candidate who was totally opposed to the Common Market, was officially endorsed by the NEC. Similarly, the secretary of the Labour Common Market Safeguards Committee, John Mills, passed the NEC's scrutiny, as did Ernest Wistrich the Director of the federalist European Movement. There was no central discrimination against pro or anti nominees, LCMSC or LCE members: every candidate chosen by an ESO was given the NEC's blessing as an official Labour party candidate for the European elections. With the absence of any effective central vetting (as Butler and Marquand remarked, the Euro-list 'carried little weight'), the NEC surrendered a potential source of influence over European selection criteria.(46) Its negative powers of validation and endorsement were a replication of the domestic procedure and, as for Westminster selections, 'no part of the selection machinery at its (the NEC's) disposal is conducive to ensuring the selection of a particular individual'.(47) Therefore, central selection criteria were inappropriate, or at least impossible to exert - the ward, branch, constituency and Euro-constituency were the areas where selection criteria and gatekeeping predominated. Even so, the NEC's conscious neglect of the Euro-elections had an important impact on the attitudes of local selectors.

This neglect was widely criticised by those engaged in the elections: the LCE post-election survey has already been discussed and its findings of 'trenchant criticism' of the NEC's political, organisational and financial role reported. A similar degree of hostility was found amongst rejected as well as selected nominees in this survey: of the 432 nominees who replied to the questionnaire, the most frequent comment (expressed by 17.4 per cent) was that the whole procedure was rushed and badly organised; the NEC was repeatedly cited as instrumental in causing the chaos. One of the more moderate critics thought the party's organisation was 'hasty and ill-prepared', another thought that the whole process 'should have been started much earlier: the party should have seen clearly that its participation was inevitable and acted accordingly'. Others singled out the decision to extend the ban on the dual mandate to prospective as well as elected candidates as especially harmful. As one aspirant on the advisory European list commented, 'the NEC decision concerning PPCs was made on 22 November 1978, after many CLPs had invited nominations'. Others were more critical in their verdicts: one non-selected nominee though it 'a farce' and a PEPC accused the NEC of being 'inept and apathetic', while others went so far as to describe the NEC's role as 'schizophrenic' and 'laughable'. Even anti-Marketeers who were selected and actually elected were not reluctant to complain: one anti-Market MEP concluded that the episode was 'a nightmare' whilst another admitted that 'the NEC never seemed to want to fight at all'. A small minority (4.6 per cent) inferred that the party's attitude was not the result of incompetence, but rather represented a conscious act of sabotage orchestrated by the anti-EEC majority of the NEC. The most scathing invective came from defeated PEPCs. One losing candidate described events as 'appalling - sometimes it seemed almost as though Transport House had deliberately arranged things so that it would be a shambles'. Another PEPC bemoaned the absence of any effective central gate-keeping and argued that the NEC should have been 'more formal and rigorous in drawing up a list of intended candiates'. The plea offered by a West Country PEPC served as a suitable epitaph: 'I hope next time the NEC will work to win'.

To balance this interpretation, it should be noted that 9.5 per cent of respondents stated that the NEC's role and selection procedures were satisfactory. However, the significant finding was that more than one in five European nominees criticized the neglect and lethargy displayed by the central organisation. While selection choice has, in practice, always been constituency-based in the Labour party, the actions of the NEC in the Euro-election were unusual for the following reasons: firstly, the absence of a selective approved list of aspirants; secondly, the technical oversight of nominations; and thirdly, the reluctant attitude generated by the NEC itself all distinguished European from Westminster selections. All three factors reduced the potential for exercising the sort of centralised candidate criteria found in the Conservative party.

Local selection criteria

Pro and anti-Marketeers: Butler and Marquand conjectured that local manipulation of selections 'was more difficult than in Westminster selection conferences, since the Euro-constituencies were so big that it was almost impossible for any single faction to deploy sufficient strength in the whole area'.(48) Partly for this reason, unions failed to dominate Euro-selections. While there was certainly no orchestrated manipulation across and or between the parliamentary constituencies within each ESO, the most crucial selection variable was unquestionably the division between pro and anti-Marketeers. This division was important in regard to both the composition of ESO delegations and the political balance of selection meeting short-lists. If the pro or anti-factions could initially control the choice of delegates, then the selection of an appropriately sympathetic candidate could be made easier.

No comprehensive data is available relating to the exact pro/anti balance of either ESO selection committees or the full delegate bodies. However, the following examples are illustrative. At what was reputedly the most anti-EEC London ESO the five short-listed nominees were all antis to a greater or lesser degree, four being signatories of the LCMSC policy statement on the direct elections. In contrast, another London ESO was evenly split between pro and anti delegates; it took five ballots for the only LCMSC nominee to defeat his rivals. Conversely, at one London seat all hardline LCMSC members were kept off the short-list. The selection of the European Movement director, Ernest Wistrich, at Cleveland indicated a pro biased ESO delegation although two of the short-list of five were self-assigned anti-Marketeers. The pro/anti sympathies of selection delegates were crucial at the earlier CLP state as well as at the full ESO. It was at this initial stage that the shape of the nominee cohort could be determined. In every Euro-constituency and at every level the anti-EEC cause was taken extremely seriously by both its advocates and opponents. Even in electorally hopeless Euro-constituencies the pro/anti distinction was the single most important selection criterion: the balance had a crucial impact upon the size and composition of the ESO short-lists, and therefore upon the political leaning of the adopted candidate.

An important stage in Labour's gate-keeping process was the decision on which nominees to short-list. Was there any pro and anti bias in the overall pattern of nominations and, more importantly, was any such bias reproduced, exaggerated or diminished in the composition of the final short-lists? Before any estimation of this gate-keeping function is possible, the general pro/anti aspirant characteristics have to be established.

Table 6.7

Pro/Anti-Market Views of Labour Aspirants and Aggregated ESO Nominations

Labour Aspirants	%	n
Pro-EEC	41.2	144
Anti-EEC	49.3	172
Unsure/Neither	9.5	33
Not Known	-	83
	100.0	432
Aggregated Nominations		
Pro-EEC	39.0	214
Anti-EEC	50.0	274
Unsure/Neither	11.0	60
Not Known		41
	100.0	589

Virtually half the respondents surveyed placed themselves firmly in the anti-Market camp. For a party committed to a policy based on fundamental re-negotiations and highly suspicious of the implications of the Treaty of Rome regarding national sovereignty, there was an extraordinarily high level of pro-EEC support. Indeed, if the unsure/neither category was placed on the pro-Market side, the pro and anti forces were almost in perfect balance. This pattern was confirmed when the aggregated nominations to the seventy-eight ESOs were similarly divided along pro and anti-EEC lines (see Table 6.7).

How were the pro and anti groups dispersed? Were the anti and pro-Marketeers concentrated or evenly divided between the seventy-eight seats? Table 6.8 distinguishes those ESOs where the pro or anti-factions had an absolute majority of all nominations submitted from those where there was parity between the two, or where a low response rate made conclusions less confident. There were some notable examples where anti-Marketeers had an overall majority of ESO nominations. No pro-EEC nominations were submitted at Yorkshire North, all but one individual nominated for Lancashire East were anti-EEC: three-quarters of the nominations received by Salop and Stafford, Devon and Hertfordshire all wore the anti-Market badege, as did two-thirds at Greater Manchester North. The most concentrated anti-Market area was Wales, where three of the four ESOs were dominated by anti-EEC forces. Six of the ten London ESOs received a majority of anti-Market nominations, making it one of the most prominent anti-Market areas in England.

Table 6.8

Pro/Anti-Market Majorities for ESO Nominations

All nominations per ESO	%	n
Pro-EEC majority	30.8	16
Anti-EEC majority	55.8	29
Parity	13.4	7
Not Known	-	26
	100.0	78

Although ESO nominations with a pro-majority were less prolific, where they did occur their level of dominance was often on a par with that of ESOs with an anti majority. For example, 70.0 per cent of nominees at London South, two-thirds at Nottingham and Leeds, eight out of thirteen at Yorkshire South West wore the pro-Community label. An equal balance of pro and anti nominations was achieved in seven seats.

Were these pro and anti characteristics translated to the ESO short-listing stage? Of the 264 short-listed ESO nominees, 90.5 per cent could be classified according to their attitude towards the EEC. The distribution is given in Table 6.9.

Table 6.9

Pro/Anti-Market Views of Short-Listed Nominations

	%	n
Pro-EEC	38.5	92
Anti-EEC	51.0	122
Unsure/Neither	10.5	25
Not Known	-	25
	100.0	264

The anti-EEC lobby maintained their control of nominations, marginally increasing their percentage from 49.3 per cent of all aspirants and exactly half of all nominations to 51.0 per cent of ESO short-listed nominees. Each ESO short-list was examined to determine whether there appeared to be any pro or anti-EEC bias in its composition. The general findings presented in Table 6.10 should be compared with those in Table 6.8 which gave the pro and anti-Market majorities for all ESO nominations. Was the pro-anti balance transposed without alteration from the nomination to the short-listing stage of the selection process?

Table 6.10

Pro/Anti-Market Majorities for ESO Short-Lists

	%	n
Pro-EEC majority	37.0	17
Anti-EEC majority	43.5	20
Parity	19.5	9
Not Known	-	32
	100.0	78

An appreciable difference was in the anti-EEC percentage which fell from 55.8 per cent of all ESO nominations to 43.5 per cent of ESO short-lists, though this may have been a consequence of the lower response rate rather than any even-handedness on the part of the local selection gate-keepers. The important point to note is that in general where a pro-Market majority existed, it was a slender one whereas an anti-Market majority was often overwhelming. A large proportion of ESOs selected only antis for their short-lists: for example, although anti-Market supporters only accounted for half of the nominations received at Essex South West, all six short-listed nominees were self-assigned antis, three of whom had signed the LCMSC policy statement. Similarly, only anti-Marketeers appeared on the short-lists at Devon, London North East, London North and Manchester North where again LCMSC members were predominant. In other seats the anti-lobby had a majority but not absolute control of nominations.

In contrast, no ESO short-list was composed entirely of pro-EEC nominees: only the ESOs of Nottingham, Cambridgeshire, Surrey, Yorkshire South West, Midlands West and Suffolk produced short-lists that were overwhelmingly in favour of Britain's membership of the Community. The pro-lobby also achieved majorities in four other seats. The short-list at London West was especially interesting: anti-Marketeers outnumbered pro-Marketeers by eight to three at the CLP nomination stage, but this advantage was reversed at the ESO selection meeting with pro-market nominees securing three of the six places on the short-list. However, the most common outcome was that anti-Marketeers dominated the short-lists.

Not only was it relatively rare for short-lists to be dominated by a pro-majority, and unknown for pro-Marketeers to be the only faction represented, even where pro-EEC candidates were selected the short-lists were usually highly competitive. Pro nominees did not have overall majorities at Cleveland, Northumbria, London East or at the Lancashire seats of East and Central yet managed to secure adoption. Nor did the mere fact of having a pro-Market majority on the short-list ensure the selection of a pro-Market candidate. In six Euro-constituencies the pro-EEC grouping failed to turn their numerical strength on the short-lists to their advantage. Their most surprising defeat was at the prized seat of Yorkshire South West, where the short-list of six comprised four members of the LCE, one LCMSC supporter and one non-aligned anti-Marketeer who became the eventual candidate. The extent of the pro-Market failure is further highlighted when the eight to four pro majority on the original long list of CLP nominations is considered. The pro-Marketeers' performance at Midlands West was as equally unimpressive, the candidacy going to Stuart Randall, the only anti on a short-list of four, although the intervention of Colin Phipps MP may have damaged the pro-lobby.

Table 6.11

Pro/Anti-Market Views of Selected Candidates

	%	n
Pro-EEC	26.6	17
Anti-EEC	53.1	34
Unsure/Neither	20.3	13
Not Known	-	14
	100.0	78

Conversely, having an anti-Market majority on the short list usually guaranteed the selection of an anti-Market candidate: there were only two exceptions to this rule. At London East the short-list was split four-three in favour of the anti-camp (three of whom supported the LCMSC) but the pro-nominee gained selection. The second exception occurred at Lancashire East where LCE member Michael Walsh was selected despite being the only pro on a short-list of five. His success was somewhat fortuitous, as two of his strongest opponnets, both LCMSC supporters, Barbara Castle and Richard Caborn, withdrew before the selection meeting, and as we have already seen, Walsh was the only pro amongst the ten nominees for this seat.

The anti-Market theme evident throughout the Labour party's local selection process was increased by the final breakdown of selected candidates into pro and anti-EEC supporters. Thus compared to the overall pro/anti EEC distribution for all nominees (Table 6.7) anti-Marketeers were marginally overrepresented on ESO short-lists: in addition, the majority of ESO short-lists favoured anti-Europeans with the final selected candidates confirming this anti-EEC trait.

To summarize, in twenty-three of the fifty-four known cases (42.6 per cent), anti-Marketeers maintained their numerical superiority at both the nomintion and short-listing stages, with nineteen (35.2 per cent) of these achieving the selection of an anti-Market candidate at the ESO selection meeting. The pro-Europeans were less successful in maintaining a hold over nomination and short-listing strategies. Twelve Euro-constituencies (22.2 per cent) had a pro-EEC majority at these initial two screening stages, yet these majorities resulted in the selection of only five pro-Market candidates (9.3 per cent). The examples of Yorkshire South West and Hereford and Worcester, where pro-Europeans controlled two-thirds of the nominations and the short-list, were more typical: both ESOs selected an anti-EEC candidate. There were three instances where anti-majorities at the nomination stage were turned into short-lists with a pro-EEC majority, and two instances where a pro-nominee majority was overturned in favour of anti-Marketeers on the selection meeting short-list. Only three Euro-constituencies retained a pro/anti balance at both screening stages prior to the ESO selection meeting.

Localism: Was local government candiadacy, residence or some notion of 'localism' a significant selection factor? One of the major differences in the recruitment and selection processes of the Labour and Conservative parties was the differing importance they each placed upon the local connections of aspirants. As has already been described, 'carpet-baggers' were the exception with approximately seven out of ten Labour aspirants limiting their ambitions to a single Euro-constituency, whereas Conservative aspirants averaged eight seat applications each: whilst not a direct measure of localism these figures suggest an important selection difference.

Another example of localism was evident in the compilation of the European list. Each of the 248 aspirants were assigned an identification number based on the Labour party's tweleve regional areas to 'enable those using the list to identify available candidates resident within a particular region'.(49) The intention seemed to be to encourage nominations not to stray beyond the broad regional categories, if not the require nominees explicitly to limit their ambitions to only local Euro-constituencies. The regional distribution of the European list was weighted in favour of London and the North of England; the Celtic fringe went almost unrepresented.

The survey also tested for a more precise measure of localism. Each respondent was asked to indicate the exact nature of any local connections which they had with the Euro-constituencies to which they had applied. The overall impression confirmed the belief that Labour aspirants were predominantly local recruits: 67.7 per cent could claim some link with the Euro-constituency they were nominated for. Approximately one-quarter claimed residential or occupational links and exactly one-third could point to candidacy as a local government councillor as either their sole or one of several local connections. In addition, 3.9 per cent had stood as PPCs or been elected as an MP for one of the parliamentary seats within the Euro-constituency. The general contrast with the Conservative aspirants was clear. The majority of Conservatives could not claim any form of local connection with the Euro-constituency of their choice.

Within this broad pattern, differences emerged when pro/anti EEC views were controlled for. In particular, aspirants of an anti-Market disposition were the least likely group to be interlopers, in the sense that they could boast the smallest percentage of aspirants who had no tanglible local ties. Anti-Marketeers were also somewhat more likely to have had some form of local government experience and less likely to have contested a parliamentary election. 36.5 per cent of anti-Marketeers compared to 31.3 per cent of EEC supporters had engaged in local politics within the Euro-constituency of their choice, whereas only 2.8 compared to 6.1 per cent of pro-Marketeers had been PPC/MPs within the area.

Another variable of some consequence was local government candidacy: 78.2 per cent of all aspirants had stood as local candidates at some time. Nor were these local government candidacies one-offs; 58.0 per cent of nominees had fought four or more local campaigns. Of those who had stood as prospective councillors, 55.0 per cent were elected with the majority serving more than seven years in office. In addition, 41.2 per cent of nominees were local government councillors at the time of the selection process for the European Parliament. Of those who had fought a local campaign, 39.4 per cent were pro-European and 50.7 per cent anti-Marketeers. Fortunately the NEC did not exclude local government councillors from competing for Europe as they did for MPs and PPCs. Had they done so, both the number of European aspirants and their relative experience in elective office would have been substantially reduced. The local government experience of the resultant Labour nominees was considerable and one of their most distinctive group characteristics.

<u>Parliamentary experience</u>: The NECs ruling outlawing sitting MPs and parliamentary candidates from European candidacy limited the size of the pool of potential aspirants: thus unlike in the Conservative party, the dual mandate could not be a pertinent selection criterion. Despite this restriction, former parliamentary experience was, in certain cases, a relevant

consideration. Seventeen of the surveyed nominee population of 432 had sat in the Commons: how did these ex-MPs fare in their quest for a seat in the European Parliament?

The most celebrated MP to stand as a European candidate was the former Cabinet Minister, the Right Hon. Barbara Castle; she had already decided to retire from Westminster at the next general election and therefore did not contravene the NEC provision relating to the dual mandate. As one of the most vociferous anti-Marketeers, Mrs Castle's nomination was criticised by several pro-Market factions. Her vast political experience and skill was evident in Mrs Castle's nomination strategy. Unlike the majority of Labour aspirants, Castle did not limit herself to merely one or two Euro-constituencies; she was nominated for six in total, all of which were projected Labour seats. She was short-listed at three including the Euro-constituency which contained her old parliamentary seat of Blackburn. Once again, time-tabling was a crucial factor in candidate selection. The NEC's insistence, that selections be conducted within a short time span inevitabley produced ESO selection meeting clashes. The meetings for two of the seats which short-listed her were both held on 11 February 1979; Castle preferred to contest Greater Manchester North and was selected there.

Sir Geoffrey de Freitas had also decided to resign his parliamentary seat of Kettering at the next general election. However, unlike Barbara Castle, he was an ardent pro-European and a former appointed MEP, and as such a bete-noir of the left wing anti-EEC element with the Labour party: he was frequently described in The Tribune as a 'Euro-fanatic' or more sardonically as 'Sir Geoffrey de Strasbourg'. Quite how earnest Sir Geoffrey's European intentions were was difficult to establish. He admitted to letting his name go forward for one or two winnable Euro-seats, but was not selected. Colin Phipps was the only Labour MP who actually complied with the NEC's ban on the dual mandate by announcing that he would not be seeking re-election for his Westminster seat of Dudley West before entering the European contest. Phipps was nominated for the projected comfortable Labour Midlands West Euro-constituency which included his old parliamentary seat among its eight parliamentary constituencies. As a member of the Labour Committee for Europe, the European Movement and the Federal Trust, Phipps was one of the more publically known pro-EEC nominees, a factor which contributed to his defeat at the selection meeting. Phipp's political aspirations within the Labour Party were formally ended in 1981 when he joined the then newly formed Social Democratic Party.

There were fourteen other nominees who at some time had sat as a member of the House of Commons: only two, Hugh Gray and Peter Jackson, were selected as prospective European candidates. Five of these former MPs were, at the time of selection, life peers: all failed to gain selection. Lord Murray of Gravesend was on the 'List of Possible Candidates' and was nominated for two seats; Baroness Fisher confined her ambitions to the local Euro-seat of Birmingham South; Lord Paget was nominated by his old CLP to the Northamptonshire ESO, but his quest for a rejuvinated political career was short-lived. Lord Bruce of Donnington, former Labour MEP, was nominated for two London seats and Lord Northfield expressed an initial interest in the European election and allowed his name to be included on the List of Possible Candidates. At an early stage in the seletion procedure his interest waned and he withdrew his potential candidacy. The only other peer to seek nomination was Lord Kennet, a former delegate to the Council of Europe and a Member of the European Parliament 1978-79.

Previous parliamentary experience was not a passport to Europe. Whether this was because local ESO selectors tended to view such aspirants with disfavour, either because of their general pro-EEC leanings, a dislike of those regarded as ambitious careerists or due to local constituency in-fighting, was unknown. Of the ex-MPs who were selected, the anti-Marketeers were the more successful, capturing the comfortable Labour seats of Birmingham North and Greater Manchester North, whereas the only Labour Committee for Europe ex-MP to be chosen was selected for the Conservative marginal of Norfolk: all the remaining former parliamentarians were all pro-Europeans and all failed to secure selection. Not surprisingly in a party that has been periodically in favour of the abolition of the House of Lords, aspirants with peerages found little favour amongst the rank and file party membership and European gate-keepers.

Parliamentary candidacy: 28.7 per cent of the 432 surveyed nominees had, at some time, been adopted as parliamentary candidates. Thirty-one European nominees contested the 1964 election, six successfully. This figure rose to thirty-four two years later, with twice as many being elected as MPs. With the Conservative victory of 1970, the number of MPs again fell to six, although forty-four future European aspirants stood for Westminster constituencies on that occasion. The first 1974 election had fifty-four European nominees standing; by October this figure for parliamentary candidates had fallen to forty-eight, of whom only three were elected.

A further twenty-two nominees were currently prospective parliamentary candidates at the start of the European selection process: only three preferred to forfeit their domestic selections and try to gain adoption for a European seat.(50) All but one of this group of twenty-two appeared on the advisory list which was published prior to the NEC decision relating to PPCs. Indeed, the NEC's late decision meant that ten of these PPCs had already progressed at least as far as the ESO nomination stage. In every case the individuals concerned withdrew their nomination from the ESOs.

It was difficult to establish the impact of nominees who were experienced as parliamentary candidates upon the formulation of local selection criteria. However, there did not appear to be any obvious discrimination against such individuals, with a large proportion gaining CLP nominations.

European list, Co-operative Panel and Trade Union sponsorship: Although the parliamentary 'A' and 'B' lists are certainly not the exclusive sources for Westminster recruitment, they have constituted a principal source of nominations. Did the European list play a similar role? Was being one of the 248 individuals on the list a selection factor? 57.9 per cent of all nominations received came from individuals from the European list.(51) This dominance was reduced to 41.5 per cent of short-listed nominees, signifying a dislike of aspirants who had shown what might be construed as European ambitions implying a pro-European stance. If such an interpretation was used it was founded in myth rather than fact. The individuals on the European list were split only 46.4 to 44.1 per cent in favour of pro-Market nominees; the list was far from being an exclusive haven for pro-Europeans. Nor does the fact that over half of all nominations came from individuals on the list necessarily imply that the list was a major recruitment source. As has already been demonstrated, the vast majority of Labour's aspirants were nominated for their local ESOs. It seems reasonable to assume that these individuals would have still been nominated had they not been on the European list. Its use as a recruitment agent was limited to the minority of aspirants who sought nominations on a wider scale. The list was often totally irrelevant to the nomination process.

The position of the Co-operative party's 'Panel of candidates for the European Assembly' was somewhat different. As was demonstrated earlier the general principles rather than the formal agreement between the Labour and Co-operative parties were transferred from the parliamentary to the European elections. The list consisted of thirty-eight individuals, twelve of whom also appeared on the European list. Despite the small size of the panel, Co-operative aspirants had a significant impact on the recruitment and selection processes with 88.2 per cent of the panel securing a CLP nomination. In total, this group obtained 9.3 per cent of all nominations. Exactly half of the panel were short-listed and six were selected as PEPCs, with two, Richard Balfe and Brian Key, elected as MEPs.

Why were Co-operative panelists disproportionately successful in gaining nominations? Was there any selection criterion that gave them an advantage over non-group promoted aspirants? The financial implications of possible Co-operative sponsorship was an underlying factor: while there was no formal agreement and financial considerations could not be discussed during the selection process, Co-operative money may have been a crucial factor - the Euro elections were appallingly under-financed and assistance towards election expenses a tempting offer. Another factor that might have helped panelists was their greater exerience of parliamentary campaigning: 65.7 per cent of known cases had stood as candidates, a marked contrast to the 23.4 per cent of the remaining surveyed nominees. What is more, four of these had been former MPs. In addition, electoral status appeared to influence Co-operative aspirants. As shown earlier, selected Co-operative candidates tended to opt for what were projected Labour seats. This characteristic was also evident at the nomination stage. Forty-two of the fifty-nine Co-operative nominations were made in projected Labour Euro-constituencies. It was apparent that the Co-operative party were reluctant to commit time, organiational resources and finance in what were essentially unwinnable Euro-constituencies. In contrast to the Westminster agreement, the Co-operative party felt less committed to contesting hopeless causes.

Finally, the pro and anti affiliations of the European Assembly panel was not a pretinent selection factor. The Co-operative list was split almost fifty-fifty in its pro and anti sympathies, though anti-Marketeers secured a greater percentage of the nominations, 54.2 per cent compared to 33.9. However, the balance was reasserted at the short-listing stage, with each camp securing eight representatives on ESO short-lists: pro-Marketeers marginally gained the ascendancy amongst PEPCs (a three to two ratio with one candidate uncommitted).

As noted earlier, trade union sponsorship constitutes a major selection factor for domestic politics but did not assume a comparable role for Europe. In consequence, trade union power to influence and shape the gate-keeping criteria was reduced. Yet the tiered structure developed for the selection of European candidates gave trade unions, and other affiliated bodies, a potentially greater source of power than for Westminster: because each CLP within the Euro-constituency could nominate up to three individuals, it was possible for union backed aspirants to gain multiple nominations, increasing their chances of gaining a place on the ESO short-list. Even if the trade union backed multiple nominations were not regarded with as much weight as ordinary ward nominations, they constituted an important selection factor as they helped to publicise specific aspirants at the Euro-level.

In summary the pro/anti controversy, the impact of localism, local government and parliamentary candidacy have been discussed, data presented and selection criteria inferred. Precise measurement of local selection criteria in the Labour party was not possible on the comprehensive scale employed for the Conservative party. To this extent, the methodological requirements of the model have only been partially realised: the processes have been examined and described and given their contextual location, yet exact criteria hypotheses remain largely untested. To compensate, the discussion of profile characteristics of all types of aspirants, rejects, nominees, winners and losers, in the following chapter goes some way to counterbalancing this omission. However, it cannot be a substitute for criteria analysis if the study of recruitment is to be enhanced; the differences between selected and non-slected aspirants are not tantamount to selection criteria, but within the confines of the data available they represent the closest approximation.

Conclusion

In a purely structural sense the European selection machinery duplicated that used for Westminster. Selections were delegate based, aspirants had to work through the traditional nomination structure and the NEC fulfilled its obligations with regard to validation and endorsement. However, beneath these structural similarities there were notable differences which effected the selection process. The reluctance of the NEC to do anything more than the procedural minimum, the absence of sponsorship and the 'A' and 'B' lists, the ban on the dual mandate and PPCs, together with low delegate participation and a general lack of enthusiasm and interest, all distinguished European from domestic selections. The overall conclusion relating to selection criteria was inescapable: Britain's memebership of the EEC was a divisive issue in the Labour party and a major selection factor in the gatekeeping process. Choice predominantly polarised around this single issue. The evidence consistently indicated that anti-Marketeers were the dominant force within the selection process; at all levels, anti-EEC majorities were the norm. Their control of the essential gate-keeping process was formidable and widespread; only in isolated areas of pro-Community sympathy could the anti-EEC tide be challenged.

NOTES

(1) Report of the Seventy Seventh Annual Conference of the Labour Party, 1978, composite resolution no. 42, p. 303, The Labour Party, 1978.
(2) NEC statement, 26.5.1978; also reprinted in Labour and Europe: recent policy statements, Transport House, The Labour Party, 1978, p.13.
(3) NEC report on Elections for the European Assembly as presented to the 1978 annual party conference, pp. 11-13.
(4) Andrew Faulds, Mark Hughes and Michael English were examples cited in Tribune, 27.10.1978.
(5) Letter sent to all CLP secretaries by the National Agent, 24.11.1978.
(6) Labour Weekly, 2.2.1979, p. 4.
(7) For the full list of constitutional exclusions see Clause X-7, The Constitution and Standing Orders of the Labour Party, as amended by the 1974 party Conference.
(8) This is not necessarily because sponsored MPs are more electorally appealing, but rather reflects the type of constituency fought - see M. Rush, The Selection of Parliamentary Candidates, London, Nelson, 1966, p. 171.
(9) I. McLean, "Party Organisation", in C. Cook and I. Taylor (eds.), The Labour Party, London, Longman, 1980, p. 42.
(10) M. Harrison, Trade Unions and the Labour Party since 1945, London, George Allen and Unwin, 1960, p. 85.
(11) A Survey on the Labour Party and the European Elections, The Labour Committee for Europe, 6.9.1979, p.7.
(12) M. Rush, op.cit., p. 167.
(13) M. Rush, op.cit., pp. 184-204, M. Harrison, op.cit., pp. 304-306, A. Ranney, Pathways to Parliament, London, Macmillan, 1965, pp. 229-235, and P. Paterson, The Selectorate, London, MacGibbon & Kee, 1967, pp. 43-44.
(14) The Co-operative sponsored PEPCs were: Brian Key (Yorkshire South), Richard Balfe (Londond South Inner), Peter Nurse (Manchester West) and Ernest Wistrich (Cleveland): Adrian Bailey (Cheshire West) and Michael Elliot (Bedforshire) were both on the European panel but did not receive any financial aid. Richard Balfe received a further 3,800 pounds from the Royal Arsenal Co-operative Society.
(15) The Common Market - the cost of membership, Labour Common Market Safeguards Committee Research Group, 1977, p. 1.
(16) Policy Statement on Direct Elections to the EEC Assembly, Labour Common Market Safeguards Committee, 10.11.1978.
(17) Letter to all LCMSC members from the secretary, John Mills, sent out with the policy statement, 10.11.1978.
(18) Tribune and Labour Weekly editions of 17.11.1978.
(19) Labour Activist, No. 2, January 1979, p. 1. The Labour Co-

ordinating Committee was a left-wing group, critical of Britain's membership of the EEC: it consisted of MPs, trade unionists, journalists and academics.

(20) Tribune and Labour Weekly editions of 12.1.1979.

(21) Labour Activist, op.cit., p. 1.

(22) The Sunday Telegraph, 7.1.1979.

(23) CGE statement of accounts presented at their AGM, 27.6.1979. Only 2,914 pounds of this grant was spent.

(24) D. Butler and D. Marquand, European Elections and British Politics, London, Longmans, 1981, p. 62.

(25) NEC Report to the 1960 Annual Party Conference, p. 24; also quoted by Rush, op.cit., p. 150.

(26) Instructions taken from the 1960 'B' list.

(27) Instructions taken from the 1978 'List of Possible Candidates for the European Assembly Elections'. However, the 'B' list issued in 1981 has adopted the same wording as the 'E' list in 1978.

(28) The Labour Party Rules for Constituency Labour Parties and Branches (1978) Clause XIV (3) (d).

(29) Rush, op.cit., p. 133.

(30) Ibid., p. 134.

(31) Constitution and Standing Orders of the Labour Party, op.cit., Clause x-4.

(32) Ibid., Clause x-7 (b).

(33) NEC Report on Elections for the European Assembly, op.cit., p.1.

(34) The Guardian, 14.5.1979.

(35) Covering letter sent to all Labour European candidates from the Labour Committee for Europe, 25.6.1979. Response rate for the survey was not particularly high, 38.5% (n=30), including the three members of the working party. The identities of respondents were disclosed to the author, but are not available for publication.

(36) A Survey on the Labour Party and the European Elections, op.cit.,pp. 9-10.

(37) Circular letter to all CLP Secretaries from the National Agent, Reg Underhill, 19.10.1978, p. 3.

(38) Ibid., p. 4.

(39) Butler and Marquand, op.cit., p. 63.

(40) 1978 NEC Report, op.cit., p. 12.

(41) Sussex East, North Wales, Mid and West Wales, South East Wales, South Wales, Sussex West, Wight and Hampshire East, Thames Valley (15 delegates); Surrey, Wessex, Devon, Somerset, Cornwall/Plymouth, The Cotswolds, Lincolnshire (12 delegates); Northumbria, Cumbria (14 delegates); and Durham, Cleveland (16 delegates).

(42) Daily Telegraph, 8.12.1978.

(43) Butler and Marquand, op.cit., p. 61.

(44) Ibid., p. 66.

(45) Butler and Marquand suggest an alternative explanation:

> 'His (Ron Leighton) name was pushed in every area of the country and he was put forward by 50 wards or branches in 16 constituencies. The fact that he was unsuccessful is an indication of the limits of the Labour Safeguard's influence'; Butler and Marquand,

op.cit., p. 61.

(46) Ibid., p. 51.

(47) Rush, op.cit., p. 143.

(48) Butler and Marquand, op.cit., p. 62.

(49) Instructions taken from the "List of possible candidates for the European Assembly Election", Transport House 1978. This procedure is also used for the parliamentary 'B' list.

(50) These three were the PPCs for Hillington (Ruislip and Northwood), Aberdeenshire West and South Worcestershire.

(51) N = 341/589 (57.9%).

7 Labour candidate and aspirant profiles

Figure 7.1 summarises the eight sub-groups within the Labour aspirant population of 432 that emerged as a result of the theoretical assumptions of the recruitment model. The first division separated the thirty-five aspirants who failed to gain a CLP nomination (either because of voluntary withdrawal or selection criteria) from the remaining 350 who secured CLP nominations. From this new population further profiles subsequently distinguished between those who made an ESO short-list and those who were rejected on biographical notes by the executive committee. The next procedure divided the short-listed nominees into two new sub-groups: those selected as PEPCs and those defeated at the ESO selection meeting. The final profile contrasted winners and losers.

The logic of the model demanded this progressive sub-division: however, the theoretical imperatives and research feasibility were not totally compatible. The entire population of Labour party aspirants was unknown: the focus of the research was directed towards those who gained at least one CLP nomination, rather than those individuals who failed to progress beyond the branch, ward or affiliated organisation stage in the nomination process. Only those individuals on the European and Co-operative lists who failed to emerge as CLP nominees could be traced: local aspirants who were rejected by CLP executive committees and GMCs remained elusive. Consequently, of the thirty-five individuals in the rejected aspirant category, 20.0 per cent were Co-operative party panelists with the remainder drawn from the Labour party's advisory list of European candidates. However, the following discussion of the aspirant group (although only based on a partial population) offers a basis for comparison. Space does not permit all the sub-groups to be examined with the same intensity. Rather the major differences or similarities between certain sub-groups are highlighted with response rates determining those that could be

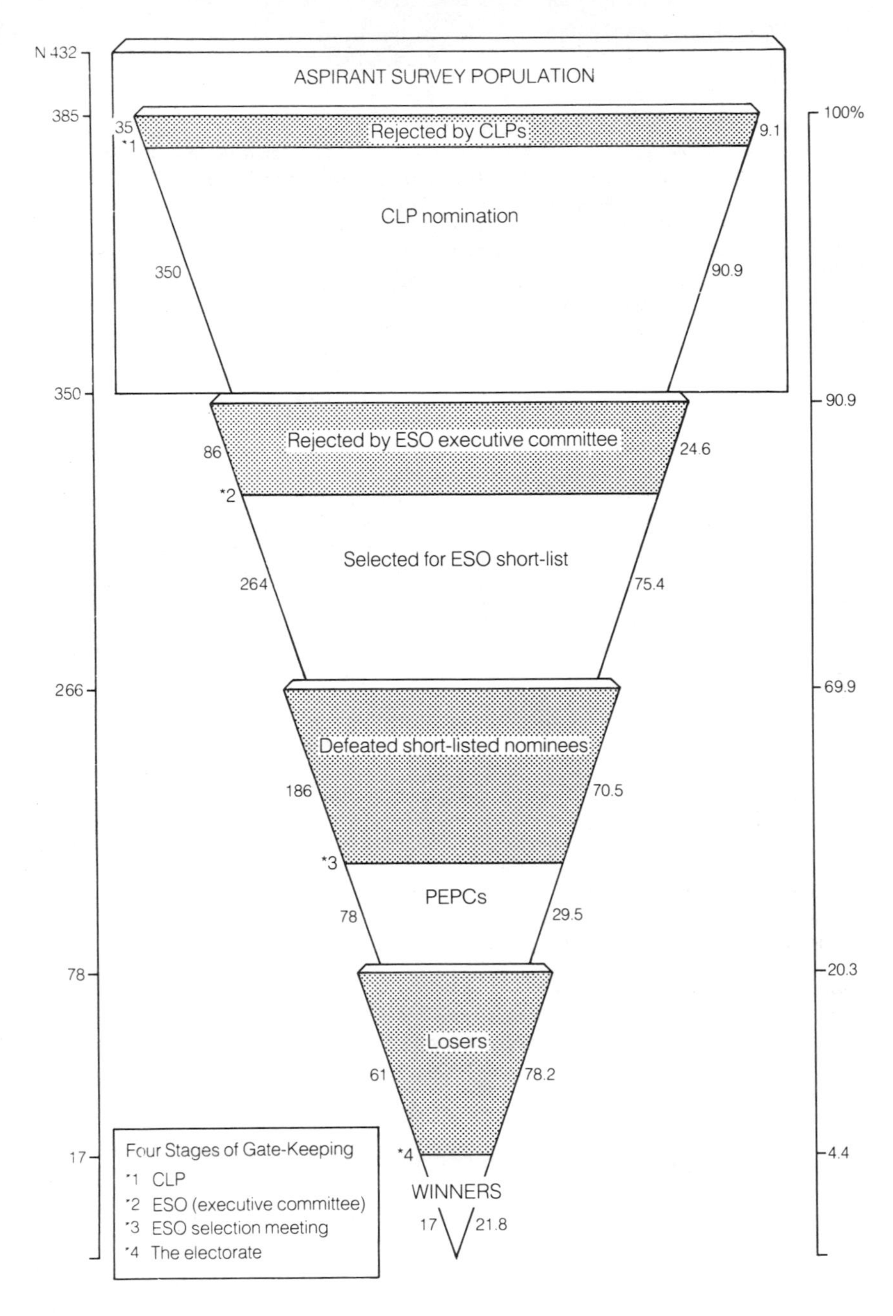

Figure 7.1 Recruitment and Selection Stages for European Aspirants: the Path from Aspirant to MEP in the Labour Party

most fruitfully analysed.

Rejected Aspirants

Less than one in ten (9.1 percent) of respondents failed to secure the necessary CLP support required for their nominations to be forwarded to the ESO. However, of the thirty-five aspirants screened out at this initial selection hurdle, not all were eliminated by constituency gate-keepers; some preferred to withdraw from the nomination process voluntarily. Seventeen withdrew their candidacies prior to the closing date for CLP nominations, seven following the NEC's ruling on PPCs. That these PPCs were not prepared to forego their domestic ambitions for Europe suggested that their candidacies for the European Parliament were not goals in themselves, but rather routes to alternative political careers. One such reluctant European stated that he put his name on the European list 'to help with my national Parliament campaign', and another Westminster PPC saw candidacy for the European Parliament 'purely as an additional opportunity in a political career'. The most bizarre reason for withdrawal was offered by an aspirant who had intended to submit her name for the Westminster 'B' list, but found herself on the European list by mistake! More generally, a variety of personal reasons, such as illness, lack of time or often an absence of any real enthusiasm for Europe were the major factors in prompting an early voluntary exit from the selection process.

Eighteen aspirants were eliminated because they failed to win a CLP nomination. Among these were two former MPs and one PPC who had resigned his Westminster adoption to run for Europe. Why were these aspirants rejected at the earliest possible stage? Were they especially poorly qualifed? The following analysis examines the complete rejected aspirant group (including voluntary withdrawals by PPCs) as well as just those who failed to secure a CLP nomination.

(a) Background characteristics: There was no appreciable difference between the two groups within the rejected aspirant category. Both were predominantly male, had a mean age of 41.8 years, were not primarily public school products and more than eight out of ten had undergone higher education, more commonly at a redbrick university rather than Oxbridge. The occupational skew was familiar, concentrating on the two highest OPCS classifications with the teaching professions the most common occupation accounting for one-fifth of all rejected aspirants and just over one-quarter of the non-nominated individuals.

(b) Previous political experience: As noted in the introduction to the chapter, seven of the rejected aspirants were forced to withdraw by the NEC ruling on eligibility. With this rider in mind, the levels for previous parliamentary candidacy for both groups were identical; 23.5 per cent of all rejected aspirant as well as non-nominated individuals had been adopted as a PPC, the only difference being that two of the latter group had been elected as MPs. Nor was there any difference for the percentage of aspirants drawn from the 'B' list of parliamentary candidates - 52.9 per cent in each case, though non-nominated aspirants were less likely to be on the list at the time of the European

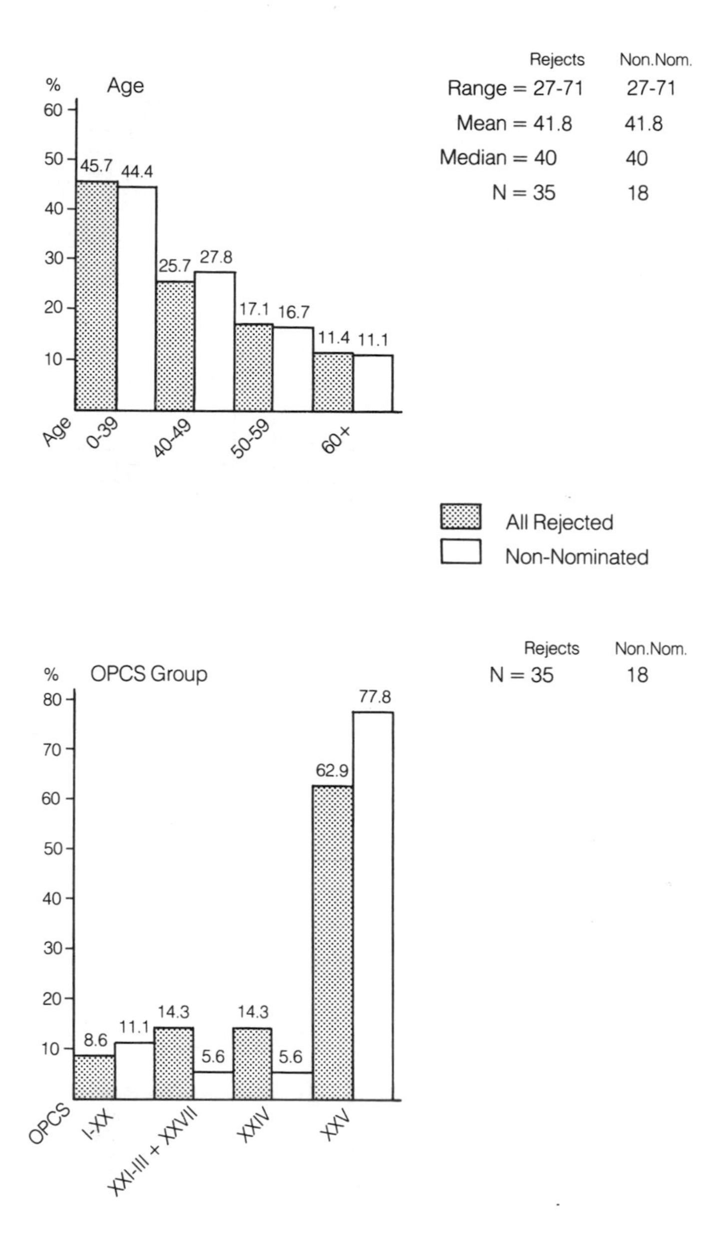

Figure 7.2 Background Characteristics of all Rejected and Non-Nominated Aspirants

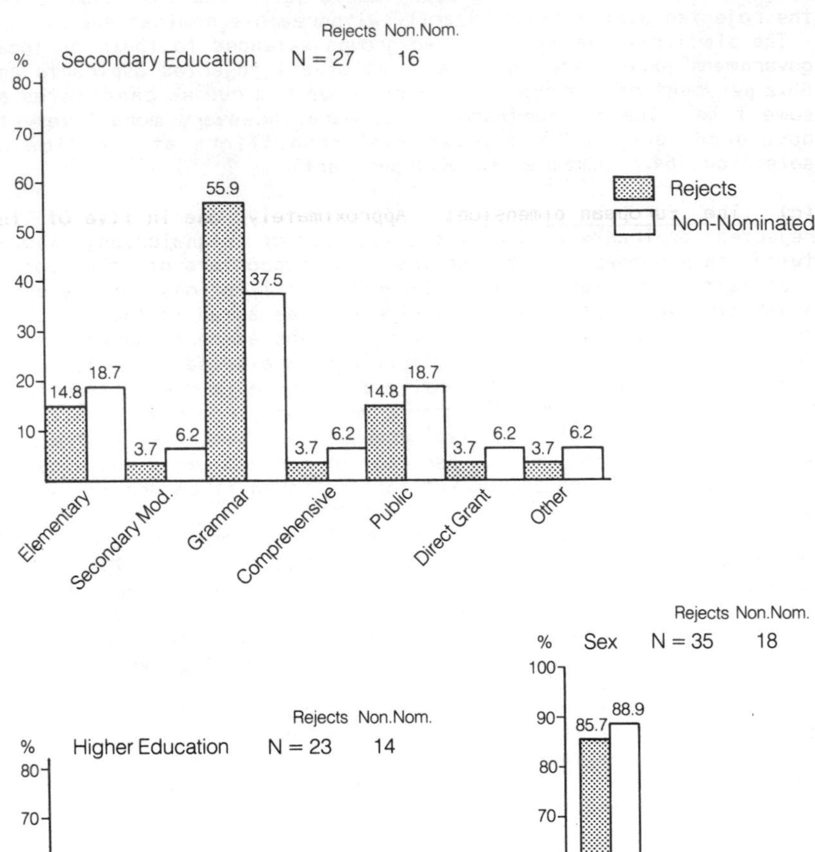

Rejects Non.Nom.
% Higher Education N = 23 14
80
70
60
50
40
30
20
10
8.7
14.3
13.0
14.3
56.5
50.0
21.8
21.4
Oxford
Cambridge
Redbrick
Other

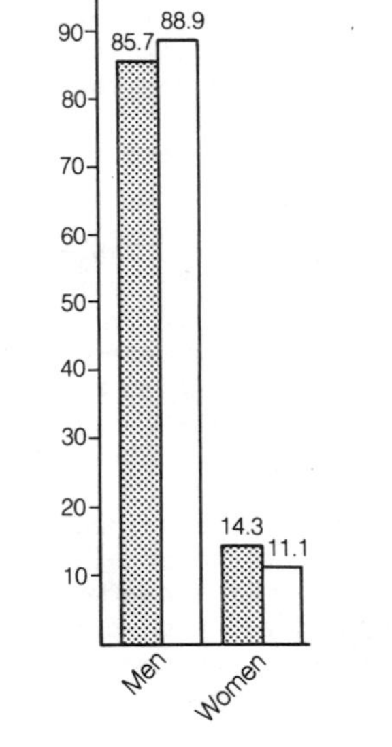

selections. Four of the five Co-operative party panelists were also in the non-nominated group: conversely, the only peer among the rejected aspirants voluntarily withdrew his nomination.

The similarity between the two groups extended to their of local government experience; 82.4 per cent of all rejected aspirants and 88.2 per cent of the non-nominated group had run as candidates at some time. The non-nominated group were, however, more likely to have been serving local government councillors at the time of selection (64.7 compared to 50.0 per cent).

(c) The European dimension: Approximately one in five of the rejected aspirants were on the LCMSC list of signatories, though twice this number felt themselves to be supporters of the policy statement. However, the anti-Market affiliations of rejected aspirants were not questioned: no one was asked if they were on the LCMSC list and only one individual was asked to answer Bryan Gould's questionnaire. These findings paralleled those for non-nominated aspirants. A substantive difference in the self-assigned European position of the two groups was found, however: only 48.0 per cent of the larger rejected group placed themselves in the pro-Market camp compared to 62.5 per cent of non-nominated individuals. It appeared that the pro-Market faction found it harder to secure CLP support.

The pro-EEC skew amongst non-nominated aspirants was not reflected in the respective attitudes of the two groups toward six European topics. Only 21.4 per cent of this group compared to 30.4 per cent of all rejects favoured the development of a European federal state; a majority of both groups favoured the reduction in the powers of the EEC over national Parliaments, were against monetary union and did not wish to see an increase in the powers of the European Parliament. The creation of transnational parties gained the popular support of six out of every ten respondents in both groups, and the move towards a uniform electoral system also had the backing of a bare majority. The attitudes of self-assigned pro-Europeans were not always consistent with the pro-Market position.

(d) Ambition: The number of PPCs in the rejected aspirant group did not seem to affect the overall patterns of motivation and ambition: PPCs were reluctant to describe their European motivations in terms of their domestic ambitions. The European dimension dominated, with pro-Marketeers tending to be disproportionately represented amongst the non-nominated group.

In summary, the two groups of rejected aspirants were largely similar in most characteristics other than prospective parliamentary candidacy. The most important difference was that aspirants with pro-European sympathies were disproportionately found in the non-nominated category, inferring an anti-Market tendency at the CLP gate-keeping selection stage. In what respects, if any, were those chosen by CLPs as their nominations to the ESOs different from the rejected aspirants surveyed?

CLP Nominees

(a) Background characteristics: 350 aspirants gained the backing of at least one CLP in their quest for European candidacy. These individuals who succeeded in having their names forwarded to the ESO executive committee tended to be older than those aspirants rejected at the CLP stage, the median age for each group being forty-five and forty respectively. This stage in the selection process was also a male domain. As found for rejected aspirants, Labour's nominees were most likely to come from grammar schools, though a high percentage had an elementary or secondary modern background. Nominees educated outside the state sector were rare, accounting for only 7.4 per cent of known cases, exactly half the figure for rejected aspirants: only three individuals had attended a Clarendon School. The contrasts with the Conservative approved list were all too apparent: 64.3 per cent had been to a public school with 30.6 per cent of these at one of the nine Clarendon institutions. 84.4 per cent of CLP nominees had undergone some form of higher education, predominantly at a redbrick university.

The preference for Labour's aspirants to be drawn from the OPCS group XXV (professional, technical workers and artists) rather than Group XXIV (administrators and managers) was reproduced for the chosen CLP nominations with two-thirds of the nominees' occupations falling in this category. The proliferation of the teaching profession in domestic parliamentary candidacy was noted by Mellors: he found that there had been a 136 per cent increase in teachers and lecturers in the ten elections since 1945, amounting to 28.1 per cent of Labour MPs in October 1974.(1) The figures for CLP Euro-nominees confirmed the importance of this path to political candidacy: 23.1 per cent of nominations went to teachers and 8.3 per cent to university teachers or lecturers in other institutions of higher or further education, the combined total accounting for almost one in every three nominees.

The next largest group of nominees were those engaged as officials of trade or professional associations, the Workers Educational Association and the Labour or Co-operative parties (OPCS group XXV). The third largest occupational category isolated executive officers in the civil service or local government (OPCS group XXI). The only substantial occupational group drawn from groups I-XX were transport workers; despite NUM sponsorship, only five workers in the coal industry were nominated to an ESO. The profession of Euro-crat, company director, and manager, typical of the Conservative aspirants were conspicuous by their virtual absence among Labour aspirants. The legal and journalist professions found some accommodation within the Labour party. Mellors' overall conclusion that the Labour party had drifted away 'from men of toil to men of ideas' was confirmed by the European nomination process.(2)

(b) Previous political experience: To be eligible for nomination, all aspirants had to have been members of the Labour party for a minimum of two years: the median number of years as a party member was nineteen. Only 9.7 per cent had been members for less than eight years, whereas the top 10.0 per cent had served the party for between thirty-three and fifty years. 30.6 per cent of nominees had stood as parliamentary candidates, though generally on only one

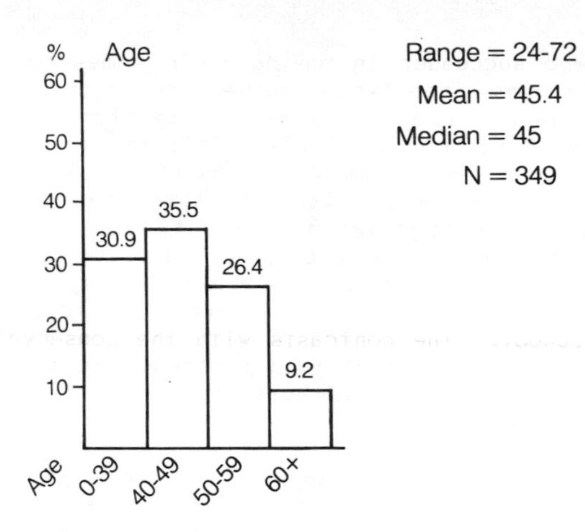

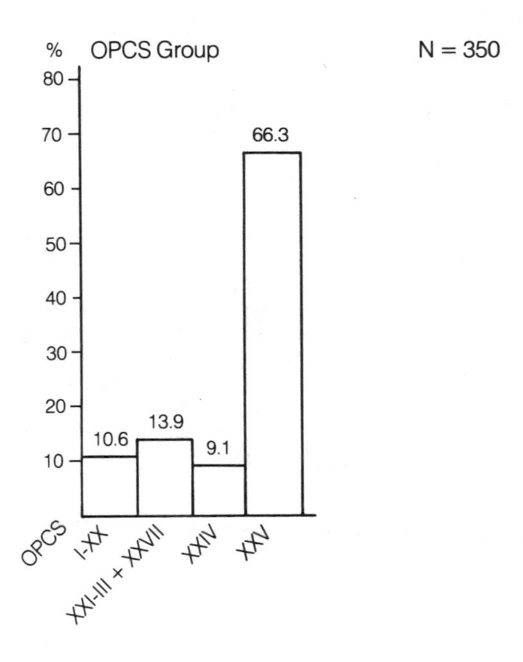

Figure 7.3 Background Characteristics of CLP Nominees

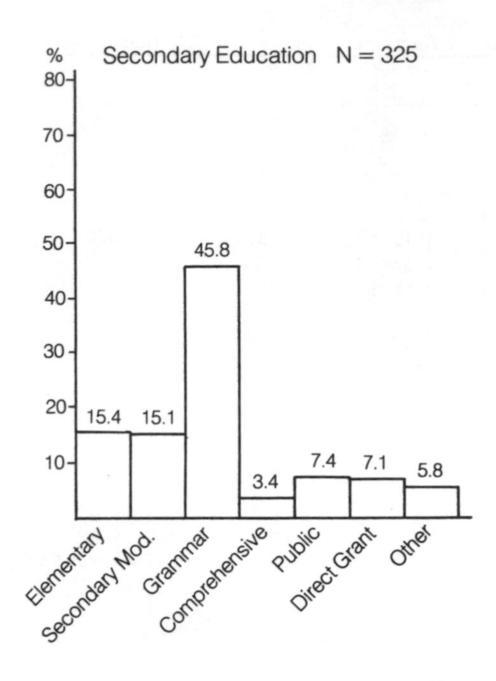
%
Secondary Education N = 325
80
70
60
50
40
30
20
10
45.8
15.4
15.1
3.4
7.4
7.1
5.8
Elementary
Secondary Mod.
Grammar
Comprehensive
Public
Direct Grant
Other

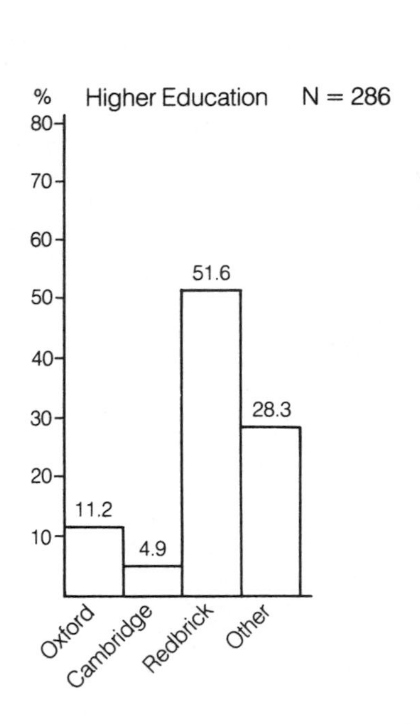
%
Higher Education N = 286
80
70
60
50
40
30
20
10
51.6
28.3
11.2
4.9
Oxford
Cambridge
Redbrick
Other

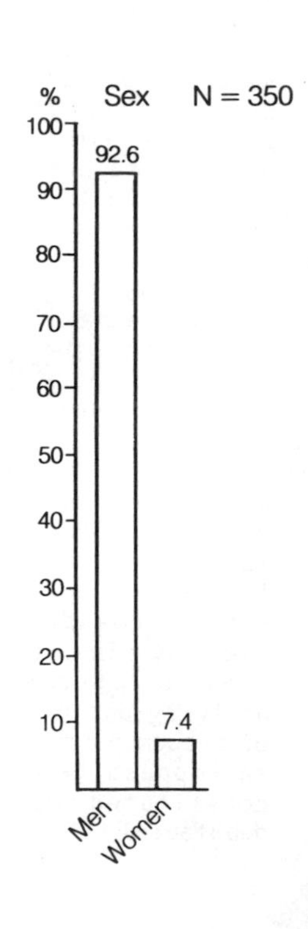
%
Sex N = 350
100
90
80
70
60
50
40
30
20
10
92.6
7.4
Men
Women

Table 7.1

Number of Parliamentary Elections Fought by CLP Nominees

No. of Elections	%	n	adjusted %
None	69.4	243	-
1	11.4	40	37.4
2	10.9	38	35.5
3	4.6	16	15.0
4	2.3	8	7.5
5-9	1.4	5	4.6
	100.0	350	100.0

or two occasions. CLP nominees also tended to be aspirants at the start of their political careers in the sense that the majority had fought at one of the three elections in the early 1970s, rather than old campaigners whose political ambitions had been suspended since the 1950s or 60s. As already noted, the NEC's declaration that PPCs were ineligible for European nomination came too late to prevent thirteen adopted parliamentary candidates from being selected as CLP nominees, with ten of these withdrawing from the European selection process rather than forfeit the chance of a possible Westminster career. In addition, fourteen of the 350 CLP nominations had served as MPs, 51.3 per cent had been on either the 'A' or 'B' parliamentary list, with 30.0 per cent still on one of these lists at the time of the European selections. 167 (67.3 per cent) of those on the advisory European list progressed beyond the CLP screening filter, as did thirty one (81.6 per cent) of the Co-operative panelists. Five peers succeeded in persuading local parties to submit their names to an ESO.

The most notable characteristic of nominated aspirants, as with those who were rejected, was their experience as local government candidates. Eight out of every ten nominees had run as a candidate. Nominees were not generally one term local government candidates but were more likely to have stood on subsequent occasions, 35.9 per cent having fought six or more campaigns. What is more, 77.4 per cent of local government candidates had at some time served as local councillors and 40.3 per cent of nominees were serving councillors at the time of selection. These factors of years service, parliamentary and local government candidacy can be used as estimators of 'apprenticeship' rather than local party activity and office-holding as suggested by Bochel in his analysis of Labour party councillors.(3) Overall, CLP nominees had served an impressive Labour party apprenticeship, although whether it constituted appropriate training for the European Parliament is debatable.

Table 7.2

Times Run as a Local Government Candidate and Years Served as a Councillor for CLP Nominees

Times Run	%	n	Years Served	%	n
Never	19.8	68	None	22.6	63
Once	10.5	36	1-3	17.6	49
Twice	9.0	31	4-6	17.2	48
3 Times	12.5	43	7-9	14.7	41
4 Times	11.9	41	10-12	9.7	27
5 Times	7.6	26	13-15	4.3	12
6 - 10 Times	20.0	69	16-18	2.1	6
11 and More	8.7	30	19-21	4.6	13
Not Known	-	6	22 and Over	7.2	20
			Not Known	-	3
	100.0	350		100.0	282

(c) The European dimension: The ratio of pro and anti-EEC support amongst CLP nominees reflected the overall trend noted throughout the analysis of Labour's European adventure: 40.9 per cent of known cases (131) professed a pro-Market commitment, compared to 49.4 per cent (158) who were opposed to UK membership; the remaining 9.7 per cent covered sceptics, unsures and those who refused to assign themselves to either option. 11.5 per cent claimed membership of the EM and 17.1 per cent the LCE, whereas 22.9 per cent were LCMSC signatories, with 52.0 per cent sympathising with the LCMSC policy statement. However, only 5.1 per cent of CLP nominees were questioned about any LCMSC affiliation and 11.6 per cent asked about Bryan Gould's questionnaire in some form.

The European attitudes of CLP nominees paralleled those for rejected aspirants: despite the fact that 40.9 per cent were self-assigned pro-Marketeers, 70.3 per cent were against the development of a federal Europe, 63.2 per cent against monetary union, 52.9 per cent against any increase in the powers of the European Parliament and 52.6 per cent in favour of a reduction in the existing powers of the Community over national parliaments. As for the rejected aspirant group, the two issues that impinged least directly upon British sovereignty, the development of transnational party organisations and a common voting system were both supported by a majority of respondents (61.5 and 52.6 per cent respectively).(4) Surprisingly, even nominees with pro-EEC sympathies tended to follow the party line in relation to the larger question of integration and the emasculation of sovereign states. The preference for a cross-national linking of parties was explained by a belief in international socialism and that the European Community could provide the basis for such a movement, even though it was regarded as fundamentally a capitalist organisation.

(d) Ambition: Whereas over half the rejected aspirants professed to being self-starters, only 38.4 per cent of nominees cited this as their single motivation, although this figure rose to 54.3 when other combinations using self-recruitment were included.

Table 7.3

Initial Stimulus for European Candidacy for CLP Nominees

Stimulus	%	n
Own Idea	38.4	121
CLP	25.7	81
Trade Union/Co-operative Party	7.9	25
Party Agents/Secretaries	1.3	4
Family/Friends	5.7	18
Own Idea Plus Agents/Secretaries	5.1	16
Own Idea Plus Trade Union/Co-operative	3.2	10
Own Idea Plus CLP	7.6	24
CLP Plus Trade Union/Co-Operative	5.1	16
Not Known	-	35
	100.0	350
All Self Starters	54.3	171

A quarter identified their initial stimulus for candidacy as emanating from a CLP; the percentage of respondents using this variable in conjunction with other explanations of motivation was 38.4 per cent. The minor role played by trade unions and the Co-operative party as recruitment agents corresponded with the earlier finding concerning sponsorship. Generally, unions did not search for suitable candidates to represent their interests in the European Parliament or assume their traditional domestic role as recruitment catalysts.

Why did these 350 individuals wish to run as potential MEPs? Again, the findings closely resembled those for rejected aspirants. The multiple responses in Table 7.4 clearly indicate that the European issue was the crucial determinant. 45.4 per cent of all nominees mentioned an anti-EEC reason in explaining their decision to run: in particular, to represent the anti-Market case, to reform the EEC or secure the UK's withdrawal and to defend national interests. Not surprisingly, there was a corresponding pro-Market response to this anti-EEC tendency which promoted the merits of UK membership, with a small percentage seeing candidacy as a trend towards the desired goal of federalism. The single most mentioned reason was to promote European socialism, which straddled both the pro and anti-Market camps.

The political aspects of motivation were interesting.

Table 7.4

Reasons for Running as an MEP Aspirant for CLP Nominees

Reason	N = 350	%	n
(i) European			
PRO:			
Interested in Europe		4.3	15
Experienced in Europe		8.3	29
UK Future is in Europe		4.0	14
To create a European Union		5.4	19
Former 'Yes' campaigner		0.6	2
Promote peace		2.3	8
To Present the Pro-EEC Case		5.7	20
		30.6	107
ANTI:			
Reform EEC/end Membership		8.3	29
Protect British Industry/Agriculture		3.7	13
Prevent a Federal States of Europe		1.4	5
Anti-European Capitalism		3.4	12
Prevent a Pro-EEC Being Selected		3.7	13
Defend British Interests		7.7	27
To Present the Anti-EEC Case		12.3	43
Former 'No' Campaigner		2.3	8
Carry Out NEC Policy		2.6	9
		45.4	159
To Serve the Area		3.4	12
Promote European Socialism		14.3	50
		17.7	62
(ii) Personal/Political			
Would Do Well/Can Contribute		6.9	24
Recruited to Stand		10.6	37
Local Candidate Needed		8.0	28
Women Candidates Needed		1.7	6
Only a 'Flagwaver'		1.1	4
Former MEP		1.1	4
Gain Experience for Westminster Candidacy		3.4	12
Failed Westminster Career		0.9	3
Logical Extension of Political Career		4.3	15
		38.0	133

Occasionally it was felt that a local nominee was needed to keep out career-orientated political opportunists seeking a secure seat. Alternatively, it was surprising that only a small number of nominees saw candidacy for the European Parliament in national career terms, either as compensation for domestic political disappointments or as a method of gaining election experience. However 10.6 per cent did fit into Schlesinger's category of 'progressive' ambition, seeing candidacy for the European Parliament as a route to Westminster.(5) How active were these individuals in seeking nominations? Just over two-thirds managed to secure CLP backing in only one Euro-Constituency, 16.9 cent in two and 5.4 per cent in three areas. Only 3.2 per cent of all nominees had their names submitted to five or more European seats.

The profile for CLP nominees can be summarised as follows: they were predominantly middle-aged, male, married, grammar school/university (non-Oxbridge) products, drawn from the OPCS group XXV with the teaching profession the most common occupation. What they lacked in parliamentary experience was compensated for by their involvement in local politics. Anti-Marketeers were in the majority as were LCMSC signatories; in addition, the European attitudes of the nominees were clearly hostile to the idea of a federal Europe or the removal of national sovereignty. Local constituency parties played a significant role as recruitment agents, though self-motivated individuals were still in the majority: trade unions did little to stimulate nominations. A belief in pro or anti-EEC doctrines was the prime reason for contesting nomination, with only one in ten treating Europe as a path to Westminster.

Rejected ESO Nominees and Short-Listed ESO Nominees

Not all CLP nominations made the final ESO selection meeting short list. Each ESO executive committee had the responsibility of recommending a short list to the full ESO delegate body for amendment or approval. Thus after the initial CLP screening, there was the executive committee hurdle to overcome. This aspect of the gate-keeping process eliminated 24.6 per cent of the nominee population of 350.

(a) Background characteristics: There was little difference between the short-listed and non-short-listed groups using the variables of sex, marital status and age; 92.4 and 93.0 per cent were male, 85.3 and 85.7 per cent married and the mean ages for each group were 44.5 and 46.7 respectively. This similarity extended to secondary education with 45.0 per cent of both groups drawn from grammar schools, although those with elementary and a non-public school education were more common among the short-listed category. While eight out of ten in both groups had undergone higher education, 54.3 per cent of those on ESO short-lists compared to 42.4 per cent of those rejected on the basis of biographical details went to a redbrick university and approximately one in seven of each group were Oxbridge graduates.

OPCS group classifications and occupation exposed the most significant difference between the two contending groups. No difference was found for the percentage of nominees in either group engaged in the broadly manual classifications I-XX, both attracting only one in ten from this area. While approximately three-quarters of all nominees came from the two highest socio-economic classifications, the balance between categories differed according to selection status. Short-listed nominees were more likely to be drawn from OPCS group XXV (68.9 per cent compared with 58.1), whereas those rejected by an ESO were more likely to be from OPCS group XXIV (15.1 compared to 7.2 per cent). Closer examination of actual occupations shed some light on these differences. Among nominees short-listed for an ESO, 25.8 per cent were teachers and a further 8.0 per cent lecturers. The corresponding figures for non-short-listed CLP nominations were 15.1 and 9.3 per cent, the sum total accounting almost entirely for the 10.0 per cent difference in the two groups' OPCS group XXV percentages. Not only were teaching professions the most prolific single occupational category, they also had a disproportionate success rate. The legal profession also emerged at this stage as an important source of political recruitment.

(b) Previous political experience: There was an equal distribution between the two nominee groups in terms of their record of party membership: both had a median of nineteen years membership. Those chosen to appear before an ESO were more likely to have had greater campaign experience as parliamentary candidates: one-third compared with a quarter had stood as candidates, with almost half of the rejected nominees who had fought only having contested one Westminster election. The eighty-six ESO short-listed nominees who were former parliamentary candidates also tended to have fought in the more recent general elections and twelve of the fourteen former MPs gained an ESO place. Three peers also progressed to the final screening stage. A bare majority of both groups had shown interest in a Westminster career at some time, their names having been included on the parliamentary 'A' or 'B' list, with three out of ten still on one of the lists in 1979, indicating conflicting, and in the Labour party, mutually exclusive objectives in terms of election to a political office. The finding also suggested that for many, Europe was merely a necessary diversion on the road to Westminster.

The negative impact of the 'Advisory List of Candidates for the European Assembly Elections' was fully exposed at the ESO gatekeeping stage. Whilst inclusion on the list may have attracted initial ward, branch or CLP interest, the list carried little weight at the Euro-constituency level: 83.7 per cent of rejected CLP nominees came from the advisory list, compard with only 36.0 per cent of ESO short-listed nominees. One explanation for this disproportionate effect was the misplaced belief that there was a pro-Market bias in the list. In contrast, membership of the Co-operative Panel appeared to be a selection advantage with twenty-two of the thirty-one panelists making an ESO short list. As intimated earlier, the prospect of sponsorship may have been a tempting influence.

In terms of political experience, local government involvement was the dominant profile characteristic for both short-listed and non-short-listed nominees: 77.9 per cent of the latter and 81.7 per cent of the former had served their political 'apprenticeships' as local government candidates. Although short-listed nominees were more likely to have contested a greater number of elections

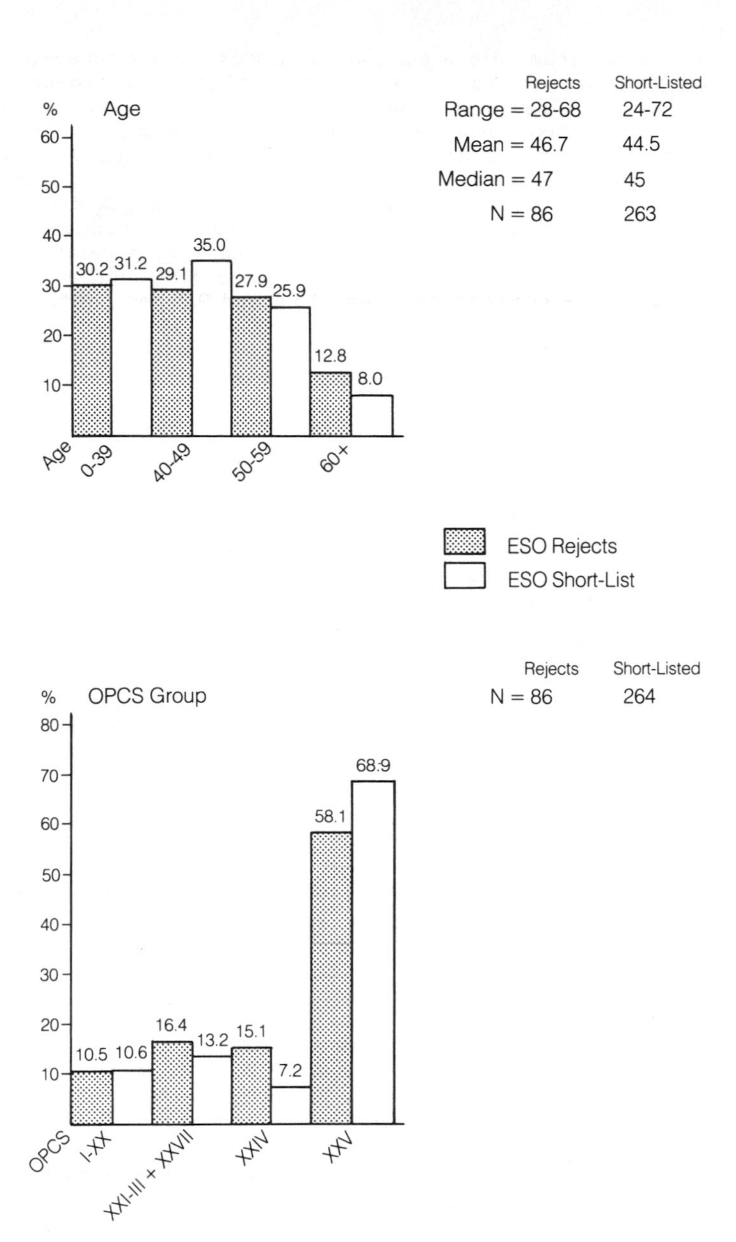

Figure 7.4 Background Characteristics of Rejected ESO Nominees and Short-Listed ESO Nominees

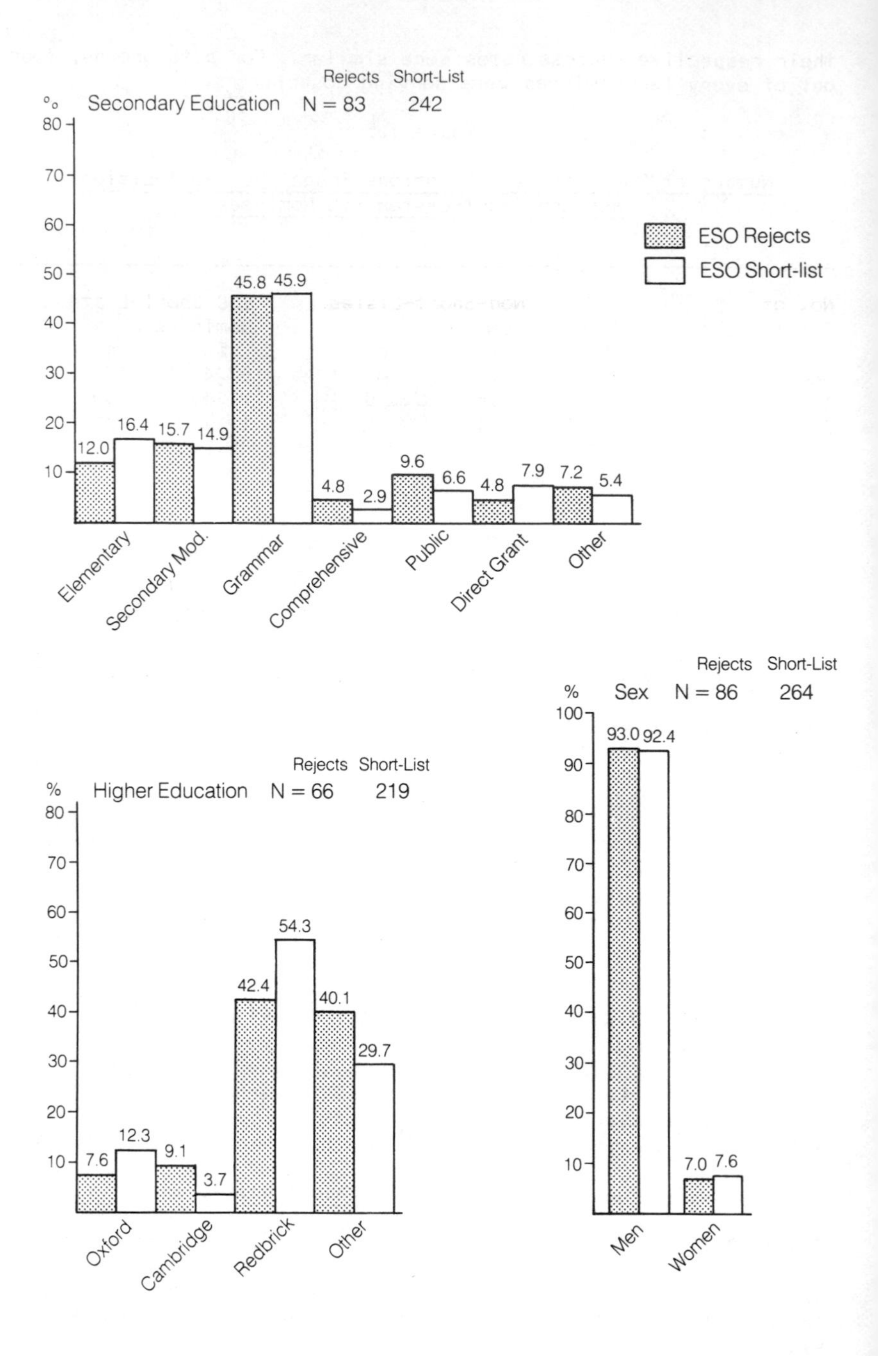
Rejects Short-List
% Secondary Education N = 83 242
ESO Rejects
ESO Short-list
12.0 16.4 15.7 14.9 45.8 45.9 4.8 2.9 9.6 6.6 4.8 7.9 7.2 5.4
Elementary
Secondary Mod.
Grammar
Comprehensive
Public
Direct Grant
Other
Rejects Short-List
% Sex N = 86 264
93.0 92.4 7.0 7.6
Men
Women
Rejects Short-List
% Higher Education N = 66 219
7.6 12.3 9.1 3.7 42.4 54.3 40.1 29.7
Oxford
Cambridge
Redbrick
Other

their respective success rates were similar. For both groups, four out of every ten nominees were serving councillors.

Table 7.5

Number of Parliamentary Elections Fought by Short-Listed and Non-Short-Listed ESO Nominees

No. of Elections	Non-Short-Listed Nominees		ESO Short-Listed Nominees	
	%	n	%	n
None	75.6	65	67.4	178
1	11.6	10	11.4	30
2	8.1	7	11.7	31
3	1.2	1	5.7	15
4	2.3	2	2.3	6
5-9	1.2	1	1.5	4
	100.0	86	100.0	264

(c) The European dimension: The most important finding in this category related to the balance between pro and anti-Marketeers. The pro faction were in the majority among individuals who were not short-listed, 48.1 per cent against 44.4 per cent. This position was clearly reversed for short-listed nominees: 51.0 classified themselves as anti-Marketeers, with only 38.5 per cent on the pro-Market side. Thus rejected ESO nominees were almost identical in their basic European position to the group of initial CLP rejects. Whereas short-listed nominees increased the anti-Market bias evident amongst the 350 CLP nominations. This latent attitude was not transferred to any group affiliation: however, short-listed nominees displayed greater support, as distinct from membership, for the LCMSC policy statement.(6) In this repect rejected aspirants and non-short-listed nominees shared the same characteristics, while those short-listed for an ESO stressed the anti-EEC theme amongst CLP nominations. The conflicting pro and anti-EEC pattern was thus heightened. Although candidates were rarely asked about affiliation to the LCMSC each nominees' European position was generally known, either through a policy statement attached to biographical notes, or from the content of their speeches to various branch, ward and CLP meetings. In addition, the LCMSC list had been published in Labour Weekly and Tribune and the names of LCMSC signatories were therefore widely available. Those eliminated by the ESO gate-keepers were clearly more European in their outlook. On every one of the issues they registered a higher pro-EEC score: in particular, the development of a trans-national party system and support for a federal Europe pointed to a significant pro-Community bias in the group. Conversely, the short-listed nominees were hostile to any such moves that might further compromise national sovereignty.

(d) Ambition: The most common initial stimulus for running for non-short-listed nominees was self-recruitment. 41.5 per cent were self-starters, rising to 54.9 per cent when this factor was used in conjunction with other catalysts. Only 22.0 per cent stated that they had been encouraged to stand by a CLP (34.2 per cent when other variables combining CLP recruitment were included). ESO short-listed nominees were slightly less likely to be pure self-starters (37.3 per cent) though their combined total was similar (54.1 per cent). A major difference was in the recruitment role played by CLPs: 27.0 per cent of those short-listed isolated a CLP as their sole recruitment stimulus, with 44.2 per cent seeing this, together with other components as a reason behind their decision to run for the European Parliament. While all ESO nominees had to have the backing of at least one CLP, not surprisingly, those who were intially encouraged to run by their CLPs were likely to proceed further in the selection race.

How did these findings on recruitment catalysts correspond to the motivations each group gave for their candidacies? There was a clear difference based on the broad pro and anti-EEC variable. One-third of the eliminated group stated that their motivation was derived from pro-European assumptions, whereas four out of ten drew on anti-Market themes in explaining their motivations. In contrast, ESO short-listed nominees were less prone to seek justification in pro-EEC terms but eager to use anti-Market rhetoric in explanations of their candidacies. As one individual put it, he ran 'to provide an alterntive to the right wing/pro-Market careerists seeking nomination', or another, who wanted 'to ensure that the LCMSC had a voice in Europe'. In particular, 14.0 per cent of ESO short-listed nominees said they were motivated by the need to represent the anti-Market view, twice the percentage for non-short-listed individuals. In addition, all thirteen CLP nominees who stood in order to prevent a pro-Marketeer from being selected were short-listed. Thus the general pro/anti bias towards short-listing as described in the previous section was also evident in the motivational responses. Interestingly, all fifteen who saw nomination for the European Parliament as an advancement of their political careers were short-listed. However, there was little difference in the percentages of short-listed and rejeted ESO nominees who possessed 'progressive' ambitions: one in ten of both groups considered European candidacy as a shortcut to Westminster.

The major findings of the short-listed/non-short-listed comparative profile can be summarised as follows. The similarities in age, sex and education were more striking than the differences: only education at public school and attendance at a non-Oxbridge university distinguished the two groups. OPCS group XXV typified the short-listed group with over one-quarter employed in the primary or secondary education sectors. Short-listed nominees were also the politically more experienced group: a greater percentage had been PPCs or MPs, they were more likely to have contested either of the 1974 elections and a greater number had been local government candidates and councillors. The vast majority of nominees who appeared on the advisory list failed to get past the ESO short-listing hurdle. Most importantly, pro/anti self-classification, LCE membership, motivation and attitudes towards six Community issues all indicated that pro-Europeans were disadvantaged at this stage of the selection process. How far were

Table 7.6

Reasons for Running as an MEP Aspirant for Short-Listed and Non-Short-Listed ESO Nominees

Reason	N = 86 ESO rejects %	n	N = 264 ESO short-list %	n
(i) European				
PRO:				
Interested in Europe	2.3	2	4.9	13
Experienced in Europe	8.1	7	8.3	22
UK Future is in Europe	9.3	8	2.3	6
To create a European Union	5.8	5	5.3	14
Former 'Yes' campaigner	1.2	1	0.4	1
Promote peace	3.5	3	1.9	5
To Present the Pro-EEC Case	3.5	3	6.4	17
	33.7	29	29.5	78
ANTI:				
Reform EEC/end Membership	9.3	8	8.0	21
Protect British Industry/Agriculture	4.7	4	3.4	9
Prevent a Federal States of Europe	1.2	1	1.5	4
Anti-European Capitalism	2.3	2	3.8	10
Prevent a Pro-EEC Being Selected	-	-	4.9	13
Defend British Interests	11.6	10	6.4	17
To Present the Anti-EEC Case	7.0	6	14.0	37
Former 'No' Campaigner	-	-	3.0	8
Carry Out NEC Policy	3.5	3	2.3	6
	39.6	34	47.3	125
To Serve the Area	2.3	2	3.8	10
Promote European Socialism	11.6	10	15.2	40
	13.9	12	19.0	50
(ii) Personal/Political				
Would Do Well/Can Contribute	5.8	5	7.2	19
Recruited to Stand	8.1	7	11.4	30
Local Candidate Needed	7.0	6	8.3	22
Women Candidates Needed	2.3	2	1.5	4
Only a 'Flagwaver'	-	-	1.5	4
Former MEP	2.3	2	0.8	2
Gain Experience for Westminster Candidacy	3.5	3	3.4	9
Failed Westminster Career	1.2	1	0.8	2
Logical Extension of Political Career	-	-	5.7	15
	30.2	26	40.6	107

these anti-Market trends evident at the next stage in the selection mechanism, the ESO selection meeting?

Defeated ESO Short-Listed Nominees and PEPCs

Before the findings are presented, two riders to this section are warranted. Firstly, at this stage in the selection procedure, the larger ESO delegate body became involved: the small band of party gate-keepers, both at the constituency and ESO level, could no longer control or shape the screening process. In consequence different factors (and less quantifiable ones) may have been crucial at this stage. A comprehensive review of variables such as speakers' addresses, their content and style as well as inter-CLP bargaining or conflict could not be estimated. Secondly, as the PEPC stage in the recruitment and selection process was reached the value of the model's approach compared to the barrenness of candidate studies was highlighted. The type of candidate chosen as a Labour PEPC can now be seen in context, matched against the characteristics of the aspirant cohort, rather than in non-comparative isolation.

(a) Background characteristics: Women were better represented amongst PEPCs: they were adopted in 10.3 per cent of the seats compared to 6.5 per cent of the defeated ESO short-listed group. PEPCs also tended to be younger, with a median age of forty-two compared with that of forty-six: in terms of age and sex, PEPCs more closely resembled the initial group of aspirant rejects rather than either the losing short-listed individuals or the larger profile of CLP nominees.

Both selected and non-selected nominees were likely to be grammar school products though the latter group contained a significant proportion with only elementary education. Only 6.0 per cent of PEPCs and 6.9 per cent of defeated nominees had a public school education. While the two groups had a similar ratio of individuals who had undergone higher education, they diverged when the actual institutions attended were examined. The PEPC profile broke down as follows: of the 89.7 who had received higher education, 64.3 per cent went to a redbrick university, and 17.1 per cent to Oxbridge. The picture for those defeated at an ESO selection meeting was somewhat different: 84.3 per cent had received higher education, of whom 49.7 per cent had been to a redbrick university and 15.4 per cent to Oxbridge. In total 81.4 per cent of PEPCs who had undergone higher education were university graduates compared to 65.1 per cent of those rejected at the selection meeting.

Occupational classifications also proved to be a significant discriminating variable. There was a marked preference for PEPCs to be from the professional, technical workers and artists category rather than be employed in manual, clerical or even administrative and managerial occupations. Within the OPCS group XXV further distinctions between the two groups were possible: 29.5 per cent of PEPCs were teachers, compared with 24.2 per cent of defeated ESO nominees, although parity was established when lecturers were included, adding 5.1 and 9.1 per cent respectively to each group.(7) Local government together with civil service executive officers and those engaged in the legal profession fared badly at the selection meetings: only 2.6 of PEPCs came from these

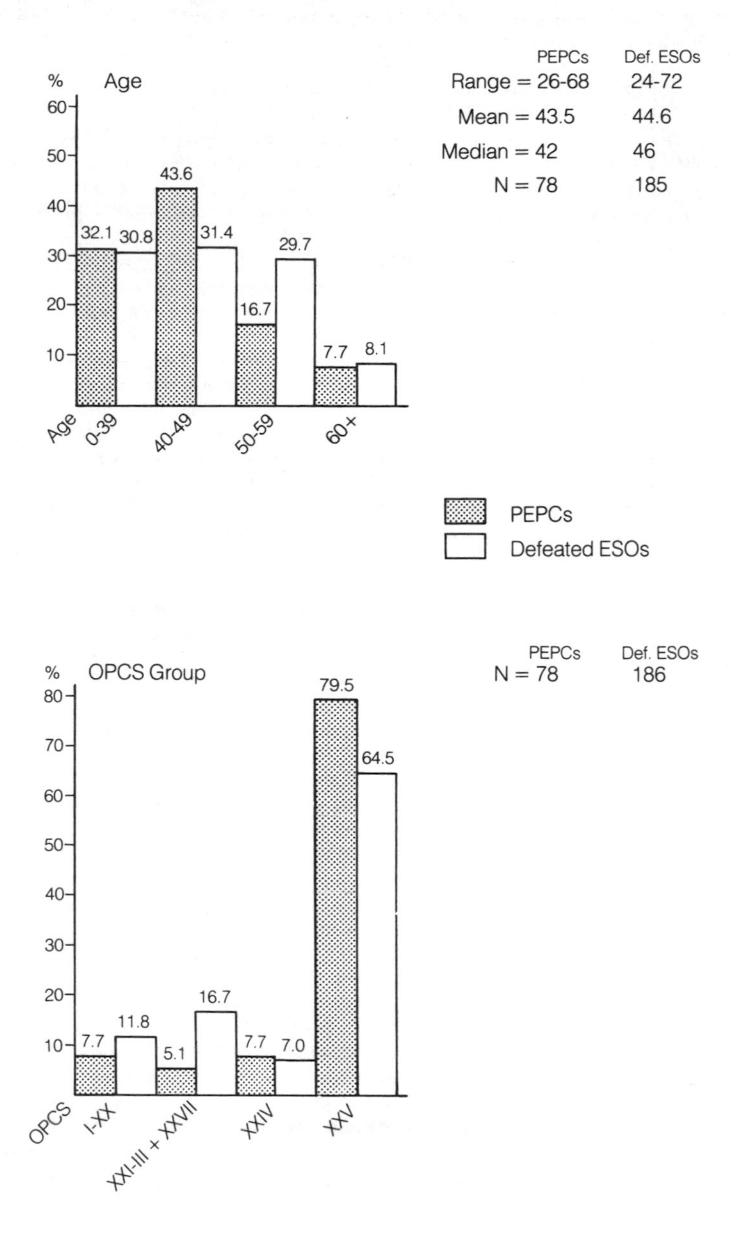

Figure 7.5 Background Characteristics of PEPCs and Defeated ESO Short-Listed Nominees

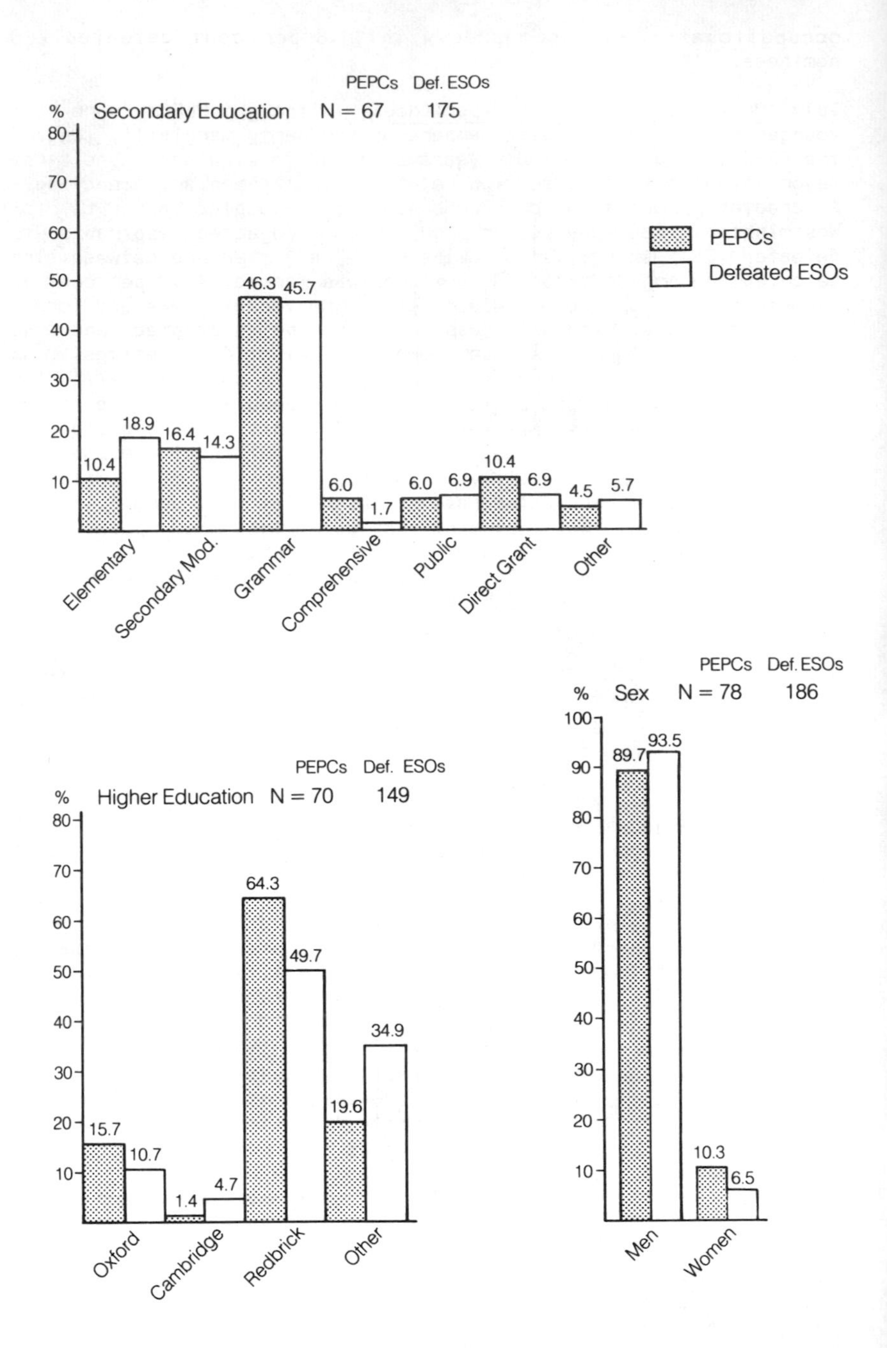

PEPCs Def. ESOs
% Secondary Education N = 67 175
80
70
60
50
40
30
20
10
PEPCs
Defeated ESOs
10.4
18.9
16.4
14.3
46.3
45.7
6.0
1.7
6.0
6.9
10.4
6.9
4.5
5.7
Elementary
Secondary Mod.
Grammar
Comprehensive
Public
Direct Grant
Other
PEPCs Def. ESOs
% Sex N = 78 186
100
90
80
70
60
50
40
30
20
10
89.7
93.5
10.3
6.5
Men
Women
PEPCs Def. ESOs
% Higher Education N = 70 149
80
70
60
50
40
30
20
10
15.7
10.7
1.4
4.7
64.3
49.7
19.6
34.9
Oxford
Cambridge
Redbrick
Other

occupational areas, compared with 11.8 per cent defeated ESO nominees.

(b) Previous political experience: Although PEPCs were the younger group they had been members of the party marginally longer, the PEPC median being twenty years compared to eighteen. The first major finding in this section related to parliamentary candidacy. A greater proportion of PEPCs had been adopted as PPCs for Westminster than any other group, from rejected aspirants to defeated ESO short-listed nominees. The difference between the selected and non-selected ESO nominees was marked, 41.0 per cent as opposed to 30.8 per cent respectively. Conversely, MPs and former MPs had a less favourable passage, three being adopted and the remaining three-quarters overlooked by selection meetings. No peers were adopted. However, when generally compared with the various disappointed groups in the aspirant population, the chosen PEPCs were more politically experienced. This finding could not have been established by looking at traditional candidate studies, confirming the model's utility. Indeed, other studies relating to Labour's European candidates have stressed that they were political minnows ignoring the fact that they were the most politically experienced of all the groups of Labour aspirants.

The discrimination against individuals from the European list found at the ESO short-listing stage was not in evidence at the selection meeting: 41.0 per cent of PEPCs were from the list compared with 33.9 per cent of losing short-listed nominees.(8) However, most ESO delegates would not have been aware which nominees were from the advisory list, and it may have been irrelevant as a selection criterion. Sixteen of the remaining twenty-two Co-operative panelists failed to become European candidates.

There was little variation between the two groups for either past or present membership of the parliamentary 'A' or 'B' lists, half of each group having been on one or other, and three out of ten still registered as Westminster hopefuls. However, an important difference was pinpointed when experience in local politics was considered. Again, the approach of the model helped to expose a PEPC profile characteristic that would otherwise have remained camouflaged. The traditional candidate literature talked of selections having 'gone, mostly, to party faithful, often with considerable experience of local government', and 'in terms of political experience Labour candidates with local council experience appear to have had greater success in their bid for office'.(9) While there was a preponderance of local government candidates among PEPCs, such an analysis failed to recognise the diminution of such aspirants throughout the recruitment and gate-keeping processes. Thus, 78.2 per cent of PEPCs compared to 83.2 per cent of losing ESO nominees had at some time been local candidates, of whom 61.5 and 66.1 per cent respectively had been elected as councillors. What is more, whereas one-third of PEPCs were serving local councillors prior to the June election, this figure rose to 43.2 per cent for the defeated group. Indeed the 33.3 percentage figure was the lowest of the six sub-groups analysed so far: even rejected aspirants could muster a total of 40.0 per cent. To summarise, PEPCs showed a tendency to have served their electoral apprenticeship fighting Westminster seats whereas non-selected aspirants were trained in local politics.

(c) The European dimension: The dichotomy separating pro and anti- Marketeers proved to be the most distinctive profile variable. Only 26.6 per cent of PEPCs described themselves as supporters of UK membership, the smallest percentage of any of the other aspirant and nominee groups examined. What is more, this paucity of pro-Europeans resulted in an ardent anti-Market majority rather than a central buffer of uncommitted candidates: 53.1 per cent of PEPCs, the highest figure for all aspirant groups, supported the anti-EEC position. Thus, once again, while other commentators have pointed to the surprisingly high level of EEC support among Labour candidates given the NEC's European manifesto, the picture that emerged from the recruitment process was one of diminishing pro-Market selection.(10) As the earlier discussion of the delegate composition of ESOs showed, grass-roots activists appeared to be even more antagonistic towards the Community than the party's gate-keeping caucuses.

In the context of the PEPC anti-Market majority, it was surprising to find higher percentages of EM and LCE members among selected rather than defeated ESO nominees. An astonishingly high percentage of PEPCs, 24.7, were members of the EM and 19.7 per cent members of the LCE: the corresponding figures for losing nominees were 7.9 and 15.2. To counter this, 29.5 per cent of PEPCs were LCMSC signatories, compared with 17.5 of those defeated at a selection meeting. 54.0 per cent of both groups indicated that they were supporters of the LCMSC policy statement. PEPCs recorded higher anti-EEC scores for five of the six Community issues tested for, confirming the other evidence of anti-Market polarization within the recruitment process. Typically, PEPCs were more extreme in their criticisms of existing Community arrangements and more resistant to any future erosion of domestic sovereignty. Thus 82.8 per cent of PEPCs were against a federal European state (a finding in some conflict with the 24.7 per cent of PEPCs who professed membership of the federalist EM) and 76.3 per cent against financial union. The findings for defeated nominees were less homogeneous with 70.9 and 61.9 per cent agreeing with the anti-Market position respectively. Only in relation to the development of cross-national party organisations did selected candidates waver from their predominantly parochial line.

(d) Ambition: The initial recruitment stimulus was a further factor that distinguished PEPCs not only from their defeated ESO adversaries, but also from all previous aspirants and nominees. Only 27.9 per cent were pure 'self-starters' although a further 23.0 per cent used this explanation in conjunction with other variables. The corresponding figures for non-selected nominees were 40.7 per cent and 15.4. PEPCs were more likely to have been recruited by a CLP than the losing nominees: the difference was 50.8 compared to 42.0 per cent for individuals in the two groups who mentioned this stimulus either on its own or in addition to other factors. Thus, more than any other group, selected candidates were examples of manufactured and promoted candidacies. They were often initially recruited by local parties and their candidacies supported by CLPs throughout the selection machinery.

Ambition seen through the European perspective dominated the motivational responses of PEPcs. While both selected and non-selected groups registered virtually identical levels for anti-Market reasons for running as a potential candidate, the imbalance of pro-EEC responses on the defeated ESO nominee side was notable: they accounted for 36.0 per cent compared with only 14.1 for PEPCs. There was also an interesting difference in the personal/ political reasons for candidacy between the two groups, with non-selected aspirants the group most likely to mention these factors (43.0 and 34.7 per cent respectively). Those who only stood in order to present the selectors with a local choice were more likely to be defeated as were those who saw candidacy in terms of campaign experience for Westminster. Individuals who adopted the approach of one nominee who, while he was 'happy to be considered for Europe', really 'would like a seat at Westminster', were the least successful. 7.0 per cent of non-selected nominees believed the European elections offered a logical extension to their political careers; for example, one non-adopted nominee thought that being an MEP would 'inevitably give an opportunity for a leadership role in the party locally and nationally'. A further 11.7 per cent regarded European candidacy as a step on the career ladder towards the Commons. Only 8.1 per cent of PEPCs were similarly seduced by domestic parliamentary aspirations. To their surprise, three of the four individuals who considered themselves as 'flagwavers' for the party rather than serious contenders for election, were chosen as PEPCs!

Nomination strategies were used to infer ambition. While not a direct measure of this factor, differences between the two groups were apparent. PEPCs opted for the more comprehensive nomination strategy: 20.6 per cent of PEPCs were nominated to four or more ESOs compared to only 7.0 per cent of those defeated at a selection meeting. PEPCs were also more successful in securing a place on more than one short list. However, the ambitions of PEPCs were predominantly parochial. Only 23.1 per cent of PEPCs had no local ties with the constituency where they were adopted.

In summary, the consequences of the pro/anti debate were most easily identifiable at this stage of the selection process. Nominees with pro-Market sympathies were less likely to be selected. PEPCs were disproprotionately LCMSC signatories, motivated by anti-EEC desires, against the existing Community structures or moves toward further integration. When faced with the delegate-based democracy of ESO selection meetings, the pro-Marketeers failed to protect their position of relative strength in the earlier stages of the European selection ordeal.

Winners and Losers

As argued in the profile of Conservative winners and losers, the composition of these two groups was the result of electoral status, the vagaries of a simple-majority-single-ballot electoral system and disproportionate turn-out, itself a consequence of apathy and ignorance on the part of the electorate. The small MEP population size exaggerated the properties of their collective profile, but even allowing for this discrepancy certain characteristics did distinguish winners from losers. The final dichotomy is summarised below.

(a) <u>Background characteristics:</u> In a number of respects winners and losers were similar. Their median age was forty-two, approximatey one in ten had only an elementary education and the percentages for Oxbridge and redbrick university education were similar. In addition, over three-quarters of MEPs and defeated PEPCs came from OPCS group XXV.

One of the major differences was in relation to female candidates. Given that only eight women were selected, half were elected accounting for 23.5 per cent of MEPs. Perhaps it was indicative of the Labour party's view that the European Parliament constituted a second rate chamber, that women fared well in comparison with Westminster elections. Alternatively, perhaps the calibre of the male aspirants was especially poor on the European circuit. Nineteen of the twenty-three teachers were defeated on 7 June as were the remaining local and civil service executive officers and members of the legal profession. The contrast with MPs drawn from the legal profession was striking. In October 1974, 11.9 per cent of Labour's 319 MPs were barristers or solicitors.

(b) <u>Previous political experience:</u> the major finding was that MEPs tended to serve their political 'apprenticeships' in local rather than national politics. Examination of former parliamentary candidacy revealed that MEPs were the less experienced group. Only 29.4 per cent of MEPs compared to 41.0 per cent of defeated PEPCs had contested an election for the House of Commons. Barbara Castle was the only MEP with legislative experience; the other two former MPs, Jackson and Gray both lost. Approximately half of each group had at some time been on one of the parliamentary lists, though 46.0 per cent of MEPs and only 29.3 per cent of losers were still included in 1979. 35.3 per cent of winners originated from the European list and 11.8 from the Co-operative panel. The figures for losers were 42.6 and 6.6 per cent respectively. However, MEPs had a greater degree of experience in local politics. 94.1 per cent of MEPs had stood as local government candidates, 82.4 per cent had been elected, with 47.1 per cent councillors at the time of their adoption as PEPCs. The corresponding figures for losing candidates were 73.8, 55.7 and 29.5 per cent.

(c) <u>The European dimension:</u> As we saw in the previous section, anti-Marketeers accounted for 53.1 per cent of all PEPCs. Winners were marginally more pro-European (29.4 per cent compared to 25.5 per cent) and a significant proportion were members of the European Movement (35.3 per cent) with only 17.6 per cent LCMSC signatories. Not only were losers more likely to assign themselves as anti-Marketeers (55.3 per cent), 32.8 per cent were LCMSC signatories, with only approximately one in five EM members. This anti-EEC theme, while typical of all PEPCs, was stronger amongst losers and yet surprisingly it was not clearly reflected in their attitudes towards the Community issues. While both groups were equally adamant in their rejection of federalism and montary union, smaller percentages of MEPs favoured the pro-EEC position of a uniform electoral system, transnationl parties and the Community's authority over national parliaments. Only the issue of extending the European Parliament's powers diverged from this pattern, and then only marginally.

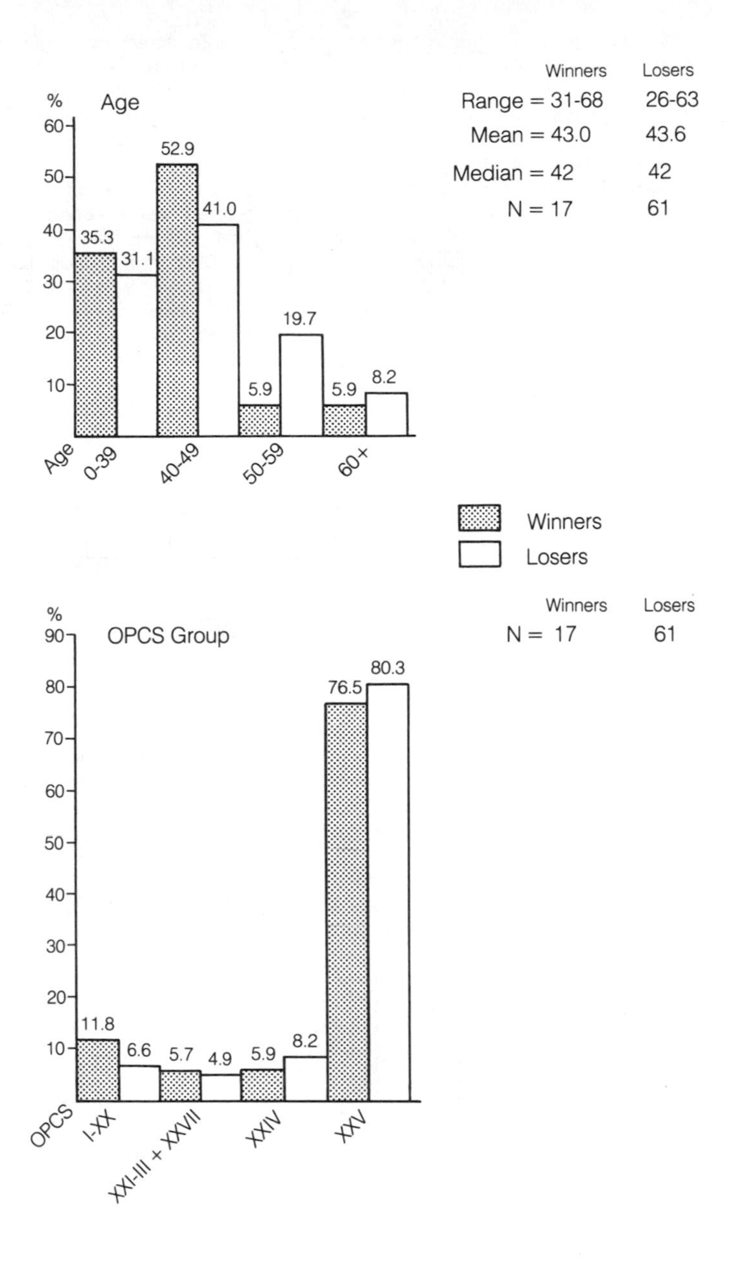

Figure 7.6 Background Characteristics of Winners and Losers

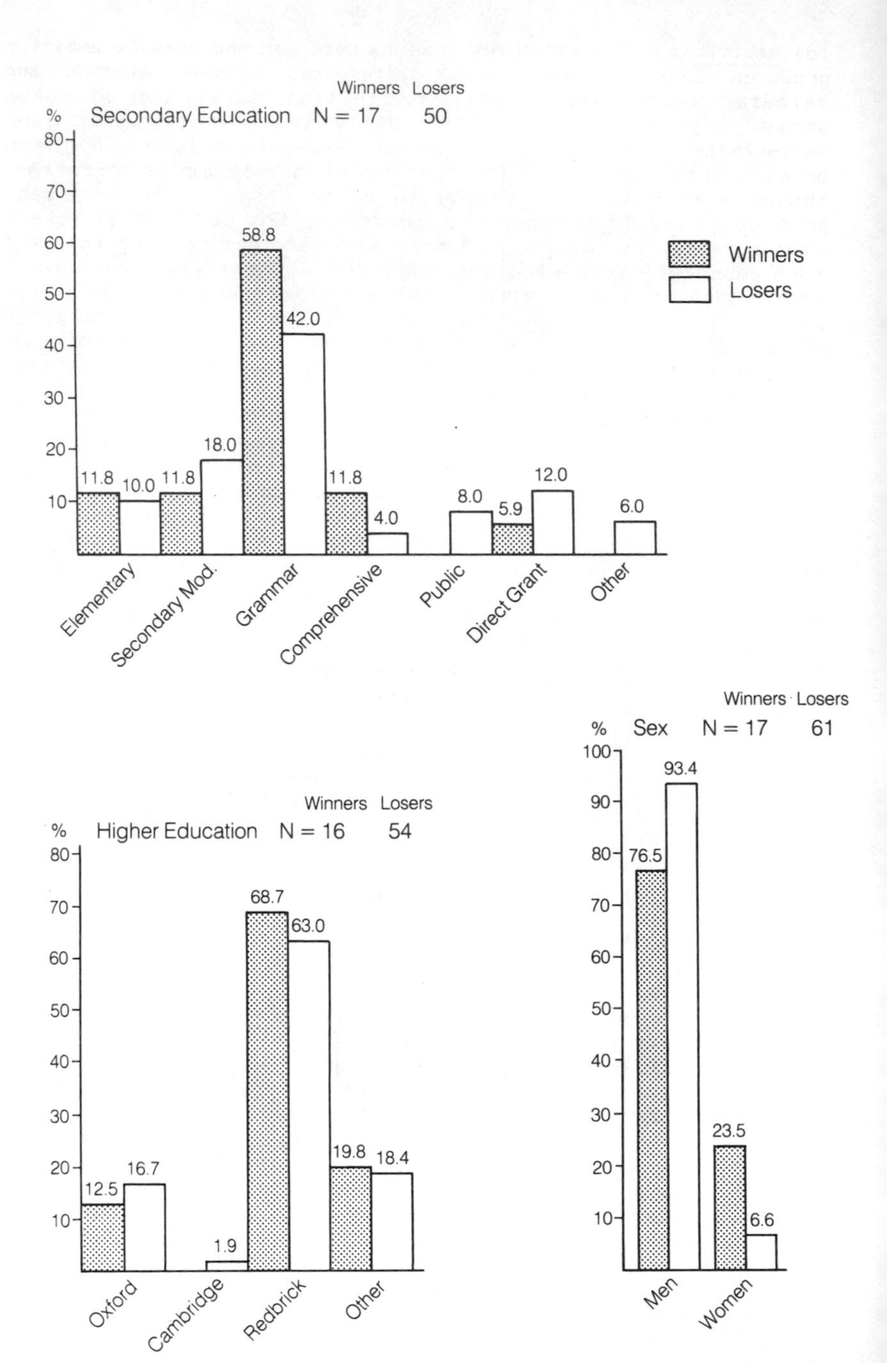
Winners Losers
% Secondary Education N = 17 50
80
70
60
50
40
30
20
10
58.8
42.0
18.0
11.8
10.0
11.8
11.8
4.0
8.0
5.9
12.0
6.0
Winners
Losers
Elementary
Secondary Mod.
Grammar
Comprehensive
Public
Direct Grant
Other
Winners Losers
% Sex N = 17 61
100
90
80
70
60
50
40
30
20
10
93.4
76.5
23.5
6.6
Men
Women
Winners Losers
% Higher Education N = 16 54
80
70
60
50
40
30
20
10
68.7
63.0
19.8
18.4
16.7
12.5
1.9
Oxford
Cambridge
Redbrick
Other

(d) Ambition: The variables used to describe and measure ambition produced some of the clearest differences between elected and defeated candidates. Firstly, the initial recruitment stimulus showed that MEPs were significantly less likely to be pure self-starters than any other group of defeated candidates, nominees or aspirants: only 13.3 per cent named this as a sole criterion, though when used in relation to other stimuli 53.3 per cent pointed to its importance. In contrast, 32.6 per cent of losers were pure self-starters, but only 47.9 per cent falling into the more generous classification. CLP recruitment was more common among defeated candidates. While the aggregated totals for personal/political reasons of candidacy were similar, defeated PEPCs included all but one of the six individuals who ran for what were domestic political reasons. Reassuringly, the three 'flagwavers' were not elected.

A significant majority of winners (70.6 per cent) described their motivations in familiar anti-EEC language.(11) One MEP for example, 'thought it essential to have anti-Market people there (the Parliament) to really push for change and to use it as a platform to explain to people in Britain what is happening there against their interests'. Another ran 'to ensure that the anti-Market view in the Labour party was fully represented'. Though less pervasive, an anti-Community theme also dominated the motivations of losing PEPCs, accounting for 40.9 per cent of responses. One candidate in particular was motivated because he 'hated the thought of little mini-Roy Jenkins characters poncing about representing the views of the Labour movement.'

It was interesting to note that while losers had a 55.3 to 47.1 per cent lead over winners in terms of anti-EEC classifiction, this self perception was not synonymous with recruitment motivation. MEPs were the only group where over half of the individuals relied upon anti-EEC dogma as a motivational source. The five PEPCs who displayed 'progressive' ambitions in that they regarded candidacy for the European Parliament as part of a career strategy for Westminster had their ambitions thwarted: the electorate chose their Conservative rivals.

MEPs were more successful in the number of nominations and short-lists they were chosen for: 63.9 per cent of losers gained only one nomination, and 78.7 per cent made just the single short-list; the corresponding figures for MEPs were 52.9 and 58.8. It may have been that the eventual winners had a more effective and efficient recruitment strategy. Many PEPCs by only showing interest in one local seat were committing themselves to certain electoral defeat from the outset. Quite remarkably there was significantly less politiking and competition for desirable seats, a consequence perhaps of a lack of ambition. Nor was the explanation based simply on parochialism: localism did not constitute a negative factor in selection. MEPs could claim to be the more local group: only 11.8 per cent failed to mention any local connection with their Euro-constituency compared with 26.2 per cent of losers.

Electoral Status

The electoral status perceptions of both aspirants and gatekeepers were shaped by the October 1974 results: how far did this influence the profile characteristics of candidates?

(a) Background characteristics: Projected Labour seats tended to prefer younger candidates: 85.4 per cent of projected Labour seats selected PEPCs aged below fifty compared with 64.7 per cent in projected Conservative seats. It was the rock solid Labour heartlands that went to the youthful candidates, securing eight of the nine safe Labour seats and all five impregnable ones. These candidates might have been expected to serve in a minimum of three parliaments. Thus secure Labour Euro-constituencies seemed to be taking a long term perspective in selecting their MEPs, given the unknown factors of re-selection and the future electoral system. 68.4 per cent of PEPCs aged fifty or more fought Conservative or SNP seats.

The distribution of women candidates was quite remarkable: one fought a Conservative semi-marginal, another an SNP marginal; the remaining six all contested Labour seats - one semi-marginal, two comfortable and three safe Labour Euro-constituencies. One-quarter of the twenty securest Labour seats selected women candidates for the European Parliament. Once again, the contrast with Westminster selections was clear-out. A second point relating to female candidates was that there seemed to be a regional variation as well as one based on electoral status. Half of the women candidates chosen came from outside England - three from Scotland and one from Wales.

Electoral status had little impact upon the remaining variables in this section. Those from grammar schools and with higher education were spread evenly across the spectrum. A similar uniformity was in evidence for the OPCS group classifications: 76.5 per cent of candidates from Conservative areas and 82.9 per cent in Labour seats came from group XXV: all but 7.3 per cent of PEPCs in Labour areas fell into the top two OPCS categories; candidates in Conservative seats were not quite so homogeneous, describing only 82.4 per cent of the thirty-four cases. Two of the candidates in the three SNP seats were also in group XXV, the other, a landowner and farmer, in group I-XX. Teachers accounted for 29.4 and 29.2 per cent of candidates from projected Conservative and Labour seats respectively, whereas three of the four employed in further or higher education fought in Conservative Euro-constituencies.

(b) Previous political experience: While the relationship was not linear, candidates in Labour seats were more likely to have been a prospective parliamentary candidate. This trend was also evident in the number of elections contested by each group: although two of the twenty-one former PPCs in Labour seats had never fought a Westminster election, they still had a 46.3 to 32.4 per cent lead over PEPCs from Conservative seats. However, there was an obvious skew towards the less experienced end of the parliamentary candidacy scale amongst Labour incumbent PEPCs, all bar three of whom had fought only one or two elections. Conversely, six of the eleven PEPCs in Conservative seats had stood in three to six contests. Thus the preference for candidates in Labour areas was for individuals with electoral experience, but not for those with a history of persistent defeat. Similarly, the projected Labour seats tended disproportionately to select parliamentary candidates from the two 1974 general elections. Two of the three PEPCs who

Table 7.7

Age, Sex, PPC and Local Government Experience of PEPCs by Electoral Status

		Electoral Status					
	N	Conservative		Labour		SNP	
		n	%	n	%	n	%
AGE							
26-39	25	9	26.5	15	36.6	1	33.3
40-49	34	13	38.2	20	48.7	1	33.3
50-59	13	8	23.5	4	9.8	1	33.3
60 and over	6	4	11.8	2	4.9	0	-
	78	34	100.0	41	100.0	3	99.9
SEX							
Male	70	33	97.1	35	85.4	2	66.7
Female	8	1	2.9	6	14.6	1	33.3
	78	34	100.0	41	100.0	3	100.0
PPC							
former PPC	32	11	32.4	21	51.2	0	-
1-2 elections fought	21	5	14.7	16	39.0	0	-
3-6 elections fought	9	6	17.7	3	7.3	0	-
	30	11	32.4	19	46.3	0	-
LOCAL GOVERNMENT							
former candidate	61	23	67.6	36	87.8	2	66.7
former councillor	48	18	52.9	29	70.9	1	33.3
serving councillor	26	12	35.3	14	34.1	0	-

had sat in the House of Commons fought comfortable Labour seats, the other the Conservative marginal of Norfolk.

The trend towards greater political experience for PEPCs in projected Labour seats extended to their past and present membership of the parliamentary lists: 58.5 per cent of PEPCs in Labour seats had been on either the 'A' or 'B' list, with 39.0 per cent current members. The corresponding figures for PEPCs in Conservative seats were 47.1 and 20.6 per cent. Labour seats also displayed a preference for candidates with local political experience: 87.8 per cent of them chose PEPCs who had been local government candidates compared with approximately two-thirds of non-Labour seats. This preference extended to the selection of local government councillors as well, 70.9 of PEPCs in Labour seats coming from this group as opposed to 52.9 per cent for Conservative seats. However, electoral status did not influence the selection of serving councillors: both Conservative and Labour seats picked one in three from this category.

(c) The European dimension: Anti-Marketeers were not just selected in the winnable Labour seats, with pro-EEC candidates symbolically sacrificed on the altar of Conservatism. In Labour seats anti-Marketeers only dominated selections in marginal and impregnable areas: however, both safe and comfortable Conservative seats attracted a similar percentage of anti-EEC candidates. Approximately a quarter of both projected seat classifications chose pro-Europeans, though only in safe Conservative seats was there a total absence of pro-Marketeers. These findings confirm the interpretation posited earlier: namely, that even in impossible electoral situations, the pro and anti divide was still a powerful and bitter selection criterion.

Electoral status had an insignificant impact upon four of the six attitudes tested for: the two exceptions were increased powers for the European Parliament, where those in Convervative seats were more hostile, and the development of a uniform electoral system. Perhaps because those in projected Conservative seats perceived that their chances of election were hindered by the present electoral system, they were twice as likely to support electoral reform than those who were more likely to benefit from the first-past-the post procedure. It was indicative that all of the PEPCs in impregnable Labour Euro-constituencies supported the status quo.

(d) Ambition: No clear pattern emerged from examining the initial stimulus for candidacy other than that PEPCs from Conservative seats were less likely to be self-starters and more likely to have been encouraged by a CLP: the figures were 44.0 and 52.0 per cent respectively, compared with 58.8 per cent and 47.1 per cent for PEPCs from Labour areas. The figures for motivation were more clear cut. PEPCs in projected Labour seats produced the following profile: 19.5 per cent claimed some type of pro-European motivation, 43.9 an anti-European reason and 41.5 per cent drew on personal/political inspirations. In contrast, of the thirty-four PEPCs who fought Conservative seats only one cited a pro-Market reason, 23.5 per cent personal/political motivation, but 52.9 per cent couched their explanations in anti-EEC language, in particular the need to present the anti-Market case to the party and the electorate. Future ambitions for Westminster did not correspond to any identifiable type of seat.

Electoral status proved to be a useful explanatory variable, but one that could only comment upon candidate not aspirant characteristics. To this extent electoral status is not central to the model's hypotheses. In summary, projected Labour seats tended to prefer younger candidates, self-starters and those with experience in parliamentary and local government elections. Neither women nor pro-Market candidates were grossly disadvantaged: they were not condemned to contesting just Conservative strongholds. Both were well represented in what were calculated as winnable Labour seats.

Conclusions

Conclusions based solely on candidate profiles are useful as far as they go, but as has been demonstrated, they may give a false or at best only a partial impression of the recruitment process. If we wish to explain candidate and legislator profiles, a sequential approach as delineated in the model is essential. The previous sections in this chapter have unearthed importnat patterns within the recruitment process, supporting the logic of the model. It has been shown that PEPCs (both winners and losers) were different from aspirants and defeated nominees across a range of characteristics and attitudes, a finding with considerable implications for both recruitment theory and legislative studies. Three major themes have demonstrated the emergent metamorphosis of profile characteristics: the broad generalisations are as follows.

Socio-demographic factors: The youngest aspirants tended to be rejected at the earliest stage, the oldest at the ESO short-listing point with the selected and elected cohorts balanced between the two. Women polarized around the two extremes displaying a tendency to be rejected out of hand or secure election. There was a steady increase in the proportion of individuals taken from OPCS group XXV as one moved up the selection ladder: 62.9 per cent of rejected aspirants were so classified; this rose to 66.3 for CLP nominees, 68.9 for ESO short-lists and 79.5 per cent for PEPCs. The success of the teaching profession accounted for this movement. The percentages of teachers at each of these selection stages were 20.0, 23.1, 25.8 and 29.5 respectively, stressing the importance of the occupation in Labour party selections.

Political factors: Contrary to popular belief, the percentage of individuals with local government experience diminshed through the party's screening process: 65.7 per cent of rejected aspirants had been councillors, as had 62.6 per cent of CLP nominees, 64.0 per cent of the short-listed were, but only 61.5 per cent of PEPCs. What is more, while four out of ten rejects, CLP and ESO short-listed nominees were serving councillors only a third of PEPCs were. Conversely, as we move up the recruitment structure, recent experience as a PPC increased. An an example, 11.4 per cent of rejects, 11.7 per cent of CLP nominees and 13.3 per cent of ESO short-lists had stood in the October 1974 election; this figure rose to 18.0 per cent for PEPCs.

Pro and anti factors: Membership of the Community, more than any other factor, helped to separate each of the successful and on unsuccessful aspirant groups. 48.0 per cent of rejected aspirants were pro-Marketeers as were 40.9 per cent of CLP nominees; 38.5 per cent made it to an ESO short-list, but only 26.6 per cent became PEPCs. There was a parallel increase in the anti-Market success rate. Whereas 46.2 per cent of rejected aspirants and 46.3 per cent of ESO rejects were LCMSC supporters, this level of support was maintained at between 52.0 and 54.0 per cent for the other six recruitment groups studied. The anti-EEC trend was reinforced in the attitudes towards federalism and monetary union: those individuals who were rejected either at the aspirant, ESO or short-listing stages were less ardently opposed to these federalist measures. The relationship was further supported when the pro and anti-Market motivations were compared.

Notes

(1) C. Mellors, The British MP, Farnborough, Saxon House, 1978, p. 76.

(2) Ibid., p. 74.

(3) J. M. Bochel, "The Recruitment of Local Councillors - a case-study", Political Studies, Vol 14, 1966.

(4) The various response rates for the six issues were - federal Europe n = 300; monetary union n = 307; Parliament's powers n = 308; EEC powers n = 302; transnational parties n = 296 and uniform electoral system n = 304.

(5) J. A. Schlesinger, Ambition and Politics; political careers in the United States, Chicago, Rand McNally, 1966, p. 10.

(6) 54.0 per cent of short-listed nominees were in favour of the LCMSC statement, 40.2 per cent against: the corresponding figures for ESO rejects were 46.3 and 50.0 per cent.

(7) Whilst the teaching professions are not usually treated separately in studies of MPs, this distinction was found to be useful for European profiles. In particular, the reliance upon teachers in the Labour party but lecturers in further and higher education in the Liberal party was noted.

(8) This figure of 41.0 per cent (n = 32) of PEPCs from the approved list conflicts with the findings of Butler and Marquand. They state that 'only 20 of 78 who where chosen and only three of the 17 actually elected, appeared on this (European) list'. D. Butler and D. Marquand European Elections and British Politics, London, Longmans 1981, p. 51.

(9) D. Butler, D. Marquand and B. Gosschalk, 'The Euro-persons', New Society, 3.5.1979, p. 260; and, I. Gordon, The Recruitment of British Candidates for the European Parliament, PSA conference paper, Hull, 1981, p. 13.

(10) For example, Butler and Marquand state when discussing PEPCs that, 'given the general mood of ordinary party members, the pro-Marketeers fared better than had seemed probable at the start', in Butler and Marquand, op.cit., p. 63. Similarly, Gordon argued that 'on the whole this attempt to prevent

supporters of the European Community being adopted failed', I. Gordon, op.cit., p. 19.

(11) No members of the Labour group in the European Parliament, unlike some of their domestic colleagues and failed European aspirants felt it necessary to defect to the pro-European SDP.

8 The Liberal party: Recruitment and party organisation

THE POLITICAL OPPORTUNITY STRUCTURE

Both the Conservative and Labour parties were characterised by a fairly restrictive attitude towards eligibility for European candidacy: Labour explicitly prohibited all those with Westminster ambitions; the Conservatives were only slightly less dogmatic with their informal yet grudging acceptance of the dual mandate. The emphasis was completely reversed in the English Liberal party: parliamentary candidacy was a positive advantage rather than an obstacle to European candidacy.(1) The Liberal's lack of success in domestic elections encouraged this open opportunity structure: there was far less chance of election in the Liberal party and the probability of the MP/MEP dual mandate occuring was therefore significantly reduced.

Paradoxically, the constraints upon the access to this open opportunity structure were no less restrictive. A European approved list was compiled by the centrally-based Candidates Committee. In directions issued to Regional Interviewing Panels by the Candidates Committee, it was repeatedly stated that before any aspirant could be considered for the European list, he had to undergo the existing vetting procedure for Westminster candidates. The Liberal party considered Westminster candidacy standards 'the minimum from which Euro-candidates should start and that knowledge of Liberal UK policy is essential for Liberal Euro-MPs to adequately represent the views of the Liberal UK voters and of the UK Liberal party in Europe.'(2) The contrast with the Labour and Conservative procedures was marked. Access to the opportunity structure was restricted, but inverted; European hopefuls without, rather than with domestic ambitions were discriminted against. Whereas Conservative aspirants who wanted to be on the Central Office approved list had to go through a similar procedure, the difference was that they had to choose between the two parliaments,

Liberals did not. To have followed the Labour party's example and excluded all sitting MPs and PPCs would have been impracticable: the pool of Liberal aspirants was limited and only by allowing a duplication of roles could a full and experienced team of Liberal contestants be produced. Having overcome the implied dual mandate question by this remedy, the timing of the general election was not a factor that appreciably inhibited the political opportunity structure. Indeed, the reverse may have been true, with candidacy for Europe an advantage, not a disadvantage for Liberal candidates with Westminster ambitions, as the European election offered an avenue for additional publicity.

The common opportunity structure variable, the electoral system, had a severe impact upon Liberal selection and recruitment. With their parliamentary attempts to introduce proportional representation thwarted, the first-past-the-post system created an electoral environment hostile to Liberal success. In none of the seventy-eight mainland Euro-constituencies were the Liberals placed first in terms of the October 1974 election results, and they were only second in six, all of which were safe or comfortable Conservative seats in the South and West of England. Even in their best Euro-constituency, Devon, the Liberals' won only 34.0 per cent of the October 1974 vote, some 11.8 per cent behind the Conservative total. The prospect of a Liberal victory in the European election was even more remote than in many Westminster seats. In consequence, a number of potential aspirants may not have emerged, seeing no point in fighting such hopeless causes. More importantly, such a discouraging electoral environment was likly to have far-reaching consequences for the resultant aspirant cohort. To reiterate the point made by Seligman, 'a permanent minority party with little hope or expectation of gaining a majority...will choose a leadship (candidates) proficient in opposing but lacking experience and/or a capacity for governing'.(3) If Seligman's hypothesis holds, the profile of Liberal aspirants ought to differ radically from that of the Conservative and Labour aspirants who had higher expectations of election.

Provisions governing the English Liberal party were not binding on either the Scottish or Welsh branches of the party. However, they too adopted a restrictive approach to European candidates. While no formal criteria for eligibility were imposed by the Scottish Liberal party, only twelve individuals were selected by the Scottish Candidates Vetting Panel to contest a special one-day selection conference. The Welsh Liberal party followed the English example more closely: they drew up an approved list of available individuals though the conditions for inclusion were less demanding. Only eleven names appeared on the list.

Thus, as in the Conservative party, the Liberals compiled a list of approved candidates, although based on very different criteria. Yet in practice their application of this central screening role was not quite so rigorous and the political opportunity structure not as closed as first appeared. Those who were on the original approved list were not the exclusive source of candidates, nor was the requirement to complete the Westminster vetting procedure a particularly onerous or difficult hurdle.

Self-Recruitment / Recruitment Agents

Liberal aspirants were predominantly self-starters: 56.5 per cent regarded the decision to run as purely their own idea with eight out of ten linking other recruitment stimuli with self motivation. The London based Liberal Party Organisation (LPO) as well as the local Liberal associations played only a minor recruitment role. The overall pattern reflected in table 8.1 was remarkably similar to the distribution for Conservative aspirants. The major difference was the absence of a recruitment role played by Liberal MPs, although given that they had only fourteen parliamentary representatives in 1978, such a finding was hardly remarkable.

Table 8.1

Initial Stimulus for European Candidacy for Liberal Aspirants

Stimulus	%	n
LPO	6.5	7
Local Associations	8.3	9
Agent	4.6	5
Own Idea	56.5	61
Own Idea and Party	21.3	23
Own Idea and Friends	2.8	3
Not Known		17
	100.0	125
All Self Starters	80.6	87

Figure 8.1 places the recruitment and selection structure of the Liberal party within the framework of the model. As will become apparent in the discussion of the Liberal party, their general lack of willing aspirants limited the potential for active recruitment both centrally and locally. The onus was essentially upon those who were self motivated. Often Euro-constituencies were grateful to receive a single nominee; a fully competitive recruitment process was a rare luxury.

The Liberal party is federally organised; there are no provisions whereby the central LPO can dictate local candidate selection, either for Westminster or Europe. The selection body in each European constituency was the sole determinant of the adopted candidate. Hence, there were no examples comparable to the Channon fiasco at Central Office. The nearest the Liberals came to such a position occurred after the May 1979 general election when their West Country MP, John Pardoe, lost his seat. It was rumoured that he might be 'given' the opportunity to stand for Europe if an adopted PEPC could be persuaded to resign his selection; however, the central LPO had no power of placement. In the event, Pardoe decided to leave his political career in abeyance. The experience

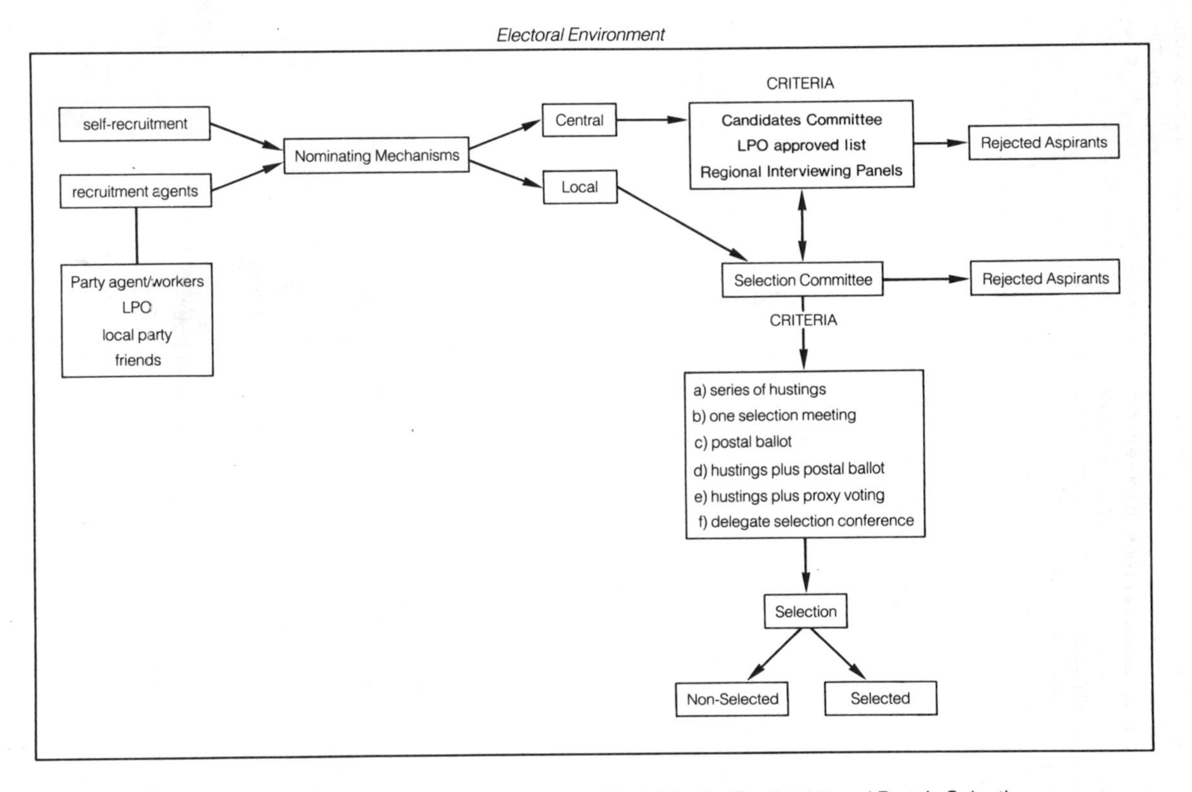

Figure 8.1 Application of the Gate-Keeping Function of the Model for the English Liberal Party's Selections

of the first European by-election held at London South West in September 1979 did indicate a power of persuasion, though not of coercion, resident with the central party organisation. It was reported that Christopher Mayhew had 'been invited by the party leader, David Steel, to stand as the party's candidate' in the by-election.(4) However, neither the leader nor the Candidates Committee possessed the authority to prescribe either the selection method or the candidate to be adopted. It was ultimately the local Euro-constituency's choice, even if their preference may have been coloured by other considerations.

The Liberals were the most pro-European of the three major parties. There was no internal party conflict between antagonistic groups as in the Labour party, and there was virtual unanimity upon the virtues of the EEC and the desirability of European federalism. Two pro-EEC groups were associated with the party: the European Movement (EM), whose financial encouragements and recruitment support have already been discussed in relation to the Labour party, and the Liberal European Action Group (LEAG). LEAG was affiliated to the EM and was the Liberal equivalent to the Conservative Group for Europe and the Labour Committee for Europe. LEAG acted as a central information service for candidates after their selection rather than as a recruitment mechanism prior to or during the selection process. This absence of factions, coupled with the party's complete commitment to Europe, reduced the impact of both the EM and LEAG; neither were overt recruitment agencies.

Formal Selection Procedures

(a) Central mechanisms

The English selection machinery: The English Liberal party's European selection machinery has to be considered in the context of their Westminster practices. Of the three major parties the Liberals operated the most open system of selection. The party constitution adopted in 1969 took a partial step towards a form of closed primary election. It stated that each constituency's selection committee should 'submit three or more names of suitable candidates to a General Meeting, but may submit fewer than three names, if, in its opinion, there are not as many as three suitable candidates among the names submitted'.(5) Such a general meeting was open to members of the association resident in that constituency. However, the decentralised structure of the Liberal party has made the application of this 'primary' concept less universal: Liberal constituency associations have considerably more independence than either constituency Labour parties or Conservative associations. Section H clause 5, gives the National Candidates Committee the power to vary this procedure where necessary. Often delegates or branch officers constitute the eligible voting members, not the constituency association's full membership. Similarly, the application of this procedure has been seriously restricted by the limited pool of potential Liberal candidates from which to draw. Not infrequently the general meeting's role is simply to endorse the only available candidate. However, the Liberal party has laid the foundations for wider selection by introducing a closed primary model. It is a closed primary in two ways: voters are limited to party members; and candidate nominations can only come via the association's executive or selection committee.(6) This latter condition tends to detract from the participatory ideals of the constitution. Each association's selection committee can only consider applicants who are either submitted by the National Candidates Committee or by a member of the association: in practice, the former tends to dominate. More importantly, the 'selectorate' characteristics of candidate selections underlie this participatory veneer. The selection committee decides which aspirants are to go forward to the general meeting and which are to be rejected. As in the Conservative and Labour parties, Liberal selections rely upon such initial gate-keeping procedures.

Not surprisingly, as the party with the nearest approximation to a primary system for Westminster candidatures, the Liberal European selection process was the most participatory. As for Westminster, the Candidates Committee was responsible for devising the selection procedures and organising a list of approved candidates. On 8 August 1978 the 'Rules for the selection of Candidates' for the European election were issued on behalf of the Candidates Committee. Regional parties were responsible for constituting the selection organisation in each Euro-constituency which were, in turn, to appoint their own selection committees. The selection committee so constituted, was empowered to invite, 'by such means as it considers apropriate ... applications from candidates whose names appear on the list of approved candidates for Europe maintained by the Candidates Committee, and, having considered all such applications, shall draw up a short-list containing not less than three persons'.(7) Only those on the approved list were eligible for selection.

The 'Rules' offered a choice of selection methods available. Selections could be by one or more selection meetings at which all members of the component Westminster constituencies were entitled to attend and vote, provided that the appropriate constituency affiliation fee had been paid in accordance with clause C(4) of the party's constitution. Where more than one meeting was held, all the votes cast were counted together at the end of the final meeting, not separately after each meeting. Members could only vote once and a secret ballot using the alternative vote system was stipulated. The 'Rules' also made provision for selection entirely by ballot. Each component Westminster constituency was obliged to appoint a returning officer to whom a list of paid-up members from affiliated constituency associations (valid from a date prescribed by the returning officer) had to be submitted. The validated list constituted the 'electors for the purpose of the ballot'.(8) Every elector was to receive details of each short-listed applicant, a ballot paper and other relevant information not less than two weeks before the closing date of the ballot. In addition, at the discretion of the returning officer, one or more meetings could be held where the short-listed individuals could speak and answer questions. Again, the ballot was determined by the alternative vote system.(9) As we shall see later, in practice there was a wider range of selection procedures adopted in the sixty-six English Liberal Euro-constituencies than set down in the 'Rules'.

As for Westminster, a list of approved candidates was drawn up by the Candidates Committee with the assistance of the Regional Interviewing Panels. The Candidates Committee felt that it was essential that 'applicants be approved in a manner at least as rigorous as that applicable to applicants for Westminster candidacy'.(10) The European application form stressed this concern. It asked for details of political experience in either parliamentary or local government elections, length of party membership and whether the applicant was a prospective parliamentary candidate. In addition to the normal background information, abilities, commitment and attitudes towards candidature was solicited. Applicants had to state why they wanted to be MEPs, their conception of Liberalism and those issues of particular concern to them; they were also required to indicate their language proficiency, experience in public speaking and list 'any special qualifications' which were germane to their claim for European parliamentary candidacy.(11)

In order to provide a reasonable choice for the sixty-six English seats it was felt that there should be between 120-150 approved Euro-candidates on the list. As Butler and Marquand argue, this number proved too small to allow a full range of choice and in consequence, the recommended number of three short-listed applicants often failed to materialise.(12) Table 8.2 demonstrates the thin spread of applications across the European constituencies. Only 112 names appeared on the English approved list, not the suggest 120-150, creating an average of less than two applications per seat.(13) Even when the additional twenty-one applicants were included the figure only rose marginally. Multiple applications on the part of the more ambitious aspirants helped to alleviate the problem, but the small size of the original list was largely responsible for causing inadequate competition.

While applicants had to undergo Westminster scrutiny prior to European approval, those already on the Westminster list did not have an automatic right to inclusion on the European list. Furthermore, 'sitting Liberal MPs, ex-Liberal MPs and Liberal peers [were] not ipso facto approved European candidates ... and subject to approval in the same manner as any other approved Westminster candidate'.(14) The actual list was devised on a regional basis, with those without domestic approval subject to a preliminary interview to gauge their suitability. All potential Euro-candidates were asked to attend briefing sessions designed to heighten their competence in EEC politics prior to the Regional Panel interviews. These interviews were arranged during the period April to July 1977. One member of the Candidates Committee sat on each of the Regional Panels in order to promote both consistency in the criteria used and in the quality of applicants chosen. The Panels could make one of four recommendations: approval; approval conditional on specified conditions; deferment for a specific time and a specific reason; and, of course, rejection. Those applicants approved by the Regional Panels were submitted for central collation by the Candidates Committee, who also acted as the final appellate body and reserved the right to review all decisions made by the Panels.

The list of approved candidates contained the names, ages, occupations, former parliamentary and current prospective candidacies of 112 individuals: how many aspirants applied for inclusion on the list is not known. The list was published by the Candidates Committee and available to every English constituency. The importance of the list cannot be over stated; the Candidates

Table 8.2

Seat Applications for Approved and Non-Approved Aspirants(15)

No. of Seat Applications	Original Approved List		Other Applicants	
	%	n	%	n
1	37.5	30	85.7	18
2	13.8	11	9.5	2
3	23.8	19	-	-
4	8.7	7	4.8	1
5	5.0	4	-	-
6 and over	11.2	9	-	-
Not Known	-	32	-	-
	100.0	112	100.0	21

Committee envisaged that it would be the sole source of candidacies. The criteria used to determine its composition was, therefore, of the greatest importance.

In spite of the Liberal stress on local autonomy, the criticisms applicable to any method that imposed a centralised limitation on choice must apply to the Liberal party's procedure. Prima facie, their position was more intransigent than that of the Conservatives, there being no specific clause by which 'locals' could contest for selection and gain late approval. The rules specified that selection committees had to limit their choice to those on the list. However, the application of this clear-cut principle was less rigidly enforced allowing a degree of flexibility in the search for appropriate candidates. While the list contained 112 aspirants, at least 131 individuals contested short-lists. The resident constitutional powers conferred on the Candidates Committee gave them an opportunity to approve 'local' aspirants if and where necessary. As one member of the Committee acknowledged, a few individuals were adopted prior to approval, although all actual candidates were eventually approved. However, the Candidates Committee, like the Conservative party Vice-Chairman, the National Union Panel and Euro-SACC, was an important central gate-keeping agent. No matter how benevolent its approach, it possessed the authority to determine the shape and outcome of recruitment and selection.

The Welsh selection machinery: Like their English partners, the Welsh Liberal party drew its candidates from its own centrally compiled approved list. Despite this restriction, the more important point was that candidate choice in Wales was principally limited by a lack of potential aspirants, not by the selection machinery employed. The Welsh approved list only contained eleven names, though not all those on the list ultimately sought selection. The dearth of interested applicants meant that the selectorate process was basically inoperative. The English and

Welsh lists were separate and autonomous lists, although there were three examples where aspirants transferred from one list to the other.(16)

The Welsh selection machinery did vary from the English example, however. Basically for reasons of finance, the concurrent referendum campaign and the geographical size of the four Welsh Euro-constituencies, it was decided that a primary open to all paid-up members was inappropriate. Selection at the short-listing stage was by a delegate conference, with each parliamentary association entitled to appoint up to fifteen non-mandated delegates. Proxy and postal voting were prohibited. Constitutionally, only affiliated constituencies were eligible to appoint delegates (i.e. those who had paid the 100 pounds affiliation fee to the National Liberal Association): in consequence, participation was severely restricted.

The Scottish selection machinery: The central selection process designed by the Scottish Liberal Party (SLP) was unique. Working from the premise that Scotland would be treated as a single eight-member Euro-constituency, the SLP initiated its selection process as early as January 1978. An approved list procedure was adopted: aspirants were asked to complete an application form before being interviewed by the Scottish Candidates Vetting Panel for approval. Apart from minor differences the application form mirrored its English counterpart. On 14 January 1978, twelve applicants approved by the Panel were invited to participate in a primary selection ballot to ascertain their rank order. The electoral college system was used, employing the same principles devised for the selection of the leader of the parliamentary Liberal party: each Scottish parliamentary constituency was given a number of votes based on their respective membership strengths.

Despite the hopes that Scotland would be treated as a single electoral district under some form of regional list system, the European Assembly Act, 1978, provided for the Scottish elections to be held under the simple majority system in eight single-member seats. Thus the SLP was faced with the dilemma of having rank ordered its eight preferred candidates, but not assigned any of them to a specific Euro-constituency. Furthermore, to compound the problem not every approved candidate stood in the primary election nor was every candidate who stood at the primary willing to be a European candidate when it became known that the elections were not to be conducted on a system of proportional representation. Six of the final eight Scottish candidates contested the primary: the two exceptions (Lord Benshie and J. Wallace) were allowed to stand as candidates because they were approved European candidates. The matching of candidates to seats was left to the delegate meetings of each European constituency.

(b) Local mechanisms

English Euro-constituencies: While the final step in the English Liberal party selection process followed a closed primary format designed to stimulate participation by the rank and file party members, the initial short-listing procedure, as in both the Conservative and Labour parties, was centred on a small band of inner party gate-keepers. The procedure established by the

Candidates Committee envisaged the Euro-constituency organisation (consisting of representatives of the component Westminster constituencies), or a selection committee appointed by this body, to act as the short-listing selectorate. As in Westminster selections, the gate-keeping function remained the exclusive domain of local elites, the only difference being that these elites were drawn from up to ten parliamentary constituencies, rather than one. Even in the Liberal party the selection committee's power to reject potential candidates was crucial. Table 8.3 displays the distribution of the total number of applications and the number of short-listed aspirants per Euro-constituency.

Table 8.3

Total Number of Applicants and the Size of Short-Lists by English Euro-Constituency

No. of Applicants	%	No. of Seats	No. on Short-list	%	No. of seats
1	5.9	3	1	9.6	5
2	7.8	4	2	19.2	10
3	9.8	5	3	36.5	19
4	21.6	11	4	26.9	14
5	13.7	7	5 and more	7.8	4
6-9	31.4	16	Not Known		14
10-15	9.8	5			
Not Known		15			
	100.0	66		100.0	66

Certain seats failed to attract sufficient applicants to make selection committee gate-keeping necessary and all the applications were forwards to the short-listing stage. This occurred in nine of the sixty-six English Euro-constituencies. A further three seats only received, or managed to solicit, one potential candidate each, and another saw its six applicants dwindle to just one by the time their selection committee convened. Thirty Euro-constituencies failed to attract more than five European aspirants (58.8 per cent of known cases) and fifteen failed to realise the short-listing quota of three laid down by the Candidates Committee. In the more competitive seats there was a higher degree of choice and local selection committees had the opportunity to choose a short-list. For example, Yorkshire North topped the list with fifteen applications, only five of whom appeared before their selection hustings, whereas in Devon the membership were allowed to choose between only two of the original nine applicants. Thus the problems associated with short-listing, as witnessed in both the Conservative and Labour selection procedures, were also evident in certain Liberal European organisations.

The Liberals' centralised approved list and local party elite short-listing ultimately gave way to the best example of selection participation for any of the major British parties that contested the European election. As explained in the previous section, the 'Rules' provided for one of two basic methods, selection by a meeting or series of meetings, or selection ballot. Both options allowed for a degree of variation in their interpretation. However, the basic principles remained clear: short-listed applicants were to contest a primary election in which all paid-up members eligible to vote could participate. The 'Rules' contained no provisions for delegate selection yet despite this, and in direct contradiction to the primary principle, seven Euro-constituencies employed such a procedure. The 'Rules' did stipulate that the Candidates Committee possessed residual authority on all aspects of procedure and empowered the committee to 'grant such dispensations from the Rules as, in particular circumstances, it may consider appropriate'.(17)

The selection of the sixty-six English prospective European candidates were made by one of six different methods ranging from a participant closed primary to delegate selection. Table 8.4 divides the selection methods into two broad groups: category A, selection by all eligible members who could vote at hustings, by post or by proxy, or some hybrid combination; and category B, delegate selection.

Table 8.4

Alternative Procedures for the Selection of English Liberal Candidates

Category	Method	Seats %	Seats n
A - Selection by paid-up members:	a) series of hustings	20.0	10
	b) one selection meeting	14.0	7
	c) postal ballot	10.0	5
	d) hustings plus postal ballot	54.0	27
	e) hustings plus proxy voting	2.0	1
		100.0	
B - Selection by Delegates:	f) selection conferences		7
	Not Known		9
			66

Delegate voting was unsatisfactory in two ways; firstly, it prevented full rank and file participation, and secondly, it resulted in relatively low turn-out figures. For example, all three Lancashire seats used the delegate system: Lancashire East had the least creditable record with only six out of a possible sixteen delegates attending their selection conference. Lancashire West selected their candidate from three applications, the decision being made by twelve individuals, though the maximum possible attendance figure was twenty-one, and at Lancashire Central twenty-three people were responsible for selecting the Liberal PEPC. Not every Euro-constituency that used the delegate system was so restrictive: Kent East allowed ten delegates for each of its eight parliamentary constituencies, with a total of sixty actually attending. Seven seats that used the paid-up member primary format failed to attract as many participants!

The five variants encompassed in category A all exhibited varying degrees of closed primary election characteristics: party members determined candidate choice (provided that two or more candidates sought selection). The Liberals were the only party to allow a postal ballot for Europe: five seats used this method exclusively. Examples of the other four selection alternatives were as follows. Sussex West was typical of seats where selection was made by a series of hustings. Three meetings were held between 29 January and 2 February at which the four short-listed applicants appeared. All members could attend any of these meetings, but only one vote could be cast per member: votes were only valid if cast at the hustings and accompanied by evidence of paid-up membership. The count was conducted after the close of the final meeting. Seven other seats conducted their selections at a single meeting. The most popular selection procedure combined hustings with the facility for a postal ballot. This took place in 54.0 per cent of known cases. Lastly, one Euro-constituency allowed selection to be made by the local membership at a single meeting coupled with proxy voting. Whilst table 8.4 illustrated the methods adopted by various Euro-constituencies, procedural intentions and selection fact often did not coincide. 'Disappearing' short-lists frequently had a chaotic effect on the best laid plans as it did with the other parties.

The primary election method for selecting Liberals was theoretically the most participant, but the actual numbers involved were generally extremely limited. As Table 8.5 indicates, in 30.8 per cent of known cases the Liberal candidate chosen to contest a Euro-constituency of approximately 500,000 electors was selected by a hundred party members or less, with 56.4 per cent by 200 or less. South Tyne and Wear were involved in one of the most limited selections: only twenty-two paid-up party members were involved in selecting the Liberal PEPC from a short-list of four. Liverpool could only muster forty votes, Midlands West forty-five and Salop and Stafford fifty. None of these selections permitted postal voting. At the opposite end of the scale, Devon attracted 186 postal and a further 134 votes at its four hustings, Wessex 175 and 322 respectively, whereas Hereford and Worcester's total of 486 all came from postal votes. The option of the postal vote clearly had an important effect on participation. Purely in terms of gross numbers, Wight and Hampshire East which also relied entirely on postal votes attracted the most voters, just under one-third of their 9,000 registered members. Cambridgeshire, another seat to use only a postal ballot, received around 1,000 votes, whereas in

Table 8.5

Total Votes Cast (Postal and Hustings) Excluding Delegate Conferences for English Euro-constituencies

Votes Cast	%	n
1-50	15.4	6
51-100	15.4	6
101-200	25.6	10
201-300	18.0	7
301-500	18.0	7
500 and more	7.7	3
Not Known		20
	100.1	
Delegate Conferences		7
		66

Northamptonshire their postal vote produced a 33.8 per cent turn-out (220 postal returns out of a possible 650). Unfortunately, comprehensive figures for each Euro-constituency's membership were unavailable: consequently it was impossible to calculate either the maximum eligible total of voters or the percentage turn-out figures for each seat. However, the examples cited were indicative of the levels of participation in the Liberals' European primaries. Although the evidence suggests that a minority of party members were involved, the primary structure and the opportunity for mass participation distinguished the Liberal approach from the other two parties.

Given the proviso that applicants had to be drawn from the approved list, the manner in which applications were attracted was another area where practices varied. The formalised application and nomination procedures characteristic of Conservative and Labour selections gave way to a looser, two-way application process in the Liberal party. For Conservatives, the onus lay squarely on the individual aspirant to apply to those seats he wished to be considered for (via Central Office, or directly): for Labour it was the responsibility of affiliated organisations to offer nominations. In the Liberal party aspirants were attracted by the Euro-constituencies writing to them directly, through adverts in Liberal News asking for applications, or by the aspirants themselves applying directly to a seat. As stated earlier, not all applicants were taken from the approved list: at least nineteen non-approved locals made selection short-lists. Once again, the ever-present Liberal handicap lay behind this flexible recruitment system - the Liberals' small pool of potential candidates. In addition the constricting size of the list was partly responsible for these intense efforts to attract applicants. Limiting the list to an average of less than two individuals per seat increased the possibility that some seats might go uncontested.

Table 8.6 indicates that there was a tendency for projected Labour seats to prefer either delegates or a single selection meeting: 34.5 per cent of Labour seats preferred one of these two options, compared with only 14.2 per cent of Liberal parties in projected Conservative seats. Participation in Labour seats was further discouraged by their greater reluctance to use postal ballots: the figures were 48.3 and 64.3 per cent for Labour and Conservative seats respectively. What is more, in those Euro-constituencies where the Liberals displaced Labour as the challenging party, selections were either by postal ballot or a series of hustings, or a combination of the two: delegate conferences or single selection meetings did not occur.

Table 8.6

Selection Methods by Electoral Status For English Euro-Constituencies

Method	Projected Labour Seats		Projected Conservative Seats		Winnable Seats	
	%	n	%	n	%	n
a) Series of Hustings	13.8	4	21.4	6	-	-
b) One Selection Meeting	17.2	5	7.1	2	40.0	2
c) Postal Ballot	6.9	2	10.7	3	-	-
d) Hustings plus Postal Ballot	41.4	12	53.6	15	40.0	2
e) Proxy Voting	3.5	1	-	-	20.0	1
f) Delegate Conferences	17.2	5	7.1	2	-	-
Not Known		3		6		1
	100.0	32	99.9	34	100.0	6

The tendency for projected Labour seats to display a less participatory attitude was reflected in the turn-out figures. Excluding the Euro-constituencies that adopted a delegate conference system, Conservative seats had a mean turn-out figure of 474.4 whereas Liberal selections in Labour seats could only muster an average of 126.7 votes per seat. The five seats where the Liberals stood the best chance of election further underlined the relationship: they had a mean turn-out figure of 843.4.(18) In 84.2 per cent of selections made by Liberal parties in projected Labour seats, the decision was made by a maximum of 200 people: the corresponding figure for Liberal selections in Conservative seats was only 30.0 per cent, and only one of the Euro-constituencies where the Liberals were in second place was a candidate chosen by less than 200 party members. It would appear that Liberal organisations were stronger in Conservative areas, encouraging greater rank and file involvement. The aspirants also seemed to view electoral status in a similar light. The mean level of applications for Labour seats was 5.5; this figure rose to 6.0 in Conservative Euro-constituencies and to 9.4 for the winnable Liberal seats.

Thus in general it would appear that Liberal organisations in Labour areas were less likely to stimulate membership participation or attract applicants than those fighting projected Conservative Euro-constituencies. However, the lower participation figures may have simply been a reflection of the lower membersip levels in these areas: there was no data available to test this explanation. Whatever the reason, the overall conclusion was clear, Liberal organisations were stronger in Conservative rather than Labour Euro-constituencies.

The selection timetable used by the Liberals was the most extended of the three major parties: the first seat chose in early January 1979, the last not until May. Precise selection dates were difficult to establish where a postal ballot was used: often the valid period for voting spanned several weeks. In all these instances, the closing date of the ballot was taken as the actual selection date. Liberal candidates who stood in Conservative seats tended to be chosen earlier: eight of the first ten seats to select were expected Conservative victories and whereas 60.8 per cent of Conservative seats had adopted their PEPC before the end of February, only 34.6 per cent of candidates in Labour seats had been selected by this date. The only seats still left to pick a candidate by April were all projected Labour Euro-constituencies. Figure 8.2 records the Liberal selection process from early January until the general election in May 1979, (the cumulative number of selections only refer to English seats). Certain features stand out. Firstly, the two Kent seats (both of which used a delegate system) were the earliest to adopt a PEPC making their selections on 12 January. However, after this flying start the Liberal performance flagged markedly. By the end of February only 48.1 per cent of Liberal candidates had been picked: the corresponding figure for Labour was 65.4 per cent and 83.1 per cent for the Conservatives. Having a large number of postal ballots tended to prolong the Liberal selection procedure and the efforts needed to involve the combined membership totals of up to ten parliamentary constituencies were time-consuming. Even so, the lethargy shown by local Liberal associations, especially in the least winnale areas, only exacerbated the delay. Some areas left it so late that there was an overlap between parliamentary selections for the General Election of May 1979 and the European selections for June of that year. One Liberal agent admitted that their European selection process only took place in the ten days prior to the General Election!

Welsh Euro-constituencies: The Welsh Liberal party were committed to selection by delegate conference: none of the four Euro-constituencies varied from this procedure. Each affiliated parliamentary constituency association was entitled to send fifteen delegates to their respective selection conferences. The potential size of each delegate selection conference was limited by the requirement that participating constituencies had to have paid the 100 pounds affiliation fee to the National Liberal Association.

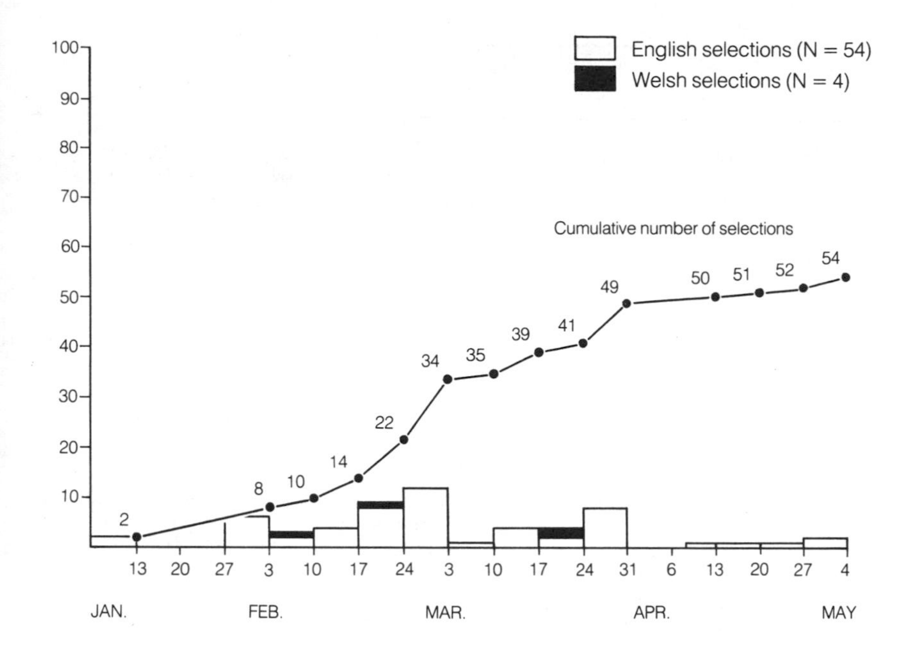

Figure 8.2 Liberal Selections by Time

Table 8.7 demonstrates this limitation and contrasts potential with actual delegate turn-out figures.

In the two most southerly Euro-constituencies potential participation was severely restircted by the affiliation clause. In South Wales only three of the nine parliamentary associations had paid the 100 pounds fee and thus selection was limited to a maximum of forty-five individuals, of whom all but one voted. In South East Wales only Ebbw Vale, Monmouth and Newport were affiliated, though here only twenty-four delegates took part. It should not be surprising even where the affiliation fee had been paid, in such weak Liberal areas participation was so low. Again, membership figures were not available, but it is doubtful whether a closed primary system, rather than one based on delegates, would have appreciably increased the numbers involved.

The Welsh list, like its English equivalent was not a rigid limitation on candidates. It constituted a useful source of capable aspirants; however, a desire to fight a Welsh seat proved to be a sufficient qualification for approval. Three last minute additions to the approved list increased the choice available to delegates marginally: two seats were contested by three individuals, the others by two each.

Table 8.7

Potential and Actual Delegate Turn-out for Welsh Euro-constituencies

Euro-constituency	No. Seats	No. of Affiliated Associations	Maximum Delegate Turn-out	Actual Delegate Turn-out	
				%	n
South East Wales	10	3	45	53.3	24
South Wales	9	3	45	97.8	44
Mid and West Wales	8	8	120	41.7	50
North Wales	9	9	135	42.2	57

In summary, the basic problem for the Liberal party, whether the English, Welsh or Scottish branch, was not primarily one of the selection structures, but of low membership and too few aspiring candidates. As demonstrated by the instances of closed primaries often the democratic process was hindered by a lack of involvement. However, the selection structures were not without fault: one critic of intra-party primaries has argued that through the maintenance of small selection committee caucuses and their exclusive power of short-listing, local 'party leaders have managed to retain considerable control over the choice of candidates while generating this aura of democratic legitimacy.'(19) In addition, some English Euro-constituency organisations were characterised by a disregard of the Candidates Committee recommendations: selections were conducted contrary to the provisions laid down. Fifteen seats failed to abide by the guidelines directive to select from short-lists of not less than three, seven operated a delegate rather than a primary selection system and most strikingly, in nine cases the candidate selected was not from the approved list as stipulted. Yet these transgressions went unsanctioned. In contrast to the tight organisational and procedural obedience displayed by the majority of Labour and Conservative selections, the Liberal party was typified by the ill-disciplined approach of Liberal associations and an indulgent acquiescence by the LPO. Such was the disarray, that the Candidates Committee appeared to be prepared to accommodate and approve even the most extreme departure from the 'Rules'.

SELECTION CRITERIA

Central

The pamphlet, Guidance to Regional Interview Panels in England, produced by the Candidates Committee set out a list of requirements interviewing panels should look for when considering aspirants for approval. As noted earlier, Westminster standards were the minimum prerequiste requirements for European candidacy. The object of the Regional interview was 'to discover a grasp of European political skills much wider and much deeper than those sought in Westminster candidates'.(20) 'Media ability' was of paramount importance: it was believed that because of the vast size of most Euro-constituencies, media exposure would be crucial to a successful campaign. In addition to a philosophical commitment to the concept of Europe, a list of eleven specific points on which to evaluate aspirants was established. These covered time and availability, language competence, European awareness, a belief in federalism and campaign experience. Each member of the Regional interviewing panels were asked to mark applicants on each of these qualities and to submit this together with the panel's overall recommendation to the Candidates Committee.

The Candidates Committee used certain criteria for excluding applicants from the list: in particular, a lack of knowledge of the EEC, a short period of party membership or an unwillingness to learn a Community language were sufficient reasons for exclusion. The committee's attitude towards allowing PPCs on the list was less than enthusiastic but, somewhat reluctantly, PPCs were not barred from the approved list. The Committee was generally happy with the overall calibre of the list; one member considered it as 'satisfactory and generally higher than that of the other two main parties'. Another felt that those on the list ranged from the exceptional to the mediocre with little political or campaign flair. Only one member thought that a significant proportion of applicants saw candidacy for the European Parliament in terms of a future Westminster career.

The federal structure of the Liberal party, together with the wide array of selection machinery used, prohibits any meaningful analysis of general local selection criteria. As for the Labour party, discussion of the Liberal's selection criteria has had to rely on inferences and individual examples: only the analysis of the Conservative's local criteria approached the methodological goals demanded by the model. In the absence of such case-studies, once again aspirant profiles constitute the only empirical tool capable of estimating the complexity of the recruitment process.

Conclusion

It could be argued that the relevance of studying Liberal selection procedures was negligible. Often there was little real choice, candidates almost being selected by default. What is more, the potential for Liberal success was limited: for the European election, just as for Westminster, it was still true that for 'the aspiring politician...the most promising vehicle of his ambition must be either the Conservative party or its Labour rival'.(21) The study of the Liberal's selection process was important for three major reasons. Firstly, the Liberal party has all too often been ignored or relegated to just a few cursory pages of commentary in the standard texts; the analysis of the 1979 European election offered by Butler and Marquand was guilty of such a fault. Secondly, the rank and file primary based selections operated by the Liberals have helped to highlight and contrast the procedures of the Conservative and Labour parties. They, more than any other party, promoted the issue of democratic participation in candidate choice, offering a viable alternative to the closed systems based on delegates or representatives. The Liberals may not boast any MEPs and their influence was muted by low membership and a limited pool of aspirants, but their diverse approach to selection was of major importance. Thirdly, to have omitted the Liberal's from the analysis would have been in direct contradiction to the assumptions and the structure of the model. It has been argued that it is fallacious and inadequate to concentrate on end-products, be they MEPs, MPs or local councillors: Liberal aspirants were as important to the fuller understanding of the recruitment process as were Labour and Conservative MEPs. To understand each stage in the selection process internal selection mechanisms have to be examined. Only by focusing analysis on this perspective can we hope to trace discernible patterns in candidate choice by identifying non-selected aspirants. The following chapter on Liberal aspirants meets these methodological and theoretical requirements and forms the final profile from which cross-party conclusions are drawn.

Notes

(1) There are separate English, Scottish and Welsh Liberal parties: they are dealt with individually in this chapter.

(2) Guidance to the Regional Interviewing Panels in England, issued by the Candidates Committee, August 1979, clause C1, p.2.

(3) L.G. Seligman, "Political Parties and the Recruitment of Political Leadership", in L.J. Edinger (ed.), Political Leadership in Industrialised Societies, Wiley, 1967, p.303.

(4) The Daily Telegraph, 14.8.1979.

(5) The Constitution of the Liberal Party (1969), Section H, clause 4(c).

(6) Lord Beaumont of Whitely, "The Selection of Parliamentary Candidates", Political Quarterly, vol. 45, 1974, pp.123-124.

(7) Rules for the Selection of Candidates for the First Direct Elections to the European Parliament, clause 2.3 (author's italics)

(8) Ibid., clause 5.3

(9) D. Butler and R. Marquand, European Elections and British Politics, Longman, 1981, p. 81, state that STV was used; however, the 'Rules' clearly state that the alternative ballot was to be used. There was evidence, however, that some Liberal Euro-constituencies did use STV, even though as a system STV was inappropriate for selecting a single candidate.

(10) Guidance, op.cit., clause A-2, p.1.

(11) There was particular concern devoted to applicant's financial status: the European candidature application form asked each applicant 'to make a full declaration of financial and business interests in accordance with the rules made by the National Executive'. In addition, four specific questions were asked: the names of their banker; whether they could 'meet the personal expenses to which [they] would be put as a Euro-candidate; whether they were a discharged or undischarged bankrupt and whether they could

devote sufficient time to 'nursing' the constituency'. The most unusual question was 'Have you, during the last ten years been convicted in a court, other than for motoring offences? Are there any proceedings pending against you?'

(12) Butler and Marquand, op.cit., p. 81.

(13) Ibid., p.81. Butler and Marquand state that the list was 150 strong; however, correspondence with the LPO Chief Agent confirmed that the English list contained only 112 names. The figure of 150 cited by Butler and Marquand may refer to the English, Welsh and Scottish lists.

(14) Guidance, op.cit., p.5.

(15) The 'original approved list' referred to the English applicants, the 'other applicants' category included those on the Welsh list.

(16) One Welsh Euro-constituency was faced with the prospect of having only one Welsh approved applicant to choose from: the constituency decided to recruit from outside the Welsh list in order to offer the delegates a contest. In the event, one applicant from the English approved list was drafted and 'approved' prior to the meeting by the Chairman of the Welsh Liberal party Executive. The individual concerned was, however, very much an also-ran. In another Welsh seat one of the three short-listed applicants was on both the English and Welsh lists. He had fought five parliamentary elections in England, but in the interim period between being approved by the English Candidates Committee and the start of the selection procedures he retired and moved to North Wales and felt it proper to apply for a Welsh rather than an English seat. Lastly, a third aspirant was short-listed for both the English seat of Cambridgeshire and the Welsh Euro-constituency of Mid and West Wales.

(17) 'Rules', op.cit., paragraph 4(b).

(18) It should be noted, however, that both the Conservative total and that for the five seats where the Liberals were placed second were exaggerated by the inclusion of the Wight and Hampshire East's turn-out figure of 3,000. However, even if this figure is excluded there remains a clear relationship between turn-out and electoral status, the reduced figures being 324.4 and 304.3 respectively.

(19) J. Obler, "Intraparty Democracy and the Selection of Parliamentary Candidates: the Belgian Case", British Journal of Political Science, vol. 4, 1974, p. 171.

(20) Guidance, op.cit., clause B2.

(21) M. Rush, The Selection of Parliamentary Candidates. Nelson, 1967, p.3.

9 Liberal candidate and aspirant profiles

The preceding chapter drew attention to the importance of the federal structure of the Liberal party. Of the 125 respondents analysed, 117 applied to English seats and the remaining eight were Welsh applicants: Scottish aspirants were not surveyed. The 117 English applicants broke down into 104 from the approved list and thirteen 'locals'. Because of the relatively small number of Welsh applicants, certain profiles were combined: thus the PEPC, non-selected and electoral status profiles relate to both English and Welsh applicants.

The European Approved List for English Euro-constituencies.

Did the English list of approved European applicants reflect the criteria set out in the Candidates Committee's Guidance for Regional Interviewing Panels in England? Data was available for 104 of the 112 individuals on the English list and an overall impression utilising as many of the criteria as possible was drawn.

One of the most important criteria was a 'philosophical commitment to Europe': only one member of the list classified himself as an anti-Marketeer. There was an equally high level of commitment found for monetary union, the development of transnational parties, extension of the powers of the European Parliament and the move towards a common electoral system, all of which can be used as partial indicators of a commitment to, or belief in, Europe. More specifically, the condition that applicants for the list must be willing to campaign for 'the ideal of a federal Europe' was met in 95.5 per cent of cases. Moreover, 56.0 per cent of known cases were members of the avowedly federalist European Movement. Motivation for running as a potential MEP confirmed this impression, with 66.3 per cent claiming a Euro-based reason for seeking selection. A further criterion was 'time and availability'. 89.2 per cent of respondents stated that they would be full-time MEPs if elected, with the remaining 10.8 per cent regarding the role of MEP as only a part-time activity. The criterion of proficiency in or willingness and ability to learn one or more of the Community languages was met to a significant degree. Lastly, the criterion of being an 'effective campaigner' was examined: 84.6 per cent were former Liberal PPCs with 58.7 per cent having contested the October 1974 election: exactly half the list were current PPCs. Only two aspirants, David Austick and Christopher Mayhew had ever sat as MPs; three others were peers. 68.4 per cent had been local government candidates, though less than half had ever been elected, and 22.0 per cent were councillors at the time of selection. Whether campaigning was 'effective' or not, there was ample evidence of campaign experience among those on the approved list. In addition, the criterion that Euro-candidates must at least possess the qualities sought in Westminster candidates was met, in that 98.8 per cent of known cases on the European list had been on the parliamentary list at some time, with 90.1 per cent currently on the list.

Unfortunately, the most important general requirement 'media ability' could not be gauged. However, despite this and other omissions, the overall impression was clear: there were no dramatic contradictions between the estabished regional panel interviewing criteria and the characteristics of individuals on the approved list.

Selected and Non-Selected Applicants

This section examines the entire aspirant population and illustrates those characteristics that differentiated the fifty seven rejected applicants from those adopted for either an English or Welsh Euro-constituency.

(a) Background characteristics: The Liberals attracted more aspirants aged under forty (39.8 per cent of the entire aspirant population) than either of the other two parties. However, youthful applicants were disproportionately represented in the rejected group: over half of this group were aged below forty and virtually one third under thirty-five. Moving up the age scale, the numbers in the rejected category visibly diminished. In comparison, the age distribution for PEPCs was fairly even, the exception being the small percentage of candidates aged over sixty. Both the means and the medians of the selected and non-selected groups confirmed that adopted candidates tended to be older. The mean ages for Liberal, Conservative and Labour PEPCs were similar (45.3, 45.1 and 43.5 respectively). However, rejected Liberal applicants were by far the youngest with a mean age of 39.8 years compared with 53.2 for Conservatives and 41.8 for CLP rejects.

OPCS group XXV dominated the occupational categories, with 69.1 per cent of PEPCs and 62.5 per cent of rejected applicants falling into this classification. Comparison with the other parties showed that Liberal PEPCs and rejected aspirants did not quite match the Labour figure of 79.5 per cent of PEPCs drawn from OPCS XXV (professional, technical workers and artists), but resembled the smaller percentage of Labour candidates from OPCS XXIV (administrators and managers) when compared with the 26.9 per cent of Conservative PEPCs who were employed in these occupations. The dominance of the teaching professions in the Liberal party followed the Labour example, though in the Liberal party lecturers rather than secondary school teachers were the more prolific: again, the impact of teaching as a recruitment occupation was crucial. The remaining Liberal applicants were largely drawn from the legal profession, journalism, finance, managerial and professional workers, all of which were distributed relatively evenly between selected and non-selected aspirants. Both ex-MPs and two peers were selected and none of the applicants were 'Euro-crats'.

As was typical for both Conservative and Labour selections, Liberal female aspirants were in a minority. Given that the number of women aspirants was derisory (accounting for only nine out of the survey total of 125) those women who did challenge for a seat were more likely to be adopted than rejected: only two of the nine failed to become PEPCs. Thus, while the number of female applicants was extremely low, their success rate was encouraging and comparable to that of both the Conservative and Labour women PEPCs.

The educational patterns for PEPCs and failed aspirants were generally similar in that grammar or public school products predominated and more than nine out of ten in both groups had received some form of higher education. PEPCs were more likely to have been to Oxbridge, some 46.2 per cent attending one of the two institutions, compared with less than one third of those rejected by a Euro-constituency. In general, the educational profile of Liberal PEPCs resembled their Conservative rather than their Labour rivals: these findings reflected the overall pattern found in studies of MPs and parliamentary candidates. The preponderance of public school candidates amongst Liberals and Conservatives was marked, though Liberal PEPCs could not quite match the predominance of the public schools evident in the Conservative party, which accounted for six out of every ten Conservative candidates. The Liberal PEPC figure for grammar schools, 34.3 per cent, was some 12.0 per cent smaller than the equivalent Labour figure.

(b) Previous political experience: 93.8 per cent of PEPCs and 95.7 per cent of non-selected aspirants had at some time been on the Westminster list of available candidates: 90.8 and 85.1 per cent respectively were on the parliamentary list prior to their European approval, satisfying, without the need of a further interview, the criterion that Westminster standards were the minimum qualifications for Europe. Experience as former parliamentary candidates most clearly distinguished Liberal aspirants from the other parties: 76.5 per cent of PEPCs and 84.2 per cent of non-selected aspirants had at some time contested a Westminster election. Nor were the majority one-off candidates, rather they tended to have a good deal of electoral experience, with some extreme examples of lengthy histories of defeat. The PEPC for Sussex West, for example, had fought every election since 1951, plus a by-election in 1961; another European candidate had stood at every election since 1955 as the Liberal candidate for Enfield-Southgate.

There was a clear tendency for European aspirants to have fought at one of the three previous general elections, with PEPCs more

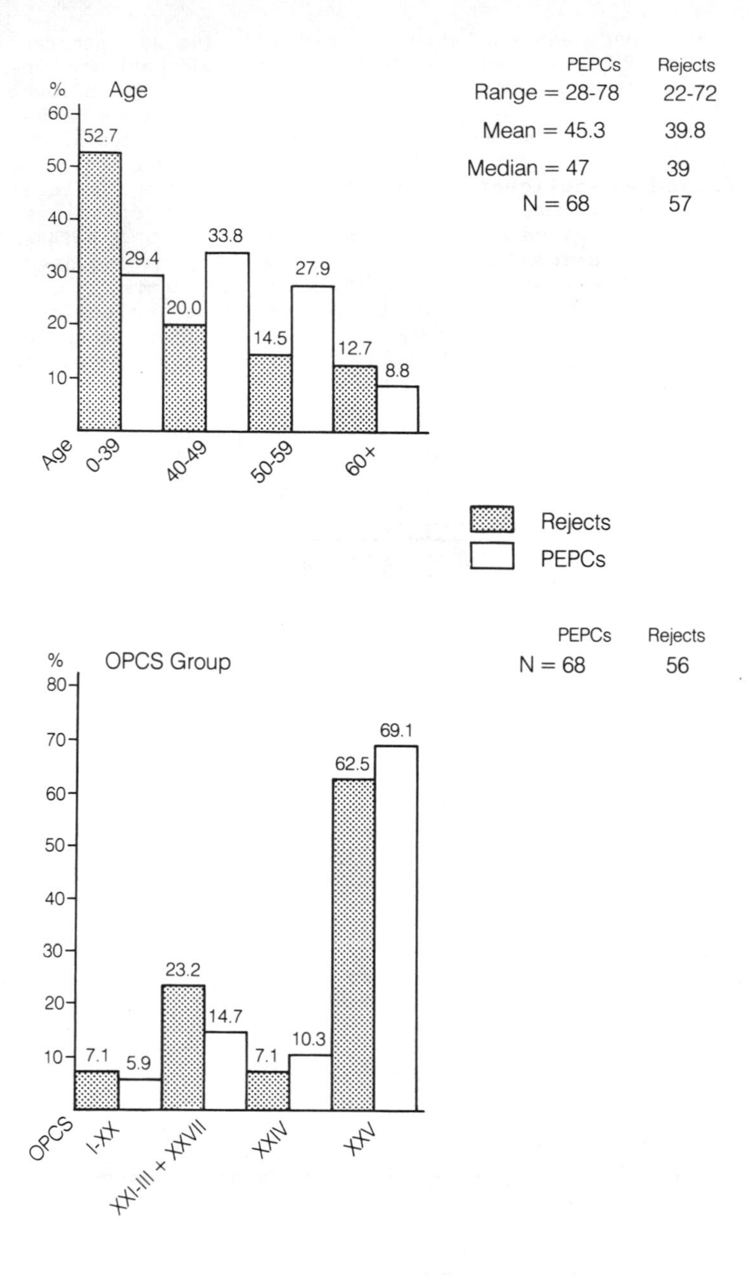

Figure 9.1 Background Characteristics of PEPCs and Rejected Liberal Applicants

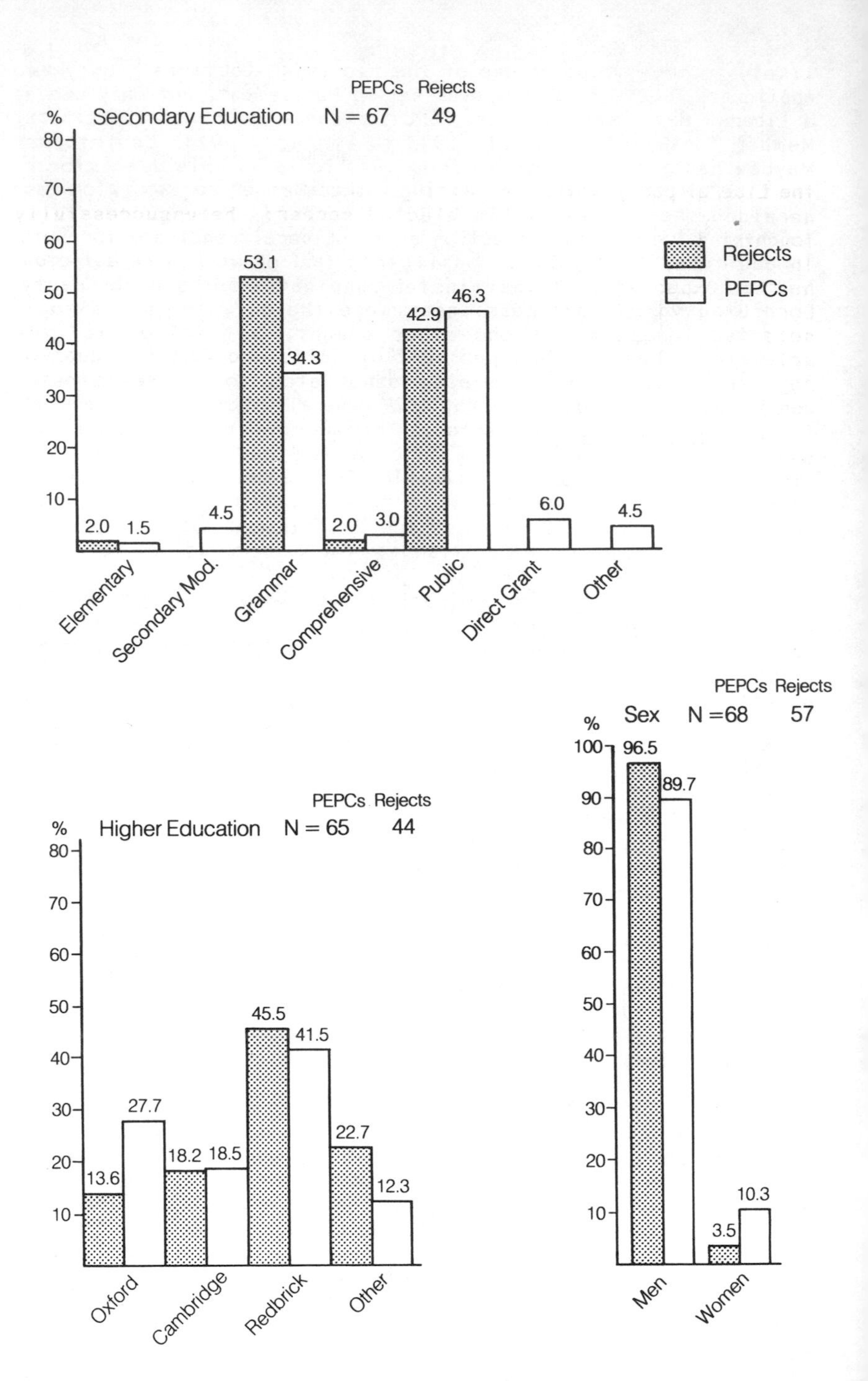
PEPCs Rejects
% Secondary Education N = 67 49
80
70
60
50
40
30
20
10
Rejects
PEPCs
2.0 1.5
4.5
53.1
34.3
2.0 3.0
42.9
46.3
6.0
4.5
Elementary
Secondary Mod.
Grammar
Comprehensive
Public
Direct Grant
Other
PEPCs Rejects
% Sex N =68 57
100
90
80
70
60
50
40
30
20
10
96.5
89.7
3.5
10.3
Men
Women
PEPCs Rejects
% Higher Education N = 65 44
80
70
60
50
40
30
20
10
13.6
27.7
18.2 18.5
45.5
41.5
22.7
12.3
Oxford
Cambridge
Redbrick
Other

likely to have stood at one of the two 1974 elections. Only two applicants, both PEPCs, had ever sat in Parliament, but only one as a Liberal MP. David Austick, PEPC for Leeds, had been the Liberal Member for Ripon from July 1973 to February 1974; Christopher Mayhew had been a Labour MP from 1945 to 1974. His defection to the Liberal party while the sitting Labour Member for Woolwich East heralded the demise of his elected career: he unsuccessfully fought the October 1974 election as the Liberal candidate for Bath. In addition, four Liberal applicants (all of whom were selected) had had experience as Westminster candidates for another party. Lord Gladwyn and Baroness Seear were the only two peers to be selected for Europe: one other sought, but failed to gain selection. Lastly, 44.1 per cent of PEPCs and 45.6 per cent of rejected applicants were also candidates for a Westminster constituency and fought the May 1979 general election for the seats in question; none were elected. The open recruitment structure with regard to parliamentary candidates, the lack of success of Liberal politicians in domestic elections, the smaller number of Liberal aspirants together with the requirement that European approved candidates had to meet the Westminster standards, meant that a duplication of the British and European political roles was inevitable.

As one would expect, in contrast to the two other major parties, Liberal European aspirants tended to have more experience as parliamentary candidates than as either local govenment candidates or councillors. Only 57.1 per cent of Liberal PEPCs had ever run as local government candidates compared with 75.0 per cent of non-selected applicants, though both groups were just as likely to have been serving councillors at the time of their selection contests (17.7 and 18.8 per cent respectively).

In summary, the overall pattern for previous political experience or apprenticeship pointed to no marked differences in the characteristics displayed by either selected or rejected Liberal aspirants. Approximately eight out of ten had stood for the House of Commons, while four out of ten were current PPCs. The only appreciable difference was that non-selected aspirants had greater experience as local government candidates but not as councillors: three out of ten from both groups were former local councillors. The more dramatic contrast was with the Labour and Conservative profiles: arguably the Liberals exhibited a greater degree of campaign experience, but it was experience gained in the context of electoral defeat not victory.

(c) European dimension: the Liberals' commitment to Europe was whole-hearted and their support for every aspect of European union virtually unanimous. For example, 58.0 per cent of PEPCs and 39.5 per cent of non-selected applicants were members of the European Movement. Only one individual in the entire aspirant population of 125 classed himself as an anti-Marketeer. Whether a greater number of anti-Marketeers were screened out by the Candidates Committee is not known. The distribution of attitudes towards five European issues reflected this homogeneity: both rejected applicants and PEPCs were overwhelmingly in favour of the creation of a federal Europe, trans-national parties, monetary union, increased powers for the European Parliament and a common voting system. Two-thirds of both groups favoured election by the single transferable vote as their preference for the uniform system to be used.

(d) Ambition: Turning the focus of analysis to the area of ambition and motivation, little difference was found between selected and non-selected aspirants in terms of their initial stimuli for running as possible candidates: 55.4 and 58.1 per cent respectively claimed to be pure self-starters, with 81.0 and 78.6 per cent combining self-recruitment with one or more external recruitment factors. Not surprisingly, the majority of motivational reasons for running for all aspirants tended to spring from a commitment to the European ideal as presented in the Programme for Europe.(1) However, PEPCs displayed a greater propensity to explain their candidacies in European terms than were rejected aspirants. This strong commitment to Europe on the part of PEPCs may have been a crucial selection factor. For example, one PEPC ran because he believed 'in Europe, and consider the development of the Community to be the most exciting and positive challenge of the second half of the 20th century'. In a similar vein, another PEPC ran because he wanted 'to see elected to the European Parliament people who are wholly committed to building a united Europe', whereas a colleague stood 'to restore the image of Britain within the Community after years of double talk and selfishness on the part of the Labour Party'.

PEPCs were also more apt to cite personal or political sources of motivation. A candidate in the South West ran 'to generate more support for the Liberal party; to re-activate poor associations'. Others had longer term motivations, either domestic or European focused (in Schlesinger's classification 'progressive' and 'static').(2) A number of PEPCs claimed that they were actively recruited. For example, one senior politician stated that he was 'really only a candidate for election to the European Parliament as a Liberal in the sense that I have said that if they really cannot find any suitable younger person, I am willing to be drafted'. In the event 'no suitable younger person' was found. Turning to non-selected applicants, one ran because he was 'a loyal party hack who does what my party needs me to do'. Another sought 'to help the Liberal cause in the UK as well as in Europe; to maximise the Liberal vote in the PR election in 1984'. Only one aspirant was critical of the EEC and motivated by a 'feeling that Britain negotiated appallingly on entry terms and need for constructive reform from within'.

Lastly, PEPCs tended to apply to more seats than rejected applicants: 42.5 per cent compared with 35.3 per cent sought adoption in three or more Euro-constituencies. Three-quarters of PEPCs could claim some form of local tie with their adopted Euro-constituency, with 39.4 per cent being a former or the current PPC for a parliamentary seat within the Euro-boundary. The figure of 29.3 per cent who could not claim any local connections was possibly inflated. Residence or parliamentary candidacy connections were strictly limited to the area within the Euro-constituency. There were several cases where PEPCs lived in an adjoining Euro-constituency (especially in London), or were PPCs for a neighbouring parliamentary district.

Electoral Status

Firstly, was Seligman's hypothesis that a party that has little expectation of winning will choose a different type of candidate from a party that is confident of election, confirmed or refuted by the Liberal's European venture?(3) Secondly, were there any differences in the kinds of Liberal PEPCs chosen to stand in projected Conservative rather than Labour Euro-constituencies in England and Wales? Of the seventy Euro-constituencies in question, thirty-four were projected Conservative and thirty-six projected Labour seats.

(a) Background characteristics: The few women who were adopted as PEPCs were more likely to be selected for Conservative rather than Labour seats (five compared with two). There was also a marked difference in the age distribution between the two categories. Candidates who contested Labour seats were the younger group, 68.5 per cent aged under fifty compared with 57.6 per cent for Conservative Euro-constituencies.(4)

Candidates selected in projected Conservative seats were the more varied occupational group, 60.6 per cent being in OPCS group XXV and a further 12.1 per cent in group XXIV. In contrast, PEPCs from Labour areas were predominantly professional, technical workers or artists (77.1 per cent). Teachers and lecturers were evenly distributed between both electoral categories, 27.3 per cent in Conservative areas and 28.6 per cent in Labour seats. Both peers who were selected fought Conservative held seats. Lastly, there was a clear differentiation according to educational backgrounds: those chosen for Labour seats tended to be grammar school and rebrick university products, whereas those who stood in Conservative seats were predominantly public school, Oxbridge products.

(b) Previous political experience: One surprising feature was that three candidates who were selected for what were regarded as 'winnable' seats for the Liberals, had only been party members for a comparatively short time. The PEPC for Cornwall and Plymouth, only joined the Liberal party in 1974, as had Christopher Mayhew (PEPC Surrey), and John Goss (PEPC Wessex): both Goss and Mayhew's short membership is explained by their former membership of the Conservative and Labour parties respectively.

Both groups displayed high, but similar, levels of experience as former parliamentary candidates (80.0 per cent in Labour seats, 78.8 per cent in Conservative). However, PEPCs adopted for Labour seats were more likely to have stood at only one election, and were also significantly more likely to have been adopted PPCs at the time of their European selection. 97.1 per cent of PEPCs in Labour seats had been and were currently on the Westminster approved list; 90.3 per cent of those in Conservative seats had been on the domestic list, with 83.9 per cent still on it at the time of selection. In terms of local government experience it was PEPCs in Labour seats who once again displayed the greater degree of involvement: 65.7 per cent of this group had fought as a local government candidate, compared with 48.5 per cent of their counterparts in Conservative seats. One third of PEPCs in Labour seats compared with 37.1 per cent in Conservative areas had been elected as a councillor at some time, with 20.0 and 15.2 per cent incumbent councillors respectively.

Table 9.1

Education by Electoral Status

	Projected Labour Seats		Projected Conservative Seats	
	%	n	%	n
Grammar	47.1	16	24.2	8
Public School	35.3	12	57.6	19
Not Known	-	1	-	-
Higher Education	94.3	33	97.0	32
Oxford	21.2	7	34.4	11
Cambridge	6.1	2	28.1	9
Redbrick	51.5	17	31.2	10
Other	21.2	7	6.3	2
	100.0	33	100.0	32

The general pattern was quite clear: the only major difference was that Liberal organisations in Labour seats tended to select candidates who were at the time of selection incumbent PPCs for a Westminster constituency: the other measures of political experience were remarkably uniform irrespective of electoral status.

(c) European dimension: Excluding the four Welsh PEPCs from analysis (all of whom fought Labour seats), in excess of 80.0 per cent of PEPCs in both Labour and Conservative Euro-constituencies came from the English list of approved candidates. Of the three main parties the Liberals showed a greater tendency to recruit their candidates from this centralised pool of aspirants. Needless to say, both groups of candidates were overwhelmingly pro-EEC. Against this background of homogeneous attitudes it was inevitable that there should be no variation between electoral categories and European attitudes.

(d) Ambition: Taking PEPCs in Labour-held seats first, 47.1 per cent declared themslves to be pure self-starters: this rose to 76.5 per cent when combined with other factors. The remaining 23.5 per cent acknowledged that the LPO, the local party or its agent had been the initial stimulus for European candidacy. PEPCs in Conservative seats displayed a greater propensity for self-recruitment, 64.5 per cent naming this reason for running exclusively, with a further 25.8 per cent using it in conjunction with other factors, totalling 90.3 per cent. Not only were PEPCs in Conservative seats more likely to have made the decision to run themselves without any external prompting, they were also more likely to possess 'progressive' ambition, regarding candidacy for the European Parliament as a route to Westminster (10.0 compared with 2.9 per cent).(5)

While PEPCs in Conservative seats were more likely to use both a European based and a personal/political reason in explaining their motivation for running, for both groups there was a high degree of conformity: commitment to a belief in Europe, a desire to help the Liberal party and confidence in one's own ability were evident in the characteristics of PEPCs in both types of seats. One distinctive feature of PEPCs who fought Conservative constituencies was that one third ran because of self-esteem: they felt that they possessed the necessary qualities to be MEPs. This self-esteem was also manifest in the number of nominations they contested: half only sought adoption in a single Euro-constituency. In contrast, although 39.4 per cent of PEPCs in Labour seats only applied to the Euro-constituency that adopted them, exactly one third applied to four or more seats in their search for European candidacy.

Lastly, Conservative seats tended to prefer PEPCs who were or had been parliamentary candidates within the boundaries of their selected seats: 45.5 per cent of Liberal PEPCs in Conservative seats compared with 31.4 per cent of those in Labour areas had such parliamentary links. Overall, PEPCs who fought Labour seats tended to have fewer public connections, with only 25.7 per cent having local government connections and a further 25.7 per cent having no links with their chosen Euro-constituency at all. The corresponding figures for Liberal PEPCs in Conservative seats were 36.4 and 21.2 per cent. This trend was heightened in the six most winnable Liberal seats, all of which were projected Conservative victories. It appeared that where the Liberals felt that they stood a real chance of winning, local ties took second place to national prominence and proven ability. Two candidates who had no links with their Euro-constituencies, Baroness Seear and Christopher Mayhew, were two of the most eminent and electorally experienced Liberal aspirants: both fought potentially winnable seats.

Conclusion

This chapter has shown that Liberal aspirants were characterized by their similarity rather than differences across a wide range of variables. In particular there were striking levels of congruence between the pro-European attitudes of rejected and selected applicants; there was little difference in the political experience of both groups in terms of their membership of the Westminster approved list, former and current parliamentary candidacies and in their experience as councillors, both past and present. Both PEPCs and rejected applicants were predominantly self-recruited. However, beneath this substantial impression of similarity, even in the Liberal party there were differences between the selected and rejected groups, although these differences tended to stem from background characteristics rather than attitudes, motivations or political experience. PEPCs were disproportionately drawn from female applicants, Oxbridge graduates, OPCS group XXV and the teaching occupations, whereas those who failed to be adopted tended to be younger, grammar school products and with a history of losing local government elections. In addition, PEPCs possessed stronger motivations for candidacy and sought adoption in a greater number of seats.

The pattern found for selected and rejected aspirants was generally replicated in the analysis of electoral status. Inevitably, there was overwhelming agreement on the European issues, similar percentages had been former parliamentary candidates and councillors with corresponding levels drawn from both the Westminster and European lists for PEPCs in both projected Conservative and Labour seats. The major differences derived from electoral status were that projected Labour seats preferred to select younger candidates, women and those with a grammar school, redbrick education. Conversely, those chosen in projected Conservative seats tended to mirror the Oxbridge and public school characteristics of Conservative PEPCs in general. Liberal candidates who stood in projected Conservative areas had been members of the party longer; were more likely to have been self-starters; apply to a larger number of Euro-constituencies; and to have either a parliamentary candidacy or local government connection with their adopted seat (although PEPCs in Labour seats were generally more likely to be adopted PPCs).

The analysis of the Liberal aspirants has supported the initial hypotheses, namely that there are important differences as well as similarities between the various groups of non-selected and selected aspirants to political office. By examining non-adopted applicants light was shed on adopted PEPCs; their attitudes, motivations, experience and background characteristics were viewed in the context of the recruitment process, not in isolation. The homogenity of the pro-European attitudes of Liberals were underlined and the differences based on parliamentary and local government candidacy as well as background factors exposed by the approach.

Notes

(1) Programme for Europe, manifesto of the European Liberals and Democrats, January 1979, p.1.

(2) J.A. Schlesinger, Ambition and Politics: political careers in the United States, Rand McNally, 1966, p.10.

(3) L.G. Seligman, "Political Parties and Recruitment of Political Leadership", In L. J. Edinger (ed.), Political Leadership in Industrialised Societies, Wiley, 1967, p.303.

(4) The age by electoral status breakdown was as follows: projected Labour seats (n=36) under 40, 37.1 per cent; 40-49, 31.4; 50-59, 31.4; 60 and over, none: projected Conservative seats (n=34), under 40, 21.2 per cent; 40-49, 36.4; 50-59, 24.2; 60 and over, 18.2 per cent.

(5) Schlesinger, op.cit., p.10.

10 The parties compared: Common themes, comparisons and recruitment differences

How successful has this study been in realising the objectives delineated in chapter 1? Firstly, in a historical sense, the study has traced the British experience of the selection of European candidates. While only concentrating on one specialized area, it has added to the richness of the election literature. In particular, it represents an alternative perspective to that forwarded by the European Elections Study and substantiates many of the general points made by Butler and Marquand in their book, European Elections and British Politics.(1)

Secondly, the data generated offers a useful guide and source for subsequent candidate studies. While this objective was not the prime goal (indeed the concentration on candidate studies has been strongly criticised throughout), European candidate profiles could usefully be juxtaposed with those of MPs or local councillors. A comparison between MEPs and Mellors' The British MP would be an interesting subsidiary aspect of the analysis.(2)

Thirdly, the role of electoral status was considered. Earlier British candidate studies have pointed to the powerful explanatory value of this approach: electoral status proved to be of equal explanatory value for European candidates. Yet despite producing important results, this approach was limited because the conclusions drawn only related to one aspect of the recruitment process, namely candidates. To have ignored electoral status or candidate profiles as aspects of the process would have been negligent; to have confined the analysis to this level would have said little about recruitment.

Fourthly, selection structures were examined. Here two aspects were considered: i) the differences between Westminster and European practices for each of the three parties; and ii) the differences in the European election structures between the parties.

i) In general, all three major parties adapted their respective domestic selection machinery for the European election. The adoption of a first-past-the-post electoral system allowed the Westminster structures to be duplicated with minimal need for alteration. The constituencies were bigger, but the organisational principles remained the same. This, coupled with the late publication of the Boundary Commissioners' final report meant that even had the parties wanted to alter their selection procedures significantly, it would have been difficult to do so. There was not sufficient time to devise and establish any radically different selection mechanisms.

The Conservatives adapted their basic Westminster structures to suit the particular needs of the European election. They relied upon an inner-party selection committee, although there were signs of a move towards greater participation with the general meeting acting as the final selection body, not the executive council as was normally the case for Westminster selection. The relationship between Central Office and constituency associations was basically maintained, although the balance somewhat revised. The Labour party's European selection machinery closely resembled the structure employed for Westminster selections which requires selections to be made by delegates and for aspirants to seek nominations. The creation of the European Selection Organisation merely super-imposed a higher but essentially identical selection mechansim on top of the existing CLP structure. Formally, the NEC performed its functions of validation and endorsement, though the application of these procedures was less than enthusiastic. The various mechanisms used by the Liberal party to select their European candidates reflected the diversity found for their Westminster selections. The option of a closed primary or a delegate system corresponded to the practices used for selecting PPCs.

Even though the European procedures used by the Labour, Conservative and Liberal parties tended to mirror those used in their Westminster selections, important variations and innovations were generated. The most important of these related to the position of a centralised 'approved' list. As for Westminster, the Conservatives drew up a European approved list. However, the restriction of the Euro-list to less than 250 candidates indicated a tigher centralised control than for domestic selections. Also, the criteria used for determining the list and the type of individuals chosen were markedly different from the Westminster situation. It was in relation to a centralised approved list that the Labour party varied the most from its domestic procedures. The absence of an 'A' or 'B' list and the 'advisory' nature of the one list that did exist constituted a major departure from its Westminster provisions and were symbolic of the Labour party's lack of interest in the elections. While the Liberal party followed its Westminster practice and drew up a list for Europe, the general lack of willing aspirants undermined this centralised selection mechanism.

ii) The contrast between the Westminster and European 'approved' list practices for each party were striking: the 'differences between parties was also an important recruitment finding. Approved lists were indispensable to both Conservatrive and Liberal selections: the vast majority of their aspirants and PEPCs came from these centralised sources. In contrast, the centralised 'advisory' list was of negligible importance in Labour party selections: the majority of their candidates were local nominees. These varying approaches to a centralised list had important consequences for recruitment and candidate selection in each party and constitute essential elements in the model.

The three parties could also be distinguished in relation to the degree of participation they allowed in the selections. Neither the Conservatives, Labour or the Welsh Liberals deviated from the notion of delegate/representative-based selections. In contrast, the English Liberal party devised a framework for rank and file participation through a closed primary selection system, although often the numbers involved limited this democratic principle. The recruitment and selection processes in each party were characterized by the way they balanced participation against centralisation: each emphasised different aspects of the equation.

All of these factors gave the Conservative, Labour and Liberal selections their own distinctive style and character and, more importantly, had a significant impact upon their actual selection outcomes. As Tobin and Keynes warned, recruitment studies that ignore structural and procedural mechanisms do so at their peril.(3) Different types of selection systems may initially attract different aspirants and internal selection mechanisms are essential in understanding why certain individuals are selected, while others are not: such a line of analysis may often be more powerful than looking for explanations in the actual selected and rejected profiles. That the three parties adopted different selection methods was in itself an important selection finding. Had either Conservative or Labour opted for a primary system, their selected cohorts may have been significantly different. The debate within the Labour party relating to grass-roots democracy and re-selection, and the Social Democratic Party's rejection of such an activist-based system are contemporary domestic examples that help to stress the importance of this factor.

An additional consideration based on the structural perspective was the role played by the 'selectorate'. In all three parties (even behind the facade of the Liberal's closed primaries) there lurked the persistent characteristic of British candidate selection - the selection committee or its inner-party equivalent. Hunt and Pendley first drew attention to 'community gate-keeping' as a recruitment variable with Patterson, Fairlie, Rush and Ranney all commenting on its application to British politics.(4) This study has further contributed to this literature: the reliance on such gate-keeping both centrally and locally was the hallmark of Conservative selections and to a lesser extent those of the Liberal party. Only the Labour party clearly relinquished its domestic role of gate-keeping for the European selections, firstly through its abdication of any centralised control of nominations and, secondly, though to a lesser extent, through the benevolent attitude at the ESO level towards short-listing. Even in the Labour party the pervasive influence of the local selectors detracted from the notion of egaliterian selection. The process of local nomination was maintained and through this mechanism gate-keeping at the Euro-constituency level was implemented.

The analysis has also contributed to the sparse literature on the

Liberal party. Liberals are rarely included in studies of British political parties, let alone been the sole focus of in-depth analysis.(5) The examintion of Liberal selection methods has never been more important: the Liberal-SDP Alliance will survive or fall on the two parties' ability to agree upon the joint selection of candidates and the distribution of seats. Their electoral pact weathered both the 1983 General Election and the 1984 direct elections to the European Parliament: however, domestically and in the European context, further analysis of Liberal and SDP selections in now required.

Besides these broader considerations, this study has focused on the limitations of traditional candidate studies, illustrated why they only constitute partial accounts of recruitment and, in response, offered an alternative approach and the necessary empirical data needed to test the hypotheses generated by the new perspective. Preference for candidate studies to the detriment of recruitment analysis has been documented at length: the limitations of the traditional British candidate approach have been contrasted with the concern for rejected aspirants as well as the winners and losers of the European election itself.

Turning to the structure of the analysis, has the model served as a heuristic device? In the past there has been an obvious discrepancy between the development of models of recruitment for British politics and the application of these models empirically. Both Gordon, and to a greater degree Collins, have presented the researcher with an operational framework for analysis.(6) However, as already noted, neither was able to test their hypotheses because they both lacked the data by which to do so. This study has presented both a useful model of recruitment and data required to test such an approach. Although it was particular in its internal mechanisms, the assumptions within the model can be transferred to a more general approach to political recruitment. The concentration upon end-products has been questioned and the necessity of analysing the entire aspirant population established theoretically and demonstrated methodologically. The simplifying assumptions of the model have served to highlight its dominant features - namely, selection filters and their corresponding criteria, the various points of exit and the resultant profile characteristics of these different groups of individuals.

Two substantive questions remain to be answered: how far have the model's hypotheses been proved and what were the main findings of the study? Has the belief that there are important differences between selected and rejected aspirants been confirmed by the data? Two separate aspects of the analysis must be kept discrete - findings that are drawn from inter-party comparisons and those based on intra-party comparisons. Thus, firstly, the major profile differences between Conservative, Labour and Liberal candidates and aspirants are discussed; secondly, the differences between each of the aspirant groups within each party are considered. These two aspects of comparison must not be confused.

The Major Profile Differences and Similarities Between Conservative, Labour and Liberal Candidates and Aspirants.

What were the major factors that distinguished the political aspirants for the three parties? Focusing on selected candidates first, the following traits emerged.

The mean ages of each group showed little difference (45.3 for Liberals, 45.1 for Conservatives and 43.5 for Labour candidates) although the Liberals selected fewer candidates aged under forty (29.9 per cent) compared with the 32.1 and 35.9 per cent for Labour and Conservative PEPCs respectively. Each party selected a roughly similar proportion of women candidates: 10.3 per cent for Labour, 12.8 for Conservatives and 15.2 per cent for the Liberals. The educational profiles produced the sharpest differences: 59.7 per cent of Conservative PEPCs and 47.0 per cent of Liberals were educated at public school compared with only 6.0 per cent of selected Labour candidates; the largest proportion of Labour's PEPCs came from grammar schools (46.3 per cent), whereas only 20.8 per cent of Conservatives did, with the Liberals occupying the midpoint with 34.8 per cent. Some form of higher education was the norm for all parties accounting for some 90.0 per cent of candidates; 50.8 per cent of Conservative and 46.5 per cent of Liberal PEPCs who had undergone higher education had Oxbridge degrees. Again, Labour's candidates proved to be the odd men out: only 17.1 per cent of them came from these two institutions - 64.3 per cent were redbrick graduates, compared with approximately four out of ten for both Conservative and Liberal candidates.

That all candidates should be drawn from the higher occupational categories was not surprising: 87.2 per cent of Labour PEPCs, 85.9 per cent of Conservatives and 79.4 per cent of Liberals fell into OPCS groups XXIV or XXV. The replacement of manual occupations by the teaching professions, local government and civil service executive jobs has been a feature of post-war Labour MPs: they were no longer 'men of toil' but rather 'men of ideas'.(7) Candidacy for the European Parliament continued this trend. Labour PEPCs were typically drawn from the educational professions: 29.5 per cent were teachers and 5.1 per cent lecturers in higher education. In contrast, only 3.9 per cent of Conservative candidates were employed in these two occupations. The Liberals proved an interesting comparison: like Labour they depended heavily upon the educational sector, though for them it was lecturers rather than primary or secondary school teachers who were the more important group (16.2 compared with 11.8 per cent respectively).

The Liberal party's reliance on its domestic political candidates for Europe was a major profile feature. Selected European Liberal candidates were almost twice as likely to have been PPCs for Westminster than either Conservative or Labour PEPCs: 84.6 per cent of Liberals had been adopted candidates for a Commons constituency; the figure for Conservative PEPCs was 47.4 and 41.0 for Labour. Whereas both the Conservative and Labour parties prohibited PPCs from standing, 44.1 per cent of the Liberal's European candidates were also adopted PPCs at the time of their selection. In contrast, the NEC's veto on domestic candidates forced the Labour party to rely almost as heavily upon candidates who had served their campaign apprenticeships in local not national politics: 78.2 per cent of their PEPCs had stood as local councillors, with 61.5 per cent achieving office. The Liberals were somewhat less locally oriented, 57.3 per cent of their PEPCs having experience as local government candidates, with 32.4 elected as councillors, whereas only 40.3 per cent of Conservative PEPCs had been local candidates and 29.5 per cent elected councillors. That less than half the Conservative PEPCs had been Westminster or local candidates reflected the nature of the approved list and the party Vice-chairman's overriding concern to secure well-qualified achievers from outside politics; Conservative PEPCs could least easily be described as party 'hacks' who had failed at other levels of political office.

The most dramatic difference between, on the one hand Conservative and Liberal PEPCs, and on the other their Labour adversaries, centred on their attitude towards membership of the European Economic Community. There was virtual unanimity in both the Conservative and Liberal ranks for support of the EEC, whereas the majority of Labour PEPCs were hostile to Britain's membership, 53.1 per cent classifying themselves as anti-Europeans and only 26.6 per cent pro-Europeans. The pro-EEC commitment of Liberal PEPCs went unquestioned when their attitudes towards the major European issues were examined. Conservative PEPCs, however, were more likely to adopt a guarded pro-European stance; they did not possess the Liberal's whole-hearted Europeanness. While a minimum of three out of four Conservative PEPCs favoured financial union, an increased role for the European Parliament, the maintenane of the EEC's supra-national authority and a move towards transnational party alignments, they shied away from any notion of federalism. Quite apart from the antagonism displayed by Labour's PEPCs towards these six issues, even the 26.1 per cent who professed to being pro-European resembled the Conservative sceptics more closely rather than the Liberal 'Euro-fanatics'. A similar percentage of Labour and Conservative PEPCs were against federalism, but in contrast to the Conservative figures, 76.3 per cent of Labour PEPCs were against monetary union, 58.6 against an increase in the European Parliament's powers, whilst only 35.6 per cent felt that the EEC's supra-national powers should be maintained rather than curbed.

Motivations again reflected the pro/anti-EEC divide among the parties and their candidates: 47.4 per cent of Labour PEPCs described their reasons for running in anti-EEC language, whereas 82.4 per cent of Liberals and 50.0 per cent of Conservative PEPCs expressed their motivations in pro-EEC statements. Stimulus for candidacy again separated Labour PEPCs from their Conservative and Liberal rivals: 64.0 per cent of Conservatives and 55.4 per cent of Liberals tended to be 'self-starters'; only one quarter of Labour's candidates were thus motivated. They were more likely to have been recruited by CLPs, trade unions or the Co-operative party. Perhaps a reflection of the Conservatives' less than whole-hearted pro-Market sympathies was that one in five of their PEPCs treated European candidacy as a useful but temporary apprenticeship on the road to Westminster. Only 8.1 per cent of Labour PEPCs and a mere 4.8 per cent of Liberals saw their European candidacies in such a light.

Lastly, the nature of the selection machinery adopted by each party directly influenced the rate of applications or nominations each parties' candidates recorded. Thus in the Conservative party, where applicants were encouraged to put themselves forward in up to a maximum of fifteen Euro-constituencies, 64.2 per cent applied to five or more and only 11.9 per cent limited their ambitions to a single seat. The mixed Liberal procedure was hampered by the small size of their list, and therefore the greater likelihood of achieving selection: only 15.2 per cent of Liberal PEPCs sought adoption in five or more seats, whereas 45.5 per cent were chosen in the only seat they applied for. The Labour party's rigid nomination structure restricted the potential for 'carpet-bagging' or at least multiple nominations. The Labour position almost exactly reversed that found for Conservative PEPCs: 61.5 per cent of Labour's PEPCs were nominated only for the seat where they were eventually adopted, with a mere 11.6 per cent seeking selection in five or more Euro-constituencies. A further consequence of these intra-party selection rules was that 49.3 per cent of Conservative PEPCs could claim no local tie with their adopted Euro-constituency. In contrast, both Liberal and Labour PEPCs were 'local' recruits. 40.3 per cent of Liberals had been or were PPCs for a parliamentary seat within the European constituency boundary, 17.9 per cent had similar local government connections, with 58.2 claiming links through residence or work: only 23.9 failed to lay claim to any tie with their Euro-constituency. Residence or work constituted the dominant local connection for Labour PEPCs (60.1 per cent), with 44.9 per cent also pointing to local government candidacy within the Euro-constituency; only 23.1 per cent of Labour PEPCs had no local ties.

The above resume has shown that Labour, Liberal and Conservative PEPCs were different in their backgrounds, political experience, European views and in their ambitions and motivations. If only selected candidates were considered this study would be guilty of the charge laid against traditional candidate studies. Thus the analysis is extended to comparing the rejected aspirants of each party. Were Labour's rejects similar to the corresponding Conservative and Liberal rejects? Did they all display the same traits, or were the three parties rejects as distinct from one another as were the adopted Labour, Conservative and Liberal European candidates? One problem is immediately apparent: which of the three different categories of Labour rejects (CLP rejected nominees, ESO rejects or defeated ESO short-listed nominees) was it appropriate to compare with the undifferentiated Conservative and Liberal rejected aspirant categories? Because both the Conservative and Liberal data tended to identify losing aspirants at the short-listing stage, the category of defeated ESO short-listed nominees was the most appropriate.

The Major Differences and Similarities Between Conservative, Labour and Liberal Rejected Aspirants.

Firstly, how did these three groups of rejected aspirants compare in terms of background characteristics? In general, the sharp divisions between Conservative and Labour candidates were reflected in the findings for rejected aspirants as well, with the Liberals hoving between the two extremes. The Conservatives had a higher percentage of women among their rejected applicants than either of the other two parties and they were also the most distinctive group in relation to educational profiles: 72.9 per cent came from public school with 54.4 per cent possessing Oxbridge degrees. In contrast, the respective figures for Liberals were 42.0 and 31.4 per cent and for rejected Labour aspirants 6.6 and 15.4 per cent. The majority of rejects (like selected candidates for all parties) came from the higher OPCS groups, although once again, Conservatives were drawn disproportionately from OPCS groups XXIV and XXV. Rejected Conservative applicants were the oldest of the three categories with a mean age of 53.2; the figure for those defeated at a Labour ESO selection meeting was 44.5 and the Liberals the youngest group of rejected aspirants with a mean age of 39.8.

Labour's rejects were the least experienced in fighting Westminster elections. Only 30.8 per cent had ever stood as PPCs, and only 11.3 per cent fought in October 1974. In contrast, 46.3 per cent of rejected Conservative applicants had contested a parliamentary election (25.4 per cent had sat as MPS), with 25.0 per cent standing as candidates in the second 1974 election. However, even the Conservative figures paled against those for Liberal aspirants, of whom 82.5 per cent had been parliamentary candidates, 45.6 per cent at the last general election. Non-selected Liberals also displayed a high degree of experience as local government candidates (75.0 per cent), though only one third had sat as councillors. 83.2 per cent of Labour's rejects had been local candidates, with virtually two-thirds having been elected. Conservative rejects were the least active in local politics, 40.3 per cent having been candidates and 29.5 per cent councillors. Thus in terms of previous political experience, Conservative, Liberal and Labour rejected Euro-aspirants were as distinct from one another as were their elected counterparts.

Turning to attitudes towards the European Community, while Liberal and Conservative rejected aspirants were virtually unanimous in their pro-EEC support only 42.9 per cent of Labour's rejects classified themselves as pro-Marketeers. Furthermore, a majority of Labour's rejected nominees were against federalism, monetary union, transnational party systems, increased powers for the European Parliament and a uniform electoral system. In contrast, a majority of both Conservative and Liberal rejected aspirants were in favour of all these issues though the support shown by the Conservatives was less clear-cut. These differences between the European attitudes of Labour's nominees and those of the rejected aspirants in the other two parties corresponded broadly to the differences found between each party's candidates, with the exception that Conservative PEPCs were hostile to European federalism whereas their losing applicants were in favour, if only marginally. Despite the Liberals almost unanimous support for the the European issues, just 50.9 per cent claimed a pro-EEC motivation for running compared with exactly 50.0 per cent of Conservatives and the rather surprisingly high figure of 36.0 per cent for rejected Labour nominees. However, while no Conservatives or Liberals mentioned any anti-EEC reasons for running, 47.3 per cent of Labour's defeated ESO short-listed nominees sought candidacy for this reason. Although rejected Labour nominees were more likely than their selected colleagues to be 'self-starters', Labour's aspirants were still the least likely of the three groups of rejected aspirants to be self-motivated. Almost twice as many Labour and Conservative rejects saw European candidacy as a route to Westminster (11.7 and 12.5 per cent respectively) than did their Liberal adversaries (6.5 per cent).

As noted in the previous section, the parties different selection mechanisms affected their respective application or nomination levels. In consequence, the ratios between the three parties found for selected candidates were basically repeated for non-selected aspirants. 67.8 per cent of rejected Conservative aspirants tried their luck in five or more seats whereas a mere 4.3 per cent of Labour's rejected and 8.8 per cent of the Liberal's put their name forward in as many Euro-constituencies.

It can be concluded that those aspirants who failed to gain adoption were as distinct from one another as were selected candidates. Rejected aspirants were not an undifferentiated mass possessing similar characteristics, experience or attitudes: party affiliation was a crucial variable.

The Major Differences Between Selected, Rejected and Elected Aspirants Within Each Party.

Having examined the main profile characteristics between parties all that remains to be done is to examine the main hypothesis of the model and to evaluate its relative success or failure. What, if any, were the differences between selected and rejected groups within each party? Has this study shown any marked differences between the candidates and their normally anonymous rejected adversaries, or were all aspirants whether selected or not, basically similar in their profiles? If there are no such differences how does this affect the initial assumption and thesis of the model?

Conservative profiles: What factors helped to discriminate between rejected aspirants, PEPCs, winners and losers? Firstly, there was a definite relationship between age and selection: the mean age for rejected Conservative aspirants was 53.2 whereas that for adopted PEPCs was 45.1. Only 9.3 per cent of non-selected applicants were aged below forty compared to a figure of 35.9 per cent for European candidates. Whether this distribution was the result of a conscious act of gatekeeping using the criterion of age or not, age constituted an important discriminating profile variable. There was no significant difference between the mean ages of winners and losers, although 44.4 per cent of losers and just one third of winners were aged under forty. Women were no less likely to be rejected than selected as candidates, but if selected they tended not to be elected: four of the eighteen defeated Conservative PEPCs, but only six of the sixty elected MEPs were female.

As noted throughout the discussions of Conservative selections, the preference for aspirants to be from public school was predominant. However, although 59.7 per cent of PEPCs were educated at public school, the figure for rejected applicants was a staggering 72.9 per cent. Once again, while the typical conclusions relating to European candidates derived from traditional candidate studies correctly stress the Conservatives' reliance on public schools as their main suppliers of political leaders they fail, by definition, to perceive that the percentage of public school candidates was smaller than that for the rejected applicant population. The possession of public school credentials was not in itself a selection asset. The general educational pattern was only partially extended when education at the university level was examined. More rejects than PEPCs (54.4 per cent as against 50.8 per cent) and more winners than losers (54.7 and 35.7 per cent) had Oxbridge degrees; the ratio was reversed when higher education at a non-Oxbridge institutions was considered.

Not only were rejected applicants more like the 'elitist' Tory stereo-type in their educational profiles than the actual European candidates, they were also disproportionately drawn from the top two OPCS occupational groups: 94.5 per cent of non-selected applicants compared with 85.9 per cent of PEPCs were classified as either administrators and managers or artists, professional or technical workers. Again, to criticise the Conservative party for selecting candidates from a narrow socio-economic range fails to recognise the overwhelming bias amongst their total applicants. That all their aspirants were drawn from a homogeneous 'class' is in itself an important, but separate point. (A rider must be added to these occupational comments: as noted in the text, the survey of Conservative aspirants probably inflated the number of MPs in the population, the majority of whom were unsuccessful in their search for a European constituency and may, therefore, have skewed the occupational balance for rejected applicants.) Other occupational differences were evident. The teaching professions tended to be associated with unsuccessful selection, or if selected, with defeat on 7 June. Only 3.9 per cent of PEPCs were either teachers or lecturers compared with 7.5 per cent of rejected applicants: what is more, none of these PEPCs were elected. Occupations more prevalent amongst PEPCs than rejected applicants were primarily the legal profession, journalism and that of 'Eurocrat'.

Conservative aspirants could be evaluated across a wide range of factors other than demographic variables, drawing out both important similarities as well as differences. Analysis of political experience as a Westminster candidate indicated that selected and non-selected aspirants were broadly similar, except that MPs tended to fall into the latter category, and winners tended to possess a greater degree of experience than defeated PEPCs. At the local political level, 40.4 per cent of rejected applicants compared with only 29.5 per cent of PEPCs had been councillors, with the figures for winners and losers 38.9 and 27.1 respectively. There was striking unanimity shown towards self-classification as a pro-Marketeer though this overall commitment was confused when the question of European federalism was considered: 51.9 per cent of rejects in contrast to only 15.4 per cent of selected candidates favoured this concept, the majority of whom were winners, not losing PEPCs. A greater percentage of PEPCs were against any reduction in the powers of the EEC (98.1 compared with 72.0 per cent) and a smaller percentage against a uniform electoral system (33.3 and 46.2 per cent).

Turning to ambition, PEPCs and MEPs were significantly more likely to be 'self-starters' than were rejected aspirants or defeated candidates: 50.0 per cent of PEPCs and 51.8 per cent of MEPs used pro-EEC motivations in explaining their candidacy in contrast to only 22.3 per cent of failed applicants and 44.4 per cent of defeated candidates. Rejected aspirants were not, in general, motivated by disappointment as Westminster candidates: indeed, PEPCs were almost four times as likely to cite this as one of their reasons for contesting the European election. However,

22.2 per cent of losers and only 1.7 per cent of winners were motivated by their domestic failures. Thus it was not surprising to find that PEPCs and losers were more likely than rejected applicants and winners to view European candidacy as a pathway to the Westminster Parliament. Lastly, rejected aspirants were no less determined in their quest for a European constituency than were winners and losers. Approximately one third of all four categories of applicants sought adoption in ten or more seats. If anything, rejected applicants tended to apply to marginally more seats; 67.8 per cent applied to five or more ECCs compared with 64.2 per cent of PEPCs, 43.8 per cent of losers and 70.6 per cent of winners.

In summary, both the need to study non-selected as well as selected aspirants has been demonstrated and the hypothesis that there are significant and important recruitment relevant differences between profiles was found to be valid for Conservative recruitment to the European Parliament. Examination of the larger aspirant cohort has shed light on a range of characteristics that would only have been partially exposed by a traditional candidate study.

Labour profiles: The survey of Labour nominees presented the best data-set for stringent testing of the model's central assumptions. Labour's three stages of selection filters created the opportunity for closer examination of the proposition that rejects were in some sense different or less well qualified than candidates. Was there any evidence of partisan gate-keeping and, if so, what criteria were employed? In particular was there a case for arguing that the pro/anti-EEC division was the crucial selection determinant explaining success and failure better than any other factor? The four groups used to illustrate and test the hypothesis were: those aspirants who were rejected prior to the CLP nomination stage; CLP nominees who failed to make an ESO short-list; those who made a short-list but were not adopted as candidates; and, the PEPCs.

Firstly, what were the relevant background similarities and differences? Aspirants who failed to gain a CLP nomination were the youngest of these four groups: their mean age was 41.8 compared with 46.7 for ESO rejects, 44.6 for defeated short-listed nominees and 43.5 for PEPCs. In addition, 45.7 per cent of those rejected outright by CLPs were aged under forty, whereas the proportions for the three other aspirant groups were all less than one third. Thus, although a sizeable percentage of PEPCs were relatively young, in general the youngest aspirants tended to fall at the first selection hurdle.

Kohn's article 'Women in the European Parliament', documented the lack of success of female candidates.(8) Within the nine EEC states 589 woman stood as candidates (17.0 per cent) with 11.0 per cent gaining election. Only twenty-five women stood in Britain (9.0 per cent); less than half were elected. Kohn records that the position for the Labour party was that half of its female PEPCs were elected, suggesting a disproportionate success rate. Examination of non-selected aspirants places the emphasis differently. While adopted women candidates stood a better chance than their male colleagues of being selected, the more important recruitment finding was the extent to which there appeared to be any sexual bias in the earlier stages of the selection process.

14.3 per cent of aspirants who failed to secure the necessary CLP nomination were women, but, if nominated, women were just as likely to be short-listed (7.6 per cent) as they were to be rejected (7.0 per cent) by the ESO. 6.5 per cent of defeated short-listed nominees were women compared with 10.3 per cent of the selected candidates. Given that the percentages of female aspirants were indefensibly small, there was no evidence that women were disadvantaged once they were within the selection process, although there was evidence to suggest that it was more difficult for them to gain a nomination.

Aspirants without a CLP nomination could also be distinguished from those excluded by ESOs, defeated at a selection conference or PEPCs in terms of their educational profiles. Rejected aspirants were more likely to be grammar or public school recruits and Oxbridge products than any of the other three groups. Although a grammar and university education was the norm for CLP nominees through to PEPCs, Labour aspirants who more closely resembled their Conservative rivals in these respects found it harder to secure a CLP nomination.

Turning to OPCS categories, here the characteristics displayed by PEPCs separated them from the disappointed aspirants: 87.2 per cent of PEPCs came from the managerial/administrative or artists, professional and technical workers categories. The group that was the closest approximation to this PEPC profile were rejected aspirants with 77.2 per cent from the top two socio-economic classifications, followed by ESO rejects with a 73.2 percentage figure and, finally, nominees who lost at the selection conference stage, of whom 71.5 per cent came from these two categories. As noted earlier, PEPCs mirrored the pattern set by MPs in that the teaching professions constituted the largest occupational block. However, being a teacher or lecturer was not necessarily a passport to selection: while 34.6 per cent of PEPCs were employed in the education sector, so were 24.4 per cent of ESO rejects and exactly one third of the non-selected nominees who contested an ESO selection conference. Lawyers, together with local government or civil service executive officers, were less likely to be selected, a larger percentage of aspirants from these occupations falling at the three selection hurdles prior to candidacy.

Aspirants with experience as parliamentary candidates stood a greater chance of being selected: 41.0 per cent of PEPCs had been PPCs, compared with 23.5 per cent of rejected aspirants, 24.4 per cent of ESO rejects and 30.8 per cent of defeated short-listed nominees. The percentage of Co-operative panelists diminished as one moved from the rejected to the selected categories. There was no real difference between the four aspirant groups with regard to membership of either the 'A' or 'B' parliamentary lists. Nor was there any preference shown for aspirants who had been either local government candidates or former councillors. However, the attrition rate for serving councillors did distinguish the selected and non-selected groups: 40.0 per cent of rejected aspirants, 40.7 per cent of ESO rejects and 43.2 per cent of defeated selection conference contestants were sitting councillors compared with only a third of PEPCs. Thus again, the diminution of local councillors through the selection machinery produced a conclusion at odds with the statements generated by ordinary candidate studies. To accuse Labour of an undue reliance on local politicians for their European candidates ignores this crucial recruitment finding and function of the filtering system.

The central axis upon which evaluation of the Labour party's recruitment rests was the pro and anti-Community controversy. What evidence was there that this selection feature was the most pervasive and influential? Analysis of the advisory list of European candidates is an appropriate starting point. Although the list divided fairly evenly between pro and anti-EEC supporters, there existed on the part of the rank and file selectors a suspicion that inclusion on the list indicated an unhealthy interest in, and by definition, acceptance of the European Parliament and Britain's membership. 55.8 per cent of those surveyed were on the European list: 85.7 per cent of aspirants who were eliminated at the first CLP screening stage were from the list; 83.7 per cent of CLP nominees rejected by an ESO were also from the list. These first two selection hurdles reduced the 55.8 per cent of hopefuls from the list to 47.7 per cent of CLP nominees and to only 36.0 per cent of ESO short-listed nominees. Only at the PEPC stage did aspirants from the list reassert themselves, capturing 41.0 per cent of the seats. Membership of the European list condemned many aspirants to an early exit from the selection system.

There was a positive decline in the success rate of pro-Europeans through the various gate-keeping stages leading to candidacy: they accounted for 48.0 per cent of aspirant rejects, 48.1 per cent of ESO rejects, 42.9 per cent of losing short-listed nominees but only 26.6 per cent of PEPCs. In the context of this anti-European backdrop, those against European federalism stood a better chance of negotiating each selection hurdle as did those who were opposed to both monetary union and any increase in the legislative role of the European Parliament. Pro-European motivations for candidacy were successively reduced at each selection barrier, particularly at the selection conference itself whereas those candidacies that were inspired by an antipathy to the EEC maintained their dominance throughout. While individual selections cannot perfectly be represented by aggregated data, the weight of evidence has indicated an anti-Market theme typical of Labour's recruitment and selection system. The plight of pro-Market PEPCs has been well-documented in other candidate studies and rumours of antagonistic anti-Market feeling at the grass-roots level were common. The data presented here has established empirically that such a pro/anti EEC dichotomy existed and had a considerable impact upon the selection process.

Across a wide range of variables, spanning background factors, political expertise, ambitions and not least attitudes towards Europe, differences between the selected and non-selected cohorts were found. The assumptions of the model were validated for the Labour party and they hypothesis that there were significant differences between selected and non-selected aspirants supported.

Liberal profiles: How far were rejected and selected Liberal aspirants different in their profile characteristics? As already demonstrated Liberal aspirants, whether selected or not, were broadly similar in terms of their national political experience, commitment to Europe and stimulus for candidacy. For example, eight out of ten in both groups had been parliamentary candidates, six out of ten had contested the October 1974 general election and 50.0 per cent of selected European candidates were also PPCs at the time of their selection compared with 44.6 of rejected aspirants. Commitment to Europe was whole-hearted: not less than 90.0 per cent of both groups favoured the pro-EEC position on all five European issues examined. However, even in a party where alignment with the concept of a federal Europe went virtually unquestioned, beneath these important similarities other variables displayed interesting variations in the profile breakdowns for selected and non-selected aspirants.

Once again, the most striking differences were in background characteristics. In summary, these differences were that women, older aspirants, Oxbridge graduates and those from OPCS groups XXIV and XXV were more likely to be adopted than rejected by Liberal selectors. The exact breakdowns were that women accounted for 10.0 per cent of PEPCs and only 3.5 per cent of rejected aspirants, and only 29.9 per cent of selected candidates were aged below forty compared with 51.8 per cent for those who did not contest the election. The two groups were also differentiated by their secondary and higher education. The percentages of adopted candidates from grammar and public schools were 34.8 and 47.0; this relationship was reversed for rejected aspirants, the figures being 52.0 and 42.0 per cent respectively. Furthermore, 46.5 per cent of the Liberal's European candidates were Oxbridge products compared with 31.4 per cent for the non-selected group. Lastly, although three-quarters of all aspirants came from OPCS groups XXIV and XXV, PEPCs were more likely to be drawn from these occupational categories (79.4 compared with 69.6 per cent).

Differences between selected and non-selected aspirants were not completely confined to background factors: candidacy at the local government level further distinguished the two groups. In contrast to the similar levels of involvement in national politics, rejected European aspirants displayed a greater degree of local political activity than their selected contemporaries: 57.3 per cent of PEPCs compared with 75.0 per cent of non-selected individuals had stood as a local candidate. However, their success rates were virtually identical with 32.4 and 33.3 per cent having been elected as councillors respectively. One final area that differentiated the two groups was motivation: PEPCs were far more likely to explain their European candidacy both in terms of pro-EEC support and their personal or political ambitions.

As far as was possible within the confines of the aggregated data generated by a postal questionnaire, crucial selection criteria have been isolated and tested. One cannot be certain whether the factors available to the social scientist are valid estimators or spurious predictors; all too often choice corresponded to those variables that were simply accessible and quantifiable. However, the argument and analysis presented have supported the recruitment theories posited (though largley untested) by other studies into legislative recruitment. As the initial literature review pleaded, if recruitment studies are to be of any value then they must attempt to explain why some individuals are selected whilst others are not. Seligman's proposition was central to this study: 'individuals are always being selected and rejected ... what happens to the losers is almost as crucial for the recruitment process as what happens to the winners'.(9) For the first time in a British recruitment study, a body of data suitable and capable of testing recruitment assumptions has been collected. The analysis of the data has largely confirmed the central core of the model, namely that there are differences between selected and rejected cohorts and that these are a consequence of external factors such as the electoral environment and opportunity structure, internal selection procedures and, most importantly, of the gate-keeping criteria employed by the inner party selectorates. The findings that traced these differences may not have said anything surprising, but that these statements were predictable does not detract from the value of the exercise. Statements concerning recruitment to the European Parliament can now be made with greater confidence in that they are based on verifiable hypotheses, rather than on circumstantial inferences or undocumented assumptions.

Notes

(1) European Journal of Political Research, vol. 8-1, 1980, is devoted to the European Elections Study's analysis of the direct elections; D. Butler and D. Marquand, European Elections and British Politics, London, Longmans, 1981.

(2) C. Mellors, The British MP, Farnborough, Saxon House, 1978.

(3) R.J. Tobin and E.E. Keynes, "Institutional Differences in the Recruitment Process: a four state study". American Journal of Political Science, vol. 19, 1975.

(4) A.L. Hunt and R.C. Pendley, "Community Gate-Keepers: and examination of political recruiters", Mid-West Journal of Political Science, vol. 16, 1971; P. Paterson, The Selectorate: the case for primary elections in Britain, London, MacGibbon and Kee, 1967; L. Fairlie, Secretary/Agents in the British Conservative and Labour Parties, unpublished Ph.D. thesis, Indianna University, 1973; M. Rush, The Selection of Parliamentary Candidates, London, Nelson, 1967; and A. Ranney, Pathways to Parliament; candidate selection in Britain, London, MacMillan, 1965.

(5) Two exceptions to this general statement are J.S. Rasmussen, The Liberal Party: a study of retrenchment and revival, London, Constable, 1965; and C. Cook, A Short History of the Liberal Party, London, MacMillan, 1984.

(6) I. Gordon, "The Recruitment of Local Politicians: an integrated approach with some parliamentary findings from a study of Labour Councillors", Policy and Politics, vol 7. 1979; and C.A. Collins, "Considerations on the Social Background and Motivation of Councillors", Policy and Politics, vol. 6, 1978.

(7) C. Mellors, op.cit., p.74.

(8) W.S.G. Kohn, "Women in the European Parliament", Parliamentary Affairs, vol. 34, 1981.

(9) L.G. Seligman, Recruiting Political Elites, New York, General Learning Press, 1971, p. 4.

Bibliography

Recruitment Books

Barber, J. D., The Lawmakers: Recruitment and Adaptation to Legislative Life, New Haven, Yale University Press, 1965.
Birch, A., Representation, London, Pall Mall, 1971.
Blondel, J., Voters, Parties and Leaders, London, Penguin, 1969.
Bottomore, T. B., Elites and Society, London, Penguin, 1979.
Buck, P. W., Amateurs and Professionals in British Politics, Chicago, Chicago Universtiy Press, 1963.
Butler, D. and D. Kavanagh, The British General Election of October 1974, London, Macmillan, 1975.
Butler, D. and D. Marquand, European Elections and British Politics, London, Longman, 1981.
Cook, C., A Short History of the Liberal Party: 1900-84, (2nd Ed.), London, MacMillan, 1984.
Cook, C. and I. Taylor, The Labour Party, London, Longman, 1980.
Crewe, I., (ed.), British Political Sociology Yearbook, Vol. I, London, Croom Helm, 1974.
Crotty, W. J., (ed.), Approaches to the Study of Party Organisation, Boston, Allyn and Bacon Inc., 1968.
Edinger, L. J., Political Leadership in Industrialised Societies, New York, Wiley, 1967.
Eldersveld, J., Political Parties: A behavioural Analysis, Chicago, Rand McNally, 1964.
Ellis, J. and R. W. Johnson, Members from the Unions, Fabian Research Series 316, 1974.
Eulau, H. and M.M. Czudnowski, Elite Recruitment in Democratic Polities: Comparative Studies Across Nations, New York, Sage, 1976.
Finer, S. E., Berrington, H. B. and D. J. Bartholomew, Backbench Opinion in the House of Commons 1955-9, London, Pergamon Press, 1961.
Greenstein, F. I. and N. W. Polsby, (eds.), Handbook of Political Science, Vol. 2, Reading, Addison-Wesley, 1975.

Guttsman, W. L., The British Political Elite, London, MacGibbon and Kee, 1965.
Harrison, M., Trade Unions and the Labour Party Since 1945, London, Allen and Unwin, 1960.
Hermann, M. C. and T. W. Milburn, A Psychological Examination of Political Leaders, New York, The Free Press, 1977.
Janosik, E., Constituency Labour Parties in Britain, London, Pall Mall Press, 1968.
Kavanagh, D., Constituency Electioneering in Britain, London, Longmans, 1970.
Kornberg, A., (ed.), Legislatures in Comparative Perspective, New York, David McKay, 1973.
Lees, J. D. and R. Kimber, (eds.), Political Parties in Modern Britain: an organisational and function guide, London, Routledge and Kegan Paul, 1972.
Mackintosh, J. P., (ed.), People and Parliament, Farnborough, Saxon House, 1978.
Marvick, D., (ed.), Political Decision-makers: recruitment and performance, Illinois, Free Press, 1961.
McKenzie, R. T., British Political Parties (2nd Ed.), London, Heinemann, 1963.
Mellors, C., The British MP, Farnborough, Saxon House, 1978.
Paterson, P., The Selectorate: the case for primary elections in Britain, London, MacGibbon and Kee, 1967.
Patterson, S. C. and J. C. Wahlke, (eds.), Comparative Legislative Behaviour: Frontiers of Research, New York, Wiley, 1972.
Prewitt, K., The Recruitment of Political Leaders: A Study of Citizen-Politicians, Indianapolis, Bobbs-Merrill, 1970.
Prewitt, K. and R. E. Dawson, Political Socialization (2nd Ed.), Boston, Little, Brown, 1977.
Prewitt, K. and A. Stone, The Ruling Elites: elite theory, power and American democracy, New York, Harper and Row, 1973.
Ranney, A., Pathways to Parliament; candidate selection in Britain, London, Macmillan, 1965.
Rasmussen, J. S., The Liberal Party: a study of retrenchment and revival, London, Constable, 1965.
Richards, P. G., Honourable Members: a study of the British backbencher, (2nd Ed.), London, Faber, 1964.
Rose, R., (ed.), Studies in British Politics: a reader in political sociology (3rd Ed.), London, Macmillan, 1976.
Rose, R., The Problem of Party Government, London, Penguin, 1976.
Roth, P., The Business Backgrounds of MPs (1975-6 Ed.), London, Parliamentary Profiles, 1975.
Rush, M., The Selection of Parliamentary Candidates, London, Nelson, 1969.
Schlesinger, J. A., Ambition and Politics; political careers in the United States, Chicago, Rand McNally, 1966.
Schwartz, D. C., Political Recruitment: an essay in theory and Research, Unpublished Ph. D. thesis, M.I.T., 1965.
Seligman, L. G., Recruitment Political Elites, New York, General Learning Press, 1971.
Seligman, L. G., Political Recruitment, Boston, Little, Brown, 1972.
Wahlke, J. C., Eulau, H., Buchanan, W., and L. Ferguson, The Legislative System, New York, John Wiley, 1962.
Walder, D., The Short List, London, Hutchinson, 1964.
Walkland, S. A. and M. Ryle, (eds.), The Commons Today, London, Fontana, 1981.

<u>Recruitment Articles</u>

Lord Beaumont of Whitley, 'The Selection of Parliamentary Candidates', <u>Political Quarterly</u>, Vol. 45, 1974.

Bell, C. G. and C. M. Price, 'Pre-legislative Sources of Representational Roles', <u>Mid-West Journal of Political Science</u>, Vol. 13, 1969.

Black, G. S., 'The Theory of Political Ambition; Career Choices and the Role of Structural Incentives', <u>American Political Science Review</u>, Vol. 66, 1972.

Black, G. S., 'A Theory of Professionalization in Politics', <u>American Political Science Review</u>, Vol. 64, 1970.

Black, V., 'Selecting for a safe seat', <u>Crossbow</u>, Vol. 4, 1960.

Bochel, J. M., 'The Recruitment of Local Councillors; a case-study', <u>Political Studies</u>, Vol. 14, 1966.

Bochel, J. and D. Denver, 'Candidate Selection in the Labour Party: what the selectors seek', <u>British Journal of Political Science</u>, vol. 13, 1983.

Bowman, L. and G. R. Boynton, 'Recruitment Patterns among local Party officials: A Model and Some Preliminary findings in Selected Locals', <u>American Political Science Review</u>, Vol. 60, 1966.

Brand, J. A., 'Party Organisation and the Recruitment of Councillors', <u>British Journal of Political Science</u>, Vol. 3, 1973.

Browning, R. P., 'The Interaction of Personality and Political System in Decisions to Run for Office: some data and a simulation technique', <u>Journal of Social Issues</u>, Vol. 24, 1968.

Browning, R. P. and H. Jacob, 'Power Motivation and the Political Personality', <u>Public Opinion Quarterly</u>, Vol. 28, 1964.

Budge, I. and D. Farlie, 'Elite background and Issue Preferences: a comparison of British and foreign data using a new technique', in I. Crewe (ed.), <u>British Political Sociology Yearbook</u>, Vol. 1, London, Croom Helm, 1974.

Budge, I. and D. Farlie, 'Political Recruitment and Dropout: Predictive Success of Background Characteristics over Five British Localities', <u>British Journal of Political Science</u>, Vol. 5, 1975.

Bullock, C. S., 'House Careerists', <u>American Political Science Review</u>, Vol. 66, 1972.

Butler, D., Marquand, D. and B. Gosschalk, 'The Euro-persons', <u>New Society</u>, 3.5.1979.

Clarke, M. G., 'National Organisation and the Constituency Association in the Conservative Party: the case of the Huddersfield Pact', <u>Political Studies</u>, Vol. 17, 1969.

Collins, C. A., 'Considerations on the Social Backgrounds and Motivation of Councillors', <u>Policy and Politics</u>, Vol. 6, 1978.

Critchley, J., 'How to get on in the Tory Party', <u>Political Quarterly</u>, Vol. 49, 1978.

Czudnowski, M. M., 'Sociocultural Variables and Legislative Recruitment', <u>Comparative Politics</u>, Vol. 1972.

Czudnowski, M. M., 'Legislative recruitment under PR in Israel; a model and case study', <u>Mid-West Journal of Political Science</u>, Vol. 14, 1970.

Czudnowski, M. M., 'Toward a New Research Strategy for the Comparative Study of Political Recruitment', <u>International Political Science Association</u>, Eight World Congress, 1970.

Czudnowski, M. M., 'Political Recruitment' in Greenstein, F. and N. Polsby, (eds.), Handbook of Political Science, Vol. 2, Reading, Addison-Wesley, 1975.
Dickson, A.D., 'MPs Re-adoption Conflicts: their causes and consequences', Political Studies, Vol. 24, 1975.
Edinger, L. J., 'Political Science and Political Biography: Reflections on the Study of Leadership', Journal of Politics, Vol. 26, 1964.
Edinger, L. J. and D. D. Searing, 'Social Background and Elite Analysis; a methodological inquiry', American Political Science Review, Vol. 61, 1967.
Eulau, H., 'Elite Analysis and Democratic Theory: the contribution of Harold D. Laswell', in Eulau, H. and M. M. Czudnowski (eds.), Elite Recruitment in Democratic Polities, New York, Sage, 1976.
Eulau, H., 'Reflections' in Whahlke, J. C. Eulau, H., Buchanan, W. and L. Ferguson, The Legislative System, New York, John Wiley, 1962.
Eulau, H. and D. Koff, 'Occupational Mobility and Political Career', Western Political Quarterly, Vol. 15, 1962.
Eulau, H. et al, 'The Political Socialization of American State legislators', Mid-West Journal of Politics, Vol. 3, 1959.
Fabian Society, 'Members from the Unions', Fabian Research Series, No. 316, 1974.
Farlie, D., Budge, I. and G. Irwin, 'Political Recruitment and drop-out; the Netherlands and USA', British Journal of Political Science, Vol. 7, 1977.
Fairlie, L. D., 'Candidate Selection Role Perceptions of Conservative and Labour Party Secretaries/Agents', Political Studies, Vol. 24, 1976.
Fiellin, A., 'Recruitment and Legislative role conceptions: a conceptual scheme and a case study', Western Political Quarterly, Vol. 20, 1967.
Fishel, J., 'Ambition and the Political Vocation: Congressional challengers in American politics', Journal of Politics, Vol. 33, 1971.
Frasure R. and A. Kornberg, 'Constituency Agents and British Party Politics', British Journal of Political Science, Vol. 5, 1975.
Goodman, J. S., Swanson, W. R. and E. E. Cornwell, 'Political Recruitment in four Selection Systems', Western Political Quarterly, Vol. 23, 1970.
Gordon, I., 'The Recruitment of Local Politicians: an integrated approach with some preliminary findings from a study of Labour councillors', Policy and Politics, Vol. 7, 1981.
Greenstein, F. I. 'The Need for Systematic Inquiry into Personality and Politics: Introduction and Overview', Journal of Social Issues, Vol. 24, 1968.
Guttsman, W. L., 'Elite Recruitment and Political Leadership in Britain and Germany Since 1950; a comparative study of MPs and Cabinets' in I. Crewe (ed.), British Sociology Yearbook, Vol. I, London, Croom Helm, 1974.
Hacker, A., 'The Elected and the Annointed; Two American Elites', American Political Science Review, Vol. 55, 1961.
Harrison, M., 'Trade Unions and the Labour Party' in Kimber, R. and J. J. Richardson (eds.), Pressure Groups in Britain: a reader, London, Dent, 1974.
Hejln, V. S. and J. P. Pisciotte, 'Profiles and Careers of Colorado State legislators', Western Political Quarterly, Vol. 21,

1968.
Hills, J., 'Life-style Constraints on Formal Political Participation - why so few women councillors in Britain?' Electoral Studies, Vol. 2, 1983.
Holland, M. 'The Selection of Parliamentary Candidates: contemporary developments and the impact of the European elections', Parliamentary Affairs, Vol. 34, 1981.
Hunt, A. L. and R. C. Pendley, 'Community Gate-Keepers: an examination of political recruiters', Mid-West Journal of Political Science, Vol. 16, 1971.
Inglehart, R. and Jacques-Rene Rabier, Gordon, I. and C. L. Strensen, 'Broader Powers for the European Parliament? The Attitudes of Candidates', European Journal of Political Research, Vol. 8, 1980.
Jacob, H., 'The Initial Recruitment of Elected Officials in the US - a model', Journal of Politics, Vol. 24, 1962.
Johnson, R. W., 'The British Political Elite, 1955-72', Archives Europeenes Sociologie, Vol. 14, 1973.
Kim, C. L., 'Political Attitudes of Defeated Candidates in an American State Election', American Political Science Review, Vol. 64, 1970.
Kim, C. L., 'Attitudinal Effects of legislative Recruitment', Comparative Politics, Vol. 7, 1974.
Kim, C. L. Green, J. and S. C. Patterson, 'Partisanship in the Recruitment and Performance of American State Legislators', in Eulau, H. and M. M. Czudnowski, (eds.), Elite Recruitment in Democratic Polities, New York, Sage, 1976.
King, A., 'The Rise of the Career Politician in Britain - And its consequences', British Journal of Political Science, Vol. 11 1981.
Kornberg, A., Clarke, H. and G. Watson, 'Towards a Model of Parliamentary Recruitment in Canada', in Kornberg, A. (ed.), Legislatures in Comparative Perspective, New York, David McKay, 1973.
Magee, B., 'Candidates - how they pick them', New Statesman, 5.2.1965.
Marcus, G., 'Psychopathology and Political Recruitment', Journal of Politics, Vol. 31, 1969.
Martin, S. L., 'The Bournemouth Affair: Britain's First Primary Election', Journal of Politics, Vol. 22, 1960.
Marvick, D., 'Political Recruitment and Party Structure', in Sills, D. (ed.), International Encyclopedia of the Social Sciences, Vol. 12, New York, Macmillan, 1968.
Marvick, 'Continuities in Recruitment Theory and Research: Toward a New Model', In Eulau, H. and M. M. Czudnowski, (eds.), Elite Recruitment in Democratic Polities, New York, Sage, 1976.
May, T., 'A Government of Meritocrats', New Society, 12.5.1977.
Newman, R. and S. Cranshaw, 'Towards a Closed Primary Election in GB', Political Quarterly, Vol. 44, 1973.
Obler, J. 'Intraparty Democracy and the Selection of Parliamentary Candidates; the Belgian Case', British Journal of Political Science, Vol. 4, 1974.
Parker, J. D., 'Classification of Candidates Motives for First Seeking Office', Journal of Politics, Vol. 34, 1972.
Paterson, P., 'Primaries: Reforming the Candidate Selection Process', in Mackintosh, J. P., MP, (ed.), People and Parliament, Farnborough, Saxon House, 1979.
Patterson, S. C., 'Characteristics of Party Leaders', Western

Political Quarterly, Vol. 16, 1963.
Patterson, S. C. and G. R. Boynton, 'Legislative Recruitment in a Civic Culture', Social Science Quarterly, Vol. 50, 1969.
Pedersen, M. M., 'Spatial Model of Political Recruitment', European Journal of Political Research, Vol. 3, 1975.
Pentley, J., 'Worms that turned: the inter-party mobility of British Parliamentary Candidates since 1945', Parliamentary Affairs, Vol. 30, 1977.
Pinto-Duschinsky, M., 'Central Office and Power in the Conservative Party, Political Studies, Vol. 20, 1972.
Prewitt, K., 'Political Socialization and Leadership in Selection', Annals of the American Academy of Political Science, Vol. 361, 1965.
Prewitt, K., 'From the Many are Chosen the Few', American Behavioural Scientist, Vol. 13, 1969.
Prewitt, K., 'Political Ambitions, Volunteerism and Electoral Accountability', American Political Science Review, Vol. 64, 1970.
Prewitt, K. and H. Eulau, 'Political Matrix and Political Representation: Prolegomenon to a new departure from an old problem', American Political Science Review, Vol. 63, 1969.
Prewitt, K. and H. Eulau, 'Social Biases in Leadership Selection, Political Recruitment and Electoral Context', Journal of Politics, Vol. 33, 1971.
Prewitt, K., Eulau, H. and B. H. Zick, 'Political Socialization and Political Roles', Public Opinion Quarterly, Vol. 30, 1966-67.
Prewitt, K. and W. Nolin, 'Political Ambitions and the Behaviour of Incumbent Politicans', Western Political Quarterly, Vol. 22, 1969.
Ramussen, J. S., 'The role of Women in British Parliamentary Elections', Journal of Politics, Vol. 39, 1977.
Ranney, A., 'Inter-constituency Movement of British Parliamentary Candidates 1951-9', American Political Science Review, Vol. 58, 1964.
Ranney, A., 'Candidate Selection and Party Cohesion in Great Britain and the United States', in Crotty, W. J. (ed.), Approaches to the Study of Party Organisation, Boston, Allyn and Bacon Inc., 1968.
Ranney, A., 'Turn-out and Representation in Presidential Primary Elections', American Political Science Review', Vol. 66, 1972.
Reif, K. and H. Schmitt, 'Nine Second Order Elections: A Conceptual Framework for the Analysis of European Election Results', European Journal of Political Research, Vol. 8, 1980.
Rush, M., 'Candidate Selection and its Impact on Leadership Recruitment' in Lees, J. D. and R. Kimber, (eds.), Political Parties in Modern Britain, London, Routledge and Kegan Paul, 1972.
Rush, M., 'Parliament and the Public; political recruitment, representation and participation' in Mackintosh, J. P. (ed.), People and Parliament, Farnborough, Saxon House, 1979.
Schlesinger, J. A., 'Lawyers and American Politics', Mid-West Journal of Political Science, Vol. 1, 1957.
Schlesinger, J. A., 'Political Career and Party Leadership', in Edinger, L. J., Political Leadership in Industrialised Societies, New York, Wiley, 1967.
Schwartz, D. C., 'Towards a theory of Political Recruitment', Western Political Quarterly, Vol. 22, 1969.

Searing, D. D., 'Comparative Study of Elite Socialization', Comparative Political Studies, Vol. 1, 1969.
Seligman, L. G., 'The Study of Political Leadership', American Political Science Review, Vol. 44, 1950.
Seligman, L. G., 'Recruitment in Politics', The American Behavioural Scientist, Vol. 1, 1958.
Seligman, L. G., 'Party Roles and Political Recruitment', Western Political Quarterly, Vol. 11, 1958.
Seligman, L. G., 'A Prefactory Study of Leadership Selection in Oregon', Western Political Quarterly, Vol. 12, 1959.
Seligman, L. G., 'Political recruitment and Party Structure; a case study', American Political Science Review, Vol. 55, 1961.
Seligman, L. G., 'Elite Recruitment and Political Development', Journal of Politics, Vol. 26, 1964.
Seligman, L. G., 'Political Parties and the Recruitment of Political Leders', in Edinger, L. J., (ed.), Political Leadership in Industrialised Societies, New York, Wiley, 1967.
Sherrod, D. R., 'Selective Perception of Political Candidates', Public Opinion Quarterly, Vol. 35, 1971.
Snowiss, L. M., 'Congressional Recruitment and Representation', American Political Science Review, Vol. 60, 1966.
St. Angelo, D. D. Dobson, 'Candidates, Issues and Political Estrangement', American Politics Quarterly, Vol. 13, 1975.
Stanyer, J., 'Electors, Candidates and Councillors: Some Technical Problems in the Study of Political Recruitment and Processes in Local Government', Policy and Politics, Vol. 6, 1977.
Tobin, R. J., 'The Influence of Nominating Systems on the Political Experiences of State Legislators', Western Political Quarterly, Vol. 28, 1975.
Tobin, R. J. and E. E. Keynes, 'Institutional Differences in the Recruitment Process: a four state study', American Journal of Political Science, Vol. 19, 1975.
Valen, H., 'The Recruitment of Parliamentary Nominees in Norway', Scandinavian Political Studies, Vol. 1, 1966.
Vallence, E., 'Women Candidates in the 1983 General Election', Parliamentary Affairs, Vol. 37, 1984.
Wilson, D. J. 'Constituency Party Autonomy and Central Control', Political Studies, Vol. 21, 1973.

Index

References from Notes indicated by 'n' after page reference

UNIVERSITY COLLEGE
LIBRARY
CARDIFF